Becoming The Person You Can Become

THE COMPLETE GUIDE TO

SELF-TRANSFORMATION

Alvin R. Mahrer, Ph.D

Bull Publishing Company
Boulder, Colorado

Published by Bull Publishing Company, Post Office Box 208, Palo Alto, California 94302-0208 (www.bullpub.com) in association with Lansing Hays Publishing LLC, 248 Prince George Street, Annapolis, Maryland 21401.

Typeset in Galliard
Printer:
Interior design: Dianne Nelson, Shadow Canyon Graphics
Cover design:
Managing editor: Linda O'Doughda
Copyeditor: Nancy Peterson

06 05 04 03 02   5 4 3 2 1

Library of Congress Cataloging-in-Publication Data

Mahrer, Alvin R.
    Becoming the person you can become: the complete guide to self-transformation / by Alvin R. Mahrer.
        p. cm.
    ISBN 0-923521-65-8
    1. Experiential psychology. 2. Self-actualization (Psychology) I. Title.

RC489.E96 M338 2001
616.89'14—dc21   2001035945

Printed in the United States of America
First Edition

TABLE OF CONTENTS

iii

A Little Bit About The Life Of The Author
And The Life Of This Book

To begin, there are a few things I would like for you to know. First, I am a reasonably mainstream psychologist and academic; that is, I don't have some intriguingly distinctive professional background. Also, this book grew little by little over almost 50 years. It did not appear suddenly and dramatically with a loud crash of cymbals.

Three early scenes come to mind when I concentrate on my life and the life of this book. In the first scene, I am about 11 years old, walking and taking excitedly with my best friend about what we might be like deep down inside. How we wished we could magically become totally different people, people who wouldn't get into such awful trouble, he with his family, me with our schoolteachers, and both of us with the big kids who beat us up.

The second scene happened either a few years earlier or later. I am huddled in the attic of my grandmother's home, absolutely enthralled by pornographic books written by someone named Sigmund Freud. Those pages take me by the hand and walk me through the excitingly arcane, subterranean world of our insides, shedding light on the hidden possibilities inside us and the inviting promise of freedom from our painful situations and the awful feelings in those painful situations.

The third scene is similar. Instead of being a little boy in my grandmother's attic hideaway, I am a doctoral student in my room at Ohio State University. Instead of reading Sigmund Freud, I am devouring underground books written by existential philosophers and philosophers of science. The feelings are similar; I am captivated by the wonders of exploring whole new and exciting worlds.

During those years, it seemed as though the wonderful sense of exploring whole new worlds was almost everywhere in the doctoral program. Carl Rogers had just left for the University of Chicago; Julian Rotter was giving birth to his seminal volume on social learning theory; and George Kelly was churning out the two volumes of his personal construct theory.

As soon as I arrived, I was so carried away by the atmosphere in the program that I happily confessed to my assigned faculty adviser the two things that placed me on immediate probationary status in the department: Becoming a solid contributor to the science and profession of clinical psychology was not a driving force in me; rather, I was desperately searching for a way to become whatever utterly new person I was capable of becoming and, hopefully, free of the mixed-up, crazy, painful feelings I had in so many situations. I also naively explained that I would be out of town one or two weekends a month because I had been earning a lot of money as a pretty good club fighter since I was an adolescent.

The next day, a formal letter summoned me to discuss with my faculty adviser my new status of being on official probation. In the meeting, my adviser quickly steered me to a kindly old fellow whose couch became my home for five hours a week over the five years of the doctoral program. I was also advised of my right to choose between being a full-time graduate student or the next welterweight champion of the world.

A month or so later, the decision was made for me by a neurologist who examined me the day after a fight that I had almost no memory of. When I informed by faculty adviser that the neurologist told me I should remain in the doctoral program because I was showing signs of minimal brain damage, I was shocked that he suddenly exploded into gales of laughter. His secretary and I could still hear his uncontrolled yelping through the closed door of his office as I backed out, totally confused over his response to my earnest concerns about my future.

I graduated in 1954 with a doctorate and two major misgivings. One was that I had almost no idea about how to do psychotherapy. I had learned a great deal about theory and research and how to walk and talk like a scientist, but I had virtually no chance to study master practitioners in action. I was used to learning by studying masters of a craft, but this seemed to be missing in my doctoral training. As a psychotherapist, I was not even a beginner, an amateur, and nowhere near being a professional with professional skills.

The second major misgiving was that I still had the same kinds of awful feelings in the same kinds of painful situations, and I still held the faint hope of somehow becoming the person I was capable of becoming. Those years of lying on the couch gave me the grateful appreciation that someone was interested in me, my thoughts, my life, everything about me, for five hours a week for so many years. That was a gift, even though I graduated from the kindly old fellow and the security of his couch as virtually the same person I was when I started.

These two misgivings proved to be the driving force behind most of my professional life, although it was only later that I understood that virtually everything I did was an attempt to answer this question: Whether I picture myself or someone I work with in what is called psychotherapy, how can a person become whatever that person is capable of becoming, and how can the person be free of painful personal situations and the painful feelings in those situations?

When I look back over my professional life, this question seems to have guided me along four intertwined professional pursuits:

1. I love studying and learning from listening to gifted practitioners. Almost as soon as I had my first job, I pleaded with fine practitioners to allow me to study and learn by listening to audiotapes of their actual work with actual patients. Over many years, I have accumulated a precious library of nearly 500 audiotapes from psychotherapists who are deservedly well-known and highly respected by their colleagues as gifted psychotherapists—even if they have not written books or held important professional offices.

2. I devour books and articles that might help answer my guiding question. For centuries, many wise people within and outside the field of psychotherapy have written about

such serious, basic issues as: what people are like; how they get to be the way they are; how truly magnificent, deep-seated change happens; how and why people have such suffering and anguish; and what a person can become. I study and learn from what the literature reveals.

3. I experiment freely in sessions with myself and, much more guardedly, with the people I work with in psychotherapy. If the field of psychotherapy trusted certain methods and techniques, I generally was eager to try them out in my own sessions with myself, whether the method or technique involved penetrating what dreams offered or examining my personal case history, using methods of relaxation or the two-chair technique, reliving traumatic childhood events or modifying the reinforcement contingencies of my behavior, using guided imagery or adopting new ways of looking at things. Gradually, I have cobbled together a way of working with myself and those in psychotherapy sessions.

4. I turned early to the philosophy of science to help pull me out of my ingrained ways of thinking and lead me into radically new ways of thinking that can perhaps answer my guiding question: How can this radically new way of thinking help me and the person I am working with in psychotherapy become what we are capable of becoming and to be free of our painful situations and the painful feelings in those situations?

These pursuits have culminated in the outside and inside faces of my professional life and the life of this book.

On the outside, my professional life has been much like that of many other psychologists. From 1954 to 1967, I was in charge of psychological training at two large training and research hospitals. In 1967, I was professor and director of the Clinical Psychology Program at Miami University in Ohio, and in 1972, I was graduate officer of a doctoral program at the University of Waterloo in Canada, moving to the University of Ottawa in 1978, where I am now Professor Emeritus. Throughout and currently, I have nurtured a small, private practice and a large passion for writing and research, so far yielding 12 books and from 200 to 300 other publications.

Some years ago, I served as president of a state psychological association and president of a division of the American Psychological Association. I was even given the National Employee of the Year award when I worked at a Veterans Administration hospital. More recently, I was proud to earn the Researcher of the Year award from the University of Ottawa, and the Distinguished Psychologist award from the American Psychological Association's Division of Psychotherapy.

On the inside, throughout all these years, the driving force has been to learn how a person can actually become the person that he or she is capable of becoming. This driving force has led me along five avenues of continuing exploration and exciting discovery.

1. To try to find a way to make sense of human beings— what we are like, how we came to be the way we are, and

why we feel what we feel and do what we do. This is what my colleagues call a theory of personality. I call my way an experiential model of human beings, an experiential psychology.

2. To sculpt out a way of doing research to uncover the secrets of psychotherapy, discover the precious changes that can occur in psychotherapy sessions, and to appreciate how gifted psychotherapists help others achieve these precious changes, breaking new ground in what psychotherapy can be. I call this a discovery-oriented approach to research in psychotherapy.

3. To add a relatively uncommon but, I believe, important and helpful element to professional training. This means that the teacher and supervisor enable the ready and willing student to delve into, explore, discover, and develop the student's own nascent, deeper framework, way of thinking, or pool of basic notions and ideas in the field of psychotherapy. I call this a discovery-oriented approach to training and supervision.

4. To study and learn from the neighboring field of the philosophy of science so that what I learn can help advance, carry forward, constructively shake up, and perhaps revolutionize psychotherapy theory, research, and practice—its very foundations, virtually everything it takes for granted, its deep-seated, ingrained problems and possibilities. I want to see if the philosophy of science can help the field of psychotherapy become what it is capable of becoming.

5. The fifth avenue of pursuit is what this book is all about. Starting in 1954, I have tried to piece together, carve out, weave together, and develop a way to help me and others become who we are capable of becoming, and to be reasonably free of our painful scenes and the painful feelings in those scenes. I have moved ahead enough to be excited about this method, so that others can use it and continue making it better. That is what this book is for. When I work with and teach a person how to go through a session that comes close to what my colleagues call psychotherapy, I refer to this as "experiential psychotherapy," but I am more comfortable thinking of it as simply teaching a person how to go through and learn how to have their own experiential sessions, their own sessions of self-transformation.

These are the five things I am proud of in my work. I am proudest of the fifth.

I hope this provides you with a brief sketch of my professional life and how this book has slowly evolved over many years.

Becoming The Person You Can Become

THE COMPLETE GUIDE TO SELF-TRANSFORMATION

p. xiv
blank

Here Is Your Guide For How To Use This Book

Chapters 5 through 8 show you how to have your own experiential sessions. If you are ready to have an experiential session, or if you want to know how to go through an experiential session, read these four chapters. There are four steps in each session. Each of these chapters deals in depth with one of the four steps.

If you want an introduction, a background, to how to have a session, read Chapters 1 through 4. When I teach people how to have their own experiential sessions, I pay attention to the questions they raise, such as: "What are the goals of experiential sessions?" "Do I need to know a lot about psychology to be able to have sessions?" "How is this different from having sessions with a professional psychotherapist?" Chapters 1 through 4 address these kinds of questions, and I know they are adequate because readers have let me know that their questions were answered.

1

Chapter 1 describes the aims and goals of having your own sessions, the changes you can achieve, and what these sessions can offer you. If you find these aims and goals to be of interest, or truly exciting, then you are likely ready to learn more about what happens in the course of each session.

Chapter 2 tells what happens inside an experiential session, that is, the steps you go through, the nuts and bolts of what a session is like. If this is appealing or exciting to you, then you are likely ready to have your own sessions of self-transformation.

Chapter 3 provides some guidelines to help you have your own sessions. It deals with such issues as when you might have sessions, whether or not you need to possess special qualities in order to have your own sessions, and some of the concerns and worries that you might have about going through these sessions.

Chapter 4 tells about the rather curious relationship between having your own sessions and the field of psychotherapy. This chapter was born out of the many questions people have raised about the field of having one's own sessions of self-transformation and the field of professional psychotherapy. (Perhaps Chapter 4 ought to bear the warning label: "Beware! This chapter contains an aggressive indictment of the field of professional psychotherapy!" The warning label is justified because the chapter deals with some serious matters raised by serious questions about the relationship between having one's own sessions and the field of professional psychotherapy.)

Following the four chapters (5 through 8) that teach you how to have your own experiential sessions, Chapter 9 tells you how to get better, and to keep getting better, at having them. In its entirety, *Becoming the Person You Can Become* is the complete guide for learning what to do, how to do it, and how to keep improving your skills in undergoing your self-transforming sessions.

p. 4
blank

1

The Goals of a Session
of Self-Transformation

Hello, and thank you for reading this chapter.

Imagine that you go into a room and have a session by yourself, one that lasts for an hour or two. Imagine that you have two goals for the session, two things that you are ready and willing to accomplish, two kinds of changes that are precious and will come out of having a session.

In this chapter, I will clearly describe the two goals that you can achieve in each session of self-transformation. I want to be clear because the goals are clear, the changes you can achieve are clear. During and after the session, the changes will be rather obvious, conspicuous, real, and clear.

I also want to be clear so that you can decide whether or not you find these goals precious, appealing, and valuable. If you are drawn toward what you can achieve in a session, it will be easier for you to read the next chapters and begin having your own sessions.

My emphasis here is on the goals you can achieve in each session, rather than the underlying theory behind, or the conceptual notions and ideas about, those goals. If you are interested, you will find a little bit of theory in some of the other chapters. If you are really interested in learning more about the theory, you are invited to read the three books that are mentioned in the final chapter.

There are two main goals; they work together, in that achieving the first goal goes a long way toward helping you achieve the second goal.

ONE GOAL IS TO BECOME THE PERSON YOU CAN BECOME

In the session, you can become a qualitatively new person. You don't become just any new person, but the person you are capable of becoming.

Picture A Qualitative Transformation In The Person You Are

The change is radical. It is a deep-seated change in the person you are. It is a genuine transformation, a qualitative shift into being a whole new person, into being the person you are capable of becoming, the person you can be. A metamorphosis occurs. You leave the session as a qualitatively different person than the person who started the session.

Picture a change that is far more and far deeper than a superficial change in something about you. The change goes further than you acting or behaving in some other way, having some new thoughts or new feelings, or solving a problem. The change includes all this, but it is much more, much deeper. It is a change in the very person you are.

The qualitative transformational change shows in the way you are, the way you walk, the way you talk, the way you behave with people, your very "presence" with people, the feelings you have, how you act and interact, the way you see things, and your outlook and perspective. And there is something much more, much deeper. There is a qualitative transformation in the person you are, the person who has that outlook, who walks and talks in that way, who has that voice quality, and who acts and interacts in those ways.

The radical shift is in the direction of becoming the person you are capable of becoming. You become more you, more of the possibilities that are in you, more of the person you can become. You do not become the kind of person that someone else wants you to become, more of what "they" believe you should be. You do not become the sort of person that you believe you should or ought to be. The direction comes from what lies deep within you, and the wellspring of the change is the inner possibilities of the person you are capable of becoming.

Picture That You Can Discover The Inner Possibilities Of The Person You Are Capable Of Becoming

Great thinkers have given us all sorts of notions about what we might find if we probed deep inside, if we explored our inner world, if we dared to go down deep inside in self-

7

exploration, in self-understanding. We may find basic needs, drives, and instincts, such as the instinct for survival, the need for sex, the drive for power, and the need for basic human security. We may find alien personalities existing deep inside, unconscious wishes and impulses, or pathological processes that form the foundation of mental illnesses and disorders. We may find a pool of original sin, basic human loving and caring, a fundamental animal nature, or forgotten early memories—or all sorts of other things.

Picture that there is a way to probe inside you to discover deeper qualities and characteristics, possible ways of being, possible ways of experiencing, possible kinds of experiencing, possibilities or potentialities for sheer experiencing. Whatever else you can imagine existing deep inside you, picture that you can discover these deeper possibilities or potentialities for experiencing.

Think of these possibilities as things inside you, things of which you are essentially unaware. Think of these as things that you can only dimly sense, that would surprise you if you discovered them.

Think of these inner possibilities or potentialities for experiencing in their neutral form, rather than in a form that can be fearful or hateful. If you fear and hate them, the inner possibilities can seem to be monstrous, frightening, grotesque, evil, bad, or something awful. On the other hand, freed of your fearful and hateful relationship, they can be discovered in a neutral form, as simply possibilities or potentialities for experiencing. Picture them as the inner possibilities of the person you are capable of becoming.

The picture is of you going deep inside yourself and discovering the kinds of deeper possibilities for experiencing that exist there. You may find possibilities for experiencing that you do not undergo in your daily life, or only rarely, or rarely with good feelings. But these possibilities are there, deep within you. Here are some examples: an experiencing of tenderness, gentleness, softness; playfulness, silliness, whimsy; violence, explosiveness, destructiveness; strength, firmness, toughness; being mischievous, devilish, wicked; being dominant, controlling, in charge; being close to, one with, intimate; being risky, daring, adventurous; an experiencing of being docile, compliant, yielding; being excited, aroused, titillated; being cold, hard, metallic; being drawn toward, attracted to, compelled by; being withdrawn, pulled away, distant, removed; being free, liberated, opened up; being bad, roguish, irreverent; experiencing independence, autonomy, self-reliance; being delicate, brittle, fragile; being captivated, wondrous, in awe; being provocative, stimulating, arousing; being invaded, entered into; being seen, exhibited, shown off; being the jewel, the special one, the precious one; being nurturing, succoring, caring for; and an experiencing of encountering, confronting, directly facing.

Picture An Inner, Deeper Possibility For Experiencing Becoming An Actual Part Of The Person You Can Become

Imagine that you discover an inner, deeper possibility for experiencing that actually becomes a qualitatively new part of the qualitatively new you. Once this deeper potentiality for experiencing becomes a part of you, you have essentially undergone a wholesale transformation into becoming a wholesale new person. You are no longer a person with that possibility for experiencing deep within you. You are much more than essentially the same person with a small, added new ingredient. The change is far more radical, extensive, and qualitative. You have essentially become a whole new person. The addition of the deeper possibility for experiencing has essentially transformed the very person whom you now are.

What had been deep inside you is now an actual part of the whole new you. The change is from possibility to actuality. The change is an "actualization" of the deeper possibilities for experiencing. The change is becoming the whole new person that the deeper possibility transforms you into being. The change is becoming the person you are capable of becoming.

For example, you discover an inner, deeper potentiality for the experiencing of tenderness, gentleness, and softness. Of course, you may have some inkling of what this is and what it means. You may even have had brushes with that kind of experiencing. But something magical happens when it becomes an actual part of the whole new you. You are no longer the same you. Something bigger has happened. Once this potentiality for experiencing becomes a genuine part of you, you are a qualitatively new person.

When inner, deeper possibilities become actual new parts of the transformed new you, there are almost always bonuses. What you experience becomes fuller, less muted, more forthcoming, more direct, more saturating, open, and complete. What you experience is more inclined to be accompanied by bodily-felt sensations of excitement, vitality, aliveness, energy, titillation, and vibrancy over more of your body and for longer periods of time. What you experience is more likely to be accompanied by feelings of joy, happiness, buoyancy, and lightness.

Becoming the person you can become means that deeper possibilities for experiencing become actual new parts of the transformed you. And there is more.

Picture An Inner, Deeper Possibility For Experiencing Becoming An Integral Part Of The Person You Can Become

Becoming a qualitatively new and transformed person means that what had existed deep inside you is now a whole new part of the whole new you. What is more, this whole new part becomes an *integral* part of the new you. It gets along well with other parts of you, and other parts of you get along well with it. Instead of hating one another, defending against one another, avoiding and pulling away from one another, being vigilant in watching over one another, the change results in the parts of you loving one another, welcoming and cherishing one another, and being playful with and accepting of one another. The change is toward a new state of inner harmony, tranquillity, working together, peacefulness, and integration.

In this new state, there is a sense of being one with yourself, liking and loving yourself, a sense of inner harmony, inner togetherness, and inner tranquillity. You feel this state. There are bodily sensations that accompany this state.

11

There is much less of the sense or state of feeling torn apart, in pieces, at war with oneself, being tortured by oneself, being overcome by awful parts of oneself, having to get away from oneself, of being broken, fragmented, disorganized, and disintegrated.

This means that you are highly in touch with, receptive and open to, what is actually occurring in you right now. You are open to the bodily sensations that are alive in you, to the thoughts and feelings that are right here, to the panorama of images and pictures that are present.

This means that there is much less of the removed you that is ever watchful, ever observing, ever vigilant, always seeing you, and having critical thoughts and reactions to yourself. Instead, you are the engaged one, the interacting one, the relating one, the doer of the doings, the experiencer of the experiencings. When you open the refrigerator to take out cold milk, you are the one who is doing this and experiencing what it is like to do this. You are not off to the side, watching the you who is doing and undergoing the experiencing. There is no part of you who is the hidden executive director, who has a stream of private thoughts about you, who judges you, and approves and disapproves of you.

This means that the parts of you enjoy and love one another so much that they can be truly honest with one another. You can actually "be" the other parts of you. You can actually move into another part of you and respond and react to how you just were. You can actually give voice to how the various parts of you respond and react to you:

"That is the dumbest thing I think I have ever heard. I have no idea what I was trying to say . . . I am so pretty! For my age, I am a truly lovely woman. Good for me!

"That was so arrogant and pompous . . . I just acted like a complete idiot. That was like being a complete idiot, right? I think I was an idiot. Do you think I was a complete idiot? Well! That was a good idea. Every so often I come up with a good idea. And that was it for a while. I like that idea . . ."

You can move into other parts of you and relate to yourself the way these other parts relate to you. You can praise yourself, be offended by yourself, see yourself as lovable, laugh at yourself, be critical of yourself, and admire yourself.

One of the goals of a session of self-transformation is to become the person you are capable of becoming. I hope you now clearly understand what this means.

Picture The Transformational Change Occurring During The Session And Remaining After The Session

During the session, in almost every session, there is a point at which you undergo the radical, qualitative, transformational shift. You literally become the person you are capable of becoming. You are this qualitatively new person for some seconds, some minutes, many minutes, or until the session comes to a close. You are the whole new person.

When the qualitative shift happens, you literally and thoroughly are the qualitatively new person. You do not usually have thoughts like: "Well, look at this! I am a qualitatively new person!" Instead, the shift is bigger and deeper; it includes the part of you that observes and takes note, even such notes as: "Well, look at this! I am a qualitatively whole new person." Truly, there is a transformational change in the very person you are.

You can remain being this whole new person when you leave the session. You can continue being this qualitatively new person in whole or in part, in little ways or in big ways, in some parts of your world or in many parts of your world, for a few minutes or for hours, days, weeks, or perhaps forever.

I hope you are clear about what this goal is, what it means to become the person you can become, to undergo genuine self-transformation. The second goal is related, and can be achieved in each session.

THE SECOND GOAL IS BEING FREE OF YOUR PAINFUL SCENES AND THE PAINFUL FEELINGS IN THOSE PAINFUL SCENES

Each session starts with you finding a scene of strong feeling, a time, incident, or situation in which the feeling in you was strong. The feeling may be pleasant and happy or it may be unpleasant and painful. The second goal involves the painful scenes and painful feelings.

There is a painful feeling that you have. It is a bad feeling, a feeling that hurts, a feeling of anguish or turmoil of some kind. It is a painful feeling. That painful feeling happens in the context of some scene, some situation. The feeling is bad and painful, and the scene or situation is bad and painful.

The marvelous goal is that, by the end of the session, you will be free of that painful feeling in that painful situation and of that painful scene or situation in which it occurs. The painful scene or situation is no longer a part of your world. It is gone. You are free of it. Even if that scene or situation is still here in your world, it is magically new, different, innocent, converted. It is no longer painful, hurtful, wrenching, agonizing, and bad. And you are free of the painful feelings. They are gone, vanished, evaporated. You are free of the painful feeling and of the painful scene in which it happens.

You are no longer the person for whom it was so important to have, to build, and to construct such painful scenes and situations. Now that you have become the qualitatively new person, it is no longer important for such painful scenes and situations to exist. Nor is it important to have such painful feelings, whatever their nature. The world of the person you are at the beginning of the session includes those painful feelings and painful scenes and situations. In the world of the qualitatively new person, it is no longer important that there be those painful feelings. It is no longer important that there be those painful scenes or situations. They float out of your world as you become the qualitatively new person.

The new world is free of people at work who hate you, who think of you as an outsider, an alien, or as someone weird. Gone too are those grinding feelings of getting even, of revenge, of showing "them."

The painful scene is when you are in the throes of doing tabooed sexual activities, secretly in your bedroom. You are racked by horrible feelings of being caught, seen by your husband and your kids. The change is being free of those painful scenes and the agonizing, wrenching feelings in the scenes.

You are free of the painful scenes in which you are with your screaming baby, and your head is pressured by horrible thoughts of muffling him, strangling him, stopping him forever by forcing the pillow over his nose and screaming mouth.

The awful scene is walking along the street, filled with so many people and so many cars, and the people are laughing at you, ridiculing you, and noticing that you are fat, ugly, a loser, an object of deserved derision. By the end of the session, these scenes and feelings are gone, vanished, over with.

The ominous scene is in the evening, when you are both getting ready for bed, and she starts whining and complaining about you. Something is wrong with you. You don't understand her. You never make love with her. You don't talk any more. And you have that same bad feeling of being numb, dead, distant, and withdrawn. It is awful. By the end of the session, those scenes and those feelings are gone. They no longer exist in your world. Your world is free of such agonizing scenes and the painful feelings in those scenes.

You still cannot believe your husband is dead. It has been more than two years, and yet everything is the same. You even kept his toothbrush, aftershave, shoes, scarf, everything. You sleep on your side of the bed. Your adult children think you are depressed and want you to "see someone," but all you can think of is that he will return someday. He did not really have that heart attack like they say. The goal of the session is that everything will be different by the time it ends. The world will no longer have, as its centerpiece, the tragedy, the loss, the sudden end of a 32-year marriage, the pain and anguish, and the utter meaninglessness of life now.

The goal is for your world to be free of the painful scenes and situations that you build, that you fill it with, and free of the painful feelings in such scenes and situations. You no longer have or build a world that includes things to defeat you mercilessly, people from whom you feel remote, people who let you down, and all sorts of scenes and situations that engender and encourage you to sink into such awful feelings, feelings that tear you apart, and that fill you with agony and pain.

When the painful scene exists in your body, the goal is to be free of that painful bodily thing. You can have painful scenes as part of your external world; that is where they usually are. But your body also houses the painful scenes and situations that it is important for you to construct, have, build. If it is important for you to have a situation containing some agent that jabs at you, picks at you, is always after you, hurts you, then your world can include a cousin, coworker, or spouse who fills that role. Or, you can have something called an ulcer.

It may be important for your world to include something that is merciless, coldly uncaring, a killing machine, something that cannot be stopped. In the face of that thing, you can feel utterly helpless, the target, the passive victim. Your world can include such unreachable, evil forces. Your world can include a person who is the incarnation of cold, killing evil. Your world can also include something called cancer.

Your body is a major part of the world in which you live, the world that you help create, build, construct. Your body can include the painful scenes, situations, and feelings that it is important for you to have and to feel. The goal is to be free of those bodily things, these scenes, situations, and feelings that are so painful.

These are the two goals of each session of self-transformation. Yes, these goals are ambitious. And yes, the second goal follows from the first. When you are being the whole new person in the session, the painful scene loses its place in the personal world of the whole new person. That painful scene has lost its painful bite. In order to give that painful scene its power and its painful feeling, you would have to return to being the person you were at the beginning of the session. The same holds true when you are being the qualitatively new person after the session, in your new personal world. Becoming the person you can become carries the bonus of being free of the painful scenes and their painful feelings. Being free of the painful scenes and their painful feelings requires first becoming the person you can become. The solution to those painful scenes of painful feelings is to let go of, to no longer be, the old person whose personal world includes those painful scenes and feelings.

I hope you now have a reasonably clear picture of the two goals of each session.

ARE THESE GOALS PRECIOUS TO YOU?

Now it is up to you. Only you can really know if these two goals are truly precious, magnificent, cherished, inspiring, something you are ready and eager to pursue throughout your whole life—or at least to take the next step and learn what happens in a session.

You may have tried other ways of achieving these two goals, or goals that are similar. You may have personal methods that you already trust and follow to achieve these or related goals. You may have undergone some wonderful religious or mystical experience. You may be a practitioner of some form of meditation. You may engage in some way of soul-searching or spiritual exploration. You may have exceptional sessions with an especially gifted psychotherapist, healer, or guru.

On the other hand, your candid reaction to the two goals may be rather neutral: They are mildly interesting, somewhat appealing.

Or, perhaps your honest reaction is that you find the goals somewhat ominous, strange, alien, somehow wrong, maybe even menacing or dangerous. Your reaction is one of being mildly offended, drawn back, questioning, skeptical, irritated, or disturbed.

If this is your reaction, you may raise all sorts of objections:

"What if I find something inside that I don't like? Do I have to become whatever I find inside? If I am so bothered by being the mother of my baby, does that mean I should give up my baby? Just how much would I have to give up? Can I decide? How do I know that I would like to be the sort of person I might become? Suppose I just do whatever I want; isn't that dangerous? Shouldn't I consider the effects on others? How do I know that I won't just start killing people, doing awful things? If I don't like what I become, can I go back?"

These are the legitimate fears and worries of the person you are. They are not the fears and worries of the person you can become. And yet, if you honestly find these two goals either only mildly interesting or ominously dangerous, you are not yet ready to proceed. Perhaps you will be ready tomorrow, in some months, or years, but not now.

Are you truly and genuinely passionate about these two goals? Do you truly and genuinely find these goals precious, magnificent, cherished, and exciting? If your answer is "Yes!" then you are ready to take the next steps toward having your own sessions. You are ready to see what happens in an experiential session of self-transformation.

2

If You Are Excited About What Happens In An Experiential Session, You Can Have Your Own Experiential Session

If you are going to have experiential sessions, it must be very special and important for you to become the person you are capable of becoming and to be free of the painful situations in your personal world. You achieve these goals by going through an experiential session. Each session is an opportunity to go through four steps, four changes. If you are passionate about going through these changes, you can have your own experiential sessions, and they will be important and precious to you. If the prospect of undergoing these in-session changes is not powerful for you, not precious or passion inspiring, then experiential sessions are probably not for you, at least not now.

In this chapter, I will introduce you to what happens during an experiential session. I will highlight the four steps, the four changes, that you go through in each session. Each of these four steps is described in working detail in Chapters 5 through 8.

Here Is A Summary Of What You Do During An Experiential Session

Please look at the figure on pages 20–21. I am proud of this figure because it shows you the big steps, as well as the sub-steps, or baby steps, to go through in an experiential session. It shows you the four steps and how to achieve each of them. If, after reading this whole book, you keep just two pages, these are the two pages to keep.

Step 1. Discover The Deeper Potential For Experiencing

The purpose of the first step is to help you discover, access, come into close touch with something deep inside you, an inner, deeper possibility or potentiality. It is a part of you that has been virtually unknown. It is like discovering a whole new part of you, a part that has been deep inside you. Think of it as a deeper potential or potentiality for experiencing.

The first step begins with you finding a time, a scene, in which the feeling is quite strong. The feeling is usually a bad one, a painful, hurtful feeling, but it may be one that is good, joyful, ecstatic. The scene is usually from your current life, but it can also be a scene from some time ago. Once you find a scene of strong feeling, you are to actually live and be in this scene as if it were immediate and real. Your feeling is also immediate, real, and strong. As you are living and being in this scene, you locate the tiny moment or instant when the strong feeling peaks. By entering into this moment or instant, there are ways for you to touch or be touched by the deeper potentiality for experiencing; you can actually undergo the deeper potentiality for experiencing. You have discovered something much deeper inside of you.

Step 2. Welcome, Accept, And Cherish
The Deeper Potential For Experiencing

The purpose of the second step is to help you accept, welcome, love, and cherish this newly discovered, deeper part of you. The typical scenario is that you have spent virtually your whole life not knowing this deeper potentiality for experiencing, hiding and disproving it, keeping it distant, unwelcomed, even loathed and hated, relating to it in fear and terror, and seeing it as grotesque, evil, monstrous, and awful. In this second step, you are to embrace it, see it as itself, enjoy it, touch and feel it, fondle it, play with it, laugh with it, and be its buddy, its friend.

Instead of ignoring what has been deep inside you, you now look at it, see it, bring it into your home, poke at it, and hold it in front of you. You have probably spent your whole life not knowing that it was there inside you, but now you fully attend to it.

23

HOW TO PROCEED THROUGH
YOUR OWN EXPERIENTIAL SESSION

STEP 1:
DISCOVER THE DEEPER POTENTIAL FOR EXPERIENCING

- Put yourself in a state of readiness for relatively strong feeling.
- Find a scene of strong feeling.
- Fully live and be in the scene of strong feeling.
- Discover the peak moment of strong feeling in the scene of strong feeling.
- In the moment of strong feeling, the deeper potential for experiencing is discovered when there is a qualitative shift in experiencing when you:
  – Fill in the missing critical detail.
  – Intensify the experiencing.
  – Penetrate down into the awful feeling.
  – Be the special other person or thing.
  – Replace the bad feeling with good feeling.

STEP 2:
WELCOME, ACCEPT, AND CHERISH THE
DEEPER POTENTIAL FOR EXPERIENCING

- Name and describe the deeper potential for experiencing.
- Acknowledge feelings about the deeper potential for experiencing.
- Savor, enjoy the momentary bodily sensations.
- Use other methods given in the manual.

STEP 3:
UNDERGO A QUALITATIVE SHIFT INTO BEING THE
DEEPER POTENTIAL FOR EXPERIENCING IN SCENES FROM THE PAST

- Find recent, earlier, and remote life scenes.
  – Use the deeper potential for experiencing to find scenes.
  – Use the general structure of the initial scene of strong feeling.
- Undergo a qualitative shift into being the whole new person in these life scenes. Do so fully, genuinely, with powerful feeling, with joyful feeling, free of all reality constraints, in the context of wholesale freedom, silliness, zaniness.

HOW TO PROCEED THROUGH
YOUR OWN EXPERIENTIAL SESSION (CONTINUED)

STEP 4:
BE THE QUALITATIVELY WHOLE NEW PERSON IN SCENES
FROM THE FORTHCOMING, NEW POST-SESSION WORLD

- Remain being the qualitatively new person.
- Find imminent scenes and situations that are outrageously unrealistic, in which the qualitatively new person can playfully and fully wallow in being the qualitatively new person

  – Extrapolate from scenes already used in the session.
  – Extrapolate from the deeper potential to generate scenes (e.g., ideal scenes; mundane scenes; fantasy-daydream scenes; impossibly inappropriate scenes; devilishly wicked scenes; would-love-to scenes).

- Playfully and fully wallow in being the qualitatively new person in the wildly unrealistic scenes and situations.
- The qualitatively new person frames scenes that are realistically fitting and appropriate.
- Rehearse and modify being the qualitatively new person in these scenes until it is just right.

  – Use bodily sensations as a criterion or guide.
  – Invite reactions from former person.
  – Insert qualitatively new person in initial scene of strong (bad) feeling.

- Commit yourself to being the qualitatively new person, with whole new ways of being and behaving, in the rehearsed scenes and situations.
- After the session, actually be the qualitatively whole new person in new ways in the new scenes and situations of the new, post-session world.

Instead of sealing off, fearing, and running from what was deep inside you, you now love it, giggle and laugh with it, make it a close friend. You feel good with it.

Step 3. Undergo A Qualitative Shift
Into Being The Deeper Potential For Experiencing
In Scenes From The Past

The purpose of the third step is for you to let go of being the person you have been, to give up and disengage from the actual person you are, to slide right out of everything that is you. You no longer are you. Instead, you are the person who is the deeper potential for experiencing. You are the living, breathing, thinking, feeling, behaving, and experiencing form of that deeper potential for experiencing. What had been deep inside is now alive, and you are it. This is the qualitative shift, a radical letting go of one person and the thorough being of a whole new person. You are no longer you. You are the deeper potential. Everything that is you is the deeper potential for experiencing, even the you who thinks about who and what you are. You have become a whole new person.

This third step begins with finding scenes and times from the past: from recently, from some time ago, or from the very beginnings of your life. In the context of these scenes and times, you then step out of being the person you have always been and emerge or become the whole new person who is the deeper potential for experiencing.

Step 4. Be The Qualitatively Whole New Person
In Scenes From The Forthcoming, New Post-Session World

In the final step of the session, you are the qualitatively whole new person. What had been deep inside you is now an integral part of the whole new person. As this qualitatively whole new person, you are ready to end the session and to live as and be this qualitatively whole new person in the qualitatively new world. Here is a most radical change: a dramatic, qualitative shift from starting the session as one person and ending it as a whole new person.

This fourth step starts by remaining the qualitatively new person that you became in Step 3. As this qualitatively new person, you look for scenes, times, situations from the next day or so, from the imminent future. These are scenes that are likely to happen or that you can help bring about. Then, as the qualitatively whole new person, you throw yourself into living and being in these forthcoming scenes, thoroughly wallowing in being the qualitatively whole new person in these scenes.

Fully being the qualitatively whole new person in these forthcoming scenes is to be carried out in the context of sheer zaniness, silliness, freedom from the constraints of reality, and utter playfulness. Then, you move into the context of reality, of what is realistically fitting and appropriate both for the whole new person whom you are and for the whole new world in which you can live. The session ends with a commitment to remain as this whole new person and to be this whole new person in an explicit scene in the next day or so in the real world.

27

*Some Of The Things You Do In An Experiential Session Are
Uncommon And Unusual Because They Have Uncommon
And Unusual Jobs To Do*

When you read about or listen to an experiential session,
you may well consider many of the things you do as uncommon, unusual, weird, bizarre, and maybe even scary or exciting. You begin by taking deep breaths, bellowing and
yelling, and screeching and thundering. You search for
moments in past scenes when strong feelings are at their
peak. You fully live in scenes of strong feeling. You undergo
radical transformations so that you sound, act, and actually
become a whole different person. You do things that are
abnormal, perhaps frowned on by most people, far outside
the realm of what you would ordinarily do.

The reason that what you do is so uncommon and
unusual is that the goals are so uncommon and unusual. In a
single session, you are to become a whole new person, the
qualitatively different person whom you are capable of
becoming. In a single session, you are to be free of the
painful scene of strong, painful feelings that was there in the
beginning of the session. These are special goals, and it takes
special methods to attain special goals.

It is uncommon and unusual to discover what has been
hidden inside you for so many years. It is uncommon and
unusual to welcome and accept what you have spent so many
years hiding and sealing off, and to accomplish this in a single
session. It is uncommon and unusual to transform into a
whole different person and to be this qualitatively new person

in the context of past scenes. Finally, it is uncommon and unusual to be this whole new person in imminent, forthcoming scenes from the real world after each session. These are special goals to achieve in each session. It is understandable that uncommon and unusual skills and steps are called for to help achieve these goals.

Many of the working methods you use in an experiential session are not common in your daily life. You do not ordinarily do these things at supper or in department stores, medical hospitals, churches, universities, or government departments, or in sessions with a counselor, psychotherapist, priest, analyst, guru, teacher, or master. In these places, and with these people, you rarely accomplish the aims and goals that you can accomplish in an experiential session.

What happens during experiential sessions does not ordinarily happen in most other circumstances, in most other sessions. What is accomplished through experiential sessions is not ordinarily accomplished in most other sessions. Perhaps it is understandable, therefore, that some of the things you do in experiential sessions are so uncommon and unusual.

Are You Excited About Going Into A Scene Of Strong Feeling And Discovering A Deeper Potential For Experiencing?

In Step 1, you first find a scene of strong feeling. Then, you do something rather strange. You enter into that scene. You live in it. You go further inside it. You actually go much further into the scene than what occurred when the scene originally took place. The scene may have taken only a few seconds or a few minutes when it actually happened. In the session, you will likely take much longer to explore inside the scene, to go down further inside it.

You study the scene from deep inside in order to discover the deeper potential for experiencing. This is the jewel, the wonderful discovery, that awaits your exploration of the scene of strong feeling.

Are you excited about finding a scene of strong feeling, entering into it, living and being in it, and then discovering the deeper potential for experiencing? Can you be excited that virtually every scene of strong feeling, if entered into and explored properly, can bring you to the discovery of a new, deeper potential for experiencing?

Some of these scenes are of a wonderful strong feeling, and others are of an intensely painful feeling. In either case, it is rare that anyone typically, deliberately, and enthusiastically plunges down inside the scene. You may commonly talk about the scene, discussing it from all angles. However, it is rare for you to be excited about the prospect of going down inside the scene and living and being in it again, more deeply and carefully than when it actually happened. Are you excited?

Experiential Sessions Are Probably Unique In Seeking To Discover The Person You Are Capable Of Becoming

The first step of each session aims to find the deeper potential for experiencing, the experiencing that you are capable of having, the experiencing that lies deep within you, a potentiality. The aim is to help discover the person you are capable of becoming. This aim is rare. It is exceedingly rare.

There may be people who poke inside you, who want to know you, who want to know what you are made of. Think of a truly close friend, an enemy who must size up the opponent, a mate or soul mate, a detective, a novelist, a person who is going to work with you on a serious mission, or a psychotherapist, anyone whose intent it is to probe inside you. These people have reasons to know you well. It is exceedingly rare, virtually unknown, however, for these people to seek to discover the kind of person you are capable of being or becoming.

These people have other agendas. One major reason is to know, to understand, the underlying causes and determinants of the person you are. Other people may know that you are a dedicated soul, a person who cannot be trusted, a firmly ambitious person, or a crackpot. They want to get at the causes, the determinants. They want to know what made or makes you the person you are. Another reason is to uncover the underlying problems, the difficulties, the inner screwups. Psychotherapists refer to these as the psychopathology, the inner conflicts, the intrapsychic pathology, the roots of the mental illness and disease, and the conflictual psychodynamics. A third reason is to know the parts of you that do not show, the aspects of you that you keep hidden, the things about you that a person would probably see if they knew you better. Then they might uncover your bad habits, the awful attitudes, the rules by which you live, the temper you really have, the peculiar things you do, the weird sexual practices, the personal oddities that do not easily show on the surface.

Lots of people want to know you, even to know you deep inside. However, it is rare for someone to seek to discover the kind of person you are capable of becoming. You may have many reasons to see what you are really like, to probe down inside. But it is exceedingly rare that the reason you seek to probe down inside is to discover what kind of qualitatively new person you are capable of becoming. Yet this is the aim of Step 1. How do you feel about this reason, about undergoing Step 1? Are you excited, impassioned about discovering what lies deep inside, about discovering the kind of person you are truly capable of becoming, even if that person is not at all like who you are now? Think about it. It is a rare reason for having a session.

Experiential Sessions Are Probably Unique In Being Able To Actually Reach What Is Deeper Inside You

Suppose that it makes sense for you to believe that there are things deep inside of you. These things may be considered qualities, characteristics, wishes, wants, or possibilities for experiencing, but the idea is that they are so deep inside that you do not know they exist or what they are. If you do believe in something deep inside, something like a possibility for experiencing sheer intimacy, or the quality of fierce and abiding loyalty, or the characteristic of vengeful hatred, then what can you do to discover what it is? How can you know whatever is truly deep down inside of you?

I would like to be able to discover this by myself, but my real quest is for a workable method, so I am also interested in what methods psychotherapists use to discover what lies deeper inside of their patients. Here are some methods, some of which I might do for myself, and some of which it probably helps for someone like a psychotherapist to use.

- Think in terms of grand polarities. If the way you are on the surface is evidence of one end of the pole, then the other end is deeper inside. For example, if you are conspicuously masculine outside, deep inside you are feminine. If your outside is the picture of weakness, then deep inside you are strong.
- Psychotherapists like to say that they know the deeper, inner qualities of people in particular groups. So, if you have been sexually abused, you are female, or a loved one died recently, psychotherapists believe they know what your deeper insides are. On the other hand, I still do not understand how psychotherapists can really know the inner, deeper characteristics of people who fall into groups.
- Psychotherapists can tell your inner, deeper qualities from things about your infancy and childhood, such as whether you were raised by your father, you were an only child, or your parents were controlling or had trouble communicating with one another. If you read about this in books, see if you can learn how, for example, being an only child means you should have this or that inner, deeper quality or characteristic. I have never found this out.

- Psychotherapists can tell what you are like deep inside if they diagnose you as, for instance, schizophrenic, suffering from a post-traumatic stress disorder, or agoraphobic. Again, it is hard to tell how psychotherapists know what the deeper insides are like for people who are given these labels.

- If you have a surface symptom, you can research what the deeper insides are like of people with that same symptom. For example, a headache means that deep inside you have repressed aggression, or a skin rash indicates tabooed sexual impulses. It is a mystery how psychotherapists found these things out in the first place.

- Some theories pronounce what all people are like deep down inside, so you can know that deep down inside you have maternal instincts, inferiority complexes, or aggressive impulses. Pick a theory and trust what it proclaims.

- Learn a decoding system, so that something that is manifest is a code for something deeper inside. For example, a hole is the code for vagina, and a snake is the code for penis.

- Take a psychological test to determine what your deeper insides are like. There are hundreds and hundreds of personality tests, although I have never found out how answering test questions in this or that way can identify your inner, deeper potentiality.

- Trust that your deeper insides will surface when you are in a state of reduced control. Let your thoughts flow freely, get high on drugs, dance with exuberance, put on a blindfold and stand in the middle of a noisy group, paint pictures without constraint, or be naked and loud in a group of other naked, loud people.

The first step of each experiential session aims to discover the possibility or potentiality for experiencing that is deep inside you. You can use other ways if you are passionate about touching and being touched by what is deeper inside you, but I believe the first step in an experiential session is better than any other way I know. Indeed, I doubt if most other ways can truly let you touch or be touched by what is deep inside you. I do believe that experiential sessions are unique in enabling you to discover what is deep inside you.

Experiential Sessions Are Probably Unique In Being Able To Actually Reach The Precious, Innermost Core Of The Person You Are

There are sessions that highlight contemplation, use guided imagery, analyze dreams, develop a strong relationship with a therapist, have you go through birth, do free association, relive powerful traumas, relive past lives, and undergo powerful emotions. The problem is that few, if any, of these methods are designed to reach that precious, innermost core of the person you are, that continuing sense of self, that sense of I-ness, that precious sense of identity.

Instead of reaching that precious, innermost core, most other methods tend to preserve that core while seeking to change something else about you. Most other sessions work at changing some way that you behave, some way that you react and respond, some thought or idea, some outlook or way you think about the person you are, or how you came to be the way you are. These other sessions seek to work on your lack of trust, over-emotionality, insecurity, anger, impulses, controls, need for affection, symptoms, compulsiveness, poor attention, history, or hypersexuality.

These other sessions fail to reach the innermost core of the person who has the behavior, the you who does the reacting and responding, and who has the thought, idea, outlook, or need for affection. Indeed, most sessions count on immunizing and preserving the innermost you, that precious sense of I-ness. You are the one who has the insight and realization, who helps change your thoughts, ideas, and behaviors. You may change all sorts of things about you, but never, ever sacrifice the precious innermost you. That is the rule in most sessions.

You are here even after they remove the baby who is born, the infected finger, or the leg. Those operations do not reach the essential you. You are here even after they remove your car, your home, your money, and your freedom. They cannot remove the innermost, precious you. You are here when the therapist says all those things, but nothing that is said can threaten or change the precious, innermost you who weighs, takes in, and listens to all those words. That precious, innermost sense of I-ness, of the you who you are, remains safely here, unreached, untouched, and unchanged.

Perhaps the only exception is when you are on the verge of dying. When the gun is pointed at your head, you have more to lose than a mere way of acting and behaving, a mere outlook or way of thinking, a mere symptom or lack of impulse control. When you face the certainty of immediate death, that precious, innermost sense of I-ness knows it has been reached; this is a whole new ball game.

In the third step of an experiential session, you are invited to move out of the innermost, precious person or self who you are and into being a radical, new, innermost self. In the fourth step, you are invited to remain being this qualitatively whole new person from now on. The stakes are almost as high as they can be. The precious, innermost core of the person you are has been reached and can undergo change. There can be a new sense of I-ness, a new sense of the person you are.

Each experiential session offers you the opportunity, the choice. Only you can accept or decline the choice. Nevertheless, what seems unique about experiential sessions is that they can actually get at, reach, affect your precious, innermost core

If What Happens In An Experiential Session Is Scary,
Maybe You Should Not Try To Have Experiential Sessions

You may feel scared when you read about what happens in an experiential session, or when you hear a tape of a teacher going through his or her own session. You may raise some sensible concerns. You may bring up some sensible objections and cite some sensible worries. You are scared. Each session starts with the practitioner getting ready to have strong feelings and to give up the minute-to-minute, civilized control over strong feelings. You bellow and blow, scream and yell, for less than a minute. Then you are ready to begin a session. Perhaps you immediately worry: "Suppose the person has a heart condition. Isn't that dangerous? Won't that push an unstable person off the deep end? What if the person has learned that screaming and yelling are not normal?"

The more you see and hear about what happens in a session, the more you pour out your worries and fears: "Maybe it's not good to dwell on times that are so traumatic. Maybe they should be left alone . . . Suppose a person gets caught in reliving bad scenes from childhood. Isn't there a danger of never getting out? What if I can't remember much of what happens? What if I find that I am someone who likes to abuse children? I am supposed to *like* that? How could I accept that, deep down, I am an ax murderer? I should just go out and kill people? If I find something deeper inside me, isn' t it dangerous if I act like that? Suppose it's against my nature, what I know is right and wrong? If I start doing crazy things in the session, how do I know that I won't do them when the session is over? It sounds like I would just start doing whatever I want, whenever I want. What about other people? Do I just stop thinking about the consequences on other people?"

These are very sensible questions. However, if they are asked with a healthy dose of fear, if you are scared by what happens in an experiential session, perhaps experiential sessions are not for you, at least not now. If your sensible questions stem from a healthy fear, and if almost any attempt to answer the questions has little or no effect on that underlying fear, then consider giving this book to someone you think would be more excitedly passionate and less worried about what happens in an experiential session.

There is something wholesomely honest in the father who says: "When I thought of a scene of strong feeling, I thought of just a few days ago. I was changing my baby daughter's diaper, and I got so scared because I was fascinated by her vulva. I even thought about touching her! It was disgusting! Thinking about scenes like that is scary. I don't know if I can do it." In contrast, it is not wholesomely honest when this concrete worry is hidden, disguised, wrapped in abstract gauze, or swathed in cerebral gossamer. Instead of mentioning his baby daughter, he launches into a lecture about how cultures vary in their rules and regulations, and the role of religion in determining infants' rights throughout history. It would have been a real feat to peel away the layers of disguise and acknowledge that he was freaked out by his repulsive fascination with his baby daughter's genitals.

There are many things for you to do in an experiential session. If these things are too scary for you, perhaps it is better for you to decline having the session.

With Rare Exception, Everyone Spends Their Whole Life
Not Doing Anything To Become What They Can Become
And To Be Free Of Their Painful Scenes.
Are You Ready To Be One Of Those Rare Exceptions?

This is the question I have asked just about everyone I could find to ask: "What do you do on a regular basis, maybe once a week, once a month, or once or twice a year, to become more of the person you are capable of becoming; to feel better; to become closer to an ideal, optimal, or good person; to be free of the painful scenes and situations in your personal life; to make things better; and to be free of the painful feelings you have?"

I have asked professional colleagues who are psychotherapists. I have chaired several panels and symposia at professional conferences and invited well-known colleagues to give their answers to this question. I have asked priests, friends, taxi drivers, novelists, professors, philosophers, cooks, plumbers, students, engineers, investment counselors, librarians, and shop owners—all sorts of real people.

Most people seem to do absolutely nothing. Some mention something that is vague, but sounds good, until you get closer to what it actually is. Then it almost evaporates into virtually nothing. "I do dream analysis." Marvelous. What do you actually do? She keeps a log of the general themes of some of her dreams. "I do self-exploration." While that sounds impressive, what he actually does is think about himself and his life while driving to and from his work. "I do meditation." I am impressed, but much less so when I find that this means she tries to let her thoughts drift while she has breakfast or goes shopping at the grocery store or reads the newspaper. "I go on a pilgrimage." Every two or three years he travels to the Alps, stays in a cabin with friends, and spends the day alone, in the mountains, at the same spot every time he goes back. There is something hallowed about returning to the same place and seeing the same view.

Some people go over and over the problem or the bad scene until it loses its pain, its hurt. When things get really awful, some people play little games that they liked when they were children, like carving things out of soap, playing checkers by oneself, or playing a harmonica. Some people indulge themselves if things fall apart. They take hours and hours to shop for a dress; spend the whole afternoon drinking port, smoking a cigar, and listening to classical music; spend hours preparing a gourmet meal; or rent an expensive sports car for the whole day and go for a long ride in the country.

Some people take time out to deliberately be alone. They spend the weekend at a camp, at a retreat, in prayer, in the bush, on a boat, in the desert. They are alone, far away from the problems and pains.

When things are really bad, some people say that they find a friend to talk things over with. This is a special friend, a close friend whom they trust, perhaps a person who is wise. What seems to be so valuable here is not the actual content of what the friend says, but rather the prized sense of having someone to talk to, someone who is there when there is a problem or a troublesome worry. Some people count on religious ritual, prayer, or reading a religious text. Some people try hard to think about the problem and to figure out when it began and what caused it. Some people work at adopting more helpful philosophies, better ways of looking at things, a more realistic or optimistic outlook, a better attitude, or a different way of thinking about things. Some people try to be solution oriented, using clever games and tricks to produce solutions for whatever is bothering them. Some people find it helpful to do such creative activities as painting, dancing, playing music, and sculpting.

There are many other things that people do to feel better, become better people, feel less bad, and get over pains and hurts. But most of them are not done regularly, and most are not impressively effective.

Most people do nothing. Except for perhaps a token few minutes, every day is spent doing nothing, certainly nothing effective, to become the person they can become and to be free of the painful scenes in their world. Take almost any day of any week in any community, and it is the rarest of persons who does anything reasonably effective to become the person he or she can become, free of the painful scenes and feelings. I want to be one of those exceedingly rare people. Do you?

"Does It Work?" Means "Are You Good Enough To Be Able To Go Through The Four Steps Of The Session?"

Psychotherapy researchers like to ask if a particular psychotherapy works. These researchers look at a patient and describe him or her as having something wrong, a psychological or psychiatric problem or condition. The patient sees things that aren't really there, feels gloomy and wants to kill herself, or has a borderline mental illness. "Does it work?"

means that if the psychotherapist administers the particular psychotherapy, will the treatment get rid of the patient's seeing things that aren't really there? Will the patient no longer feel gloomy and want to kill herself? Does the patient no longer have the borderline mental illness?

In an experiential session, one goal is to discover a deeper potential for experiencing and to integrate that as part of the whole new person you become in the fourth step. A related goal is to find a scene of strong feeling and, if it is a painful scene with painful feelings, be free of that painful scene and painful feeling.

"Does it work?" means "Are you good enough to be able to go through the four steps of the session?" The test is really a test of knowing enough and being skilled enough to go through each of the four steps. If the answer is yes, that means you are able to go through the four steps. If the answer is no, you have more learning to do. The test is a test of knowing enough and being competent enough. It is not a test of the methods of going through the four steps. It is not a test of whether the four steps work. It is a test of your knowledge and ability.

"It Works" Means "In The Session, You Were Able To Become The Person You Can Become And To Be Free Of The Painful Scene And Feelings." How Can These Magnificent Changes Continue From Then On, Outside The Session?

In Step 4, you will become the whole new person that you are capable of becoming, based on the deeper potential for experiencing that you discovered in the first step. You are also free of the painful scene of strong, painful feeling that you began the session with. The session is really over when you carry out the homework, that is, when you live as and are the whole new person, undergoing the new experiencing, in some scene or situation after the session, in the real world. Then, the session is over. You have completed the four steps, and now, some hours after the session, you are undergoing the new experiencing, being the new person and behaving and experiencing life as the new person. You are doing your homework.

Instead of asking, "Does it work?" the more meaningful questions are: "How can these magnificent changes remain? How can they be made a solid part of the new person from now on?" If you were the whole new person in the session and while doing your homework after the session, how can you remain the whole new person? How can you be the whole new person more fully, more enjoyably, in more and more situations, and for years to come? If, by the end of the session, you were free of the painful scenes and the painful feelings in the scenes, how can you remain free after the session? How can you be free of the painful scene and the painful feeling in that scene, from now on?

Asking "Does it work?" does not make much sense. If you go through the four steps, you will have become the person you are capable of becoming, and you will be free of painful scenes. The more meaningful question is, "How can I make the changes last, spread out, and be more accompanied by good feelings?" Answering this question will make the experiential method better and better.

If You Are Truly Passionate About What Happens In An Experiential Session, Then You Can Have Your Own Experiential Sessions

The purpose of this chapter is not to give you an in-depth, nuts-and-bolts, careful description of how to go through an experiential session. That is the job of Chapters 5 through 8. Instead, the purpose is to give you a sound overview of what happens in an experiential session so you can decide if there is a glow of passion in you for having these sessions. This is the purpose of introducing you to experiential sessions.

Now it is up to you. Is there a glow of excitement, enthusiasm, and passion about having your own sessions? If so, then you can have your own experiential session.

blank

3

Here Are Some Guidelines Before Having Experiential Sessions

The specific details of how to have your own experiential sessions are given in Chapters 5 through 8. The purpose of this chapter is to first present some helpful guidelines.

THIS BOOK IS A COMPLETE GUIDE, UNLESS YOU ARE CURIOUS TO KNOW MORE

This book is a complete guide for people who are interested in having their own experiential sessions, including those who know little or nothing about experiential sessions. Whether or not you are familiar with experiential sessions, you are certainly entitled to wonder if this is the only book you will need.

The answer is yes. This book is a complete guide. However, some people want to know even more than what is covered in this book. They are curious, either in the beginning, when they are just learning about having their own sessions, or later, after they have become fairly proficient at having their own sessions. For those of you who are still curious, you are invited to take a look at one or more of the three books mentioned below (the publishing details are given in Chapter 9) to supplement this guide for having your own experiential sessions.

You might be curious about the general philosophy underlying experiential sessions, the experiential conceptualization of human beings, the experiential model or picture of what people are like, where it all comes from in the first place, how an infant is created and becomes a person, how personal and social worlds are constructed, how and why people act the way they do, how and why good and bad feelings happen, and what a person can become—most of the deep issues and questions that have been debated since philosophers and other thinkers have been fascinated with the in-depth understanding of themselves and human beings in general. If you are especially curious about the experiential positions on these issues and answers to these questions, please read a book that presents the experiential philosophy and psychology (Mahrer, 1989a), a revision of a book originally published in 1978.

Experiential sessions can include working with your dreams. *Becoming The Person You Can Become* includes enough information for you to have experiential sessions working with your dreams. However, if you are curious to learn much more about the experiential way of understanding and using dreams, both in having your own experiential sessions and doing experiential psychotherapy, please read a book that is wholly dedicated to providing the experiential approach to the age-old fascination with dreams and their use (Mahrer, 1989b).

If you are a psychotherapist, you may be curious about experiential psychotherapy, including its conceptualization and practice. Although I have written a number of books during the slow and gradual course of evolving an experiential psychotherapy, I think I have evolved it about as far as I am able to in a book published rather recently (Mahrer, 1996).

Becoming the Person You Can Become is complete enough, however, to guide you through your own experiential sessions.

As I wrote this book, the person I had in mind was one who was genuinely interested in having his or her own sessions. Later, I had a twinge of worry because I had included almost no citations to the works of other practitioners, scientists, and researchers. My first inclination was to add a respectable number of references at appropriate places in the text. That inclination did not last long. Whereas citations might make the book appear more sophisticated and respectable, my main concern was to tell you how to have your own experiential sessions; if a citation, a quotation, or a reference helped, I would include it. Because I have not included many, I leave the book open to criticism that there are virtually no references.

It is also helpful to study tapes of people who are good at having their own experiential sessions. This book is all you need to be able to have your own sessions, but it is also helpful to study experiential sessions of people who are rather good at having their own sessions. I have made audiotapes of two of my sessions. I believe it is helpful to listen carefully to my sessions, the sessions of another experiential teacher, or those of another person who seems to be rather good at having experiential sessions.

Sooner or later, either as you read this book or begin to have your own experiential sessions, it is a good idea to study tapes of actual sessions carried out by practitioners who are fairly good at having their own sessions.

THROUGHOUT THIS BOOK, I WILL REFER TO YOU AS THE "STUDENT" OR "PRACTITIONER"

When I picture you having your own session, I think of you as the "practitioner." That word seems to be appropriate whether you are just learning or are relatively accomplished. When I think of you as the person who is seeking to learn how to have your own sessions, I will use the word "student."

When I am in a group of people who are interested in learning how to have their own experiential sessions, I think of myself as a "teacher." I also think of myself as a teacher when I am with one person who is seeking to learn how to have a session, and I am guiding, coaching, teaching, or showing that person how to go through a session.

When I am in a room with one person, and I show this person how to proceed through a session, working closely with him or her in going through the session, I am the person's guide. I am the person's teacher. The experiential psychotherapist is perhaps best referred to as the experiential teacher or teacher-therapist.

If the person is intent on learning how to have a session, I think of that person as a "student." If the person has little or no intent to have their own experiential session, I think of myself as the experiential teacher-therapist, because most of what I do is a matter of teaching, showing, guiding, and coaching that person on what to do and how to do it. I am still puzzled about what word to use to refer to the person I am working with. If the person is not here as a student, the word "student" is inappropriate, but words like "client" or "patient" have never seemed right to me, especially since so much of what I do is to be the teacher who shows the person what to do and how to do it. Perhaps the word "person" is a little better than "client" or "patient."

My First Job Is To Give You A Proper Introduction To Experiential Sessions; If You Have A Passionate Interest, My Next Job Is To Show You How To Have Your Own Sessions

Having your own experiential sessions usually means having a session every few weeks or so, for the rest of your life. If you are going to make these sessions a part of your life, they should be important to you; you should have a serious passion for experiential sessions. You now have a picture of the two goals of having a session and of what happens inside a session. I want to bring you even closer to what an experiential session is like. If, after a proper introduction, you still have a passionate interest in having experiential sessions, then you are ready to learn how.

A proper introduction means reading Chapters 1 through 4. Read these chapters to see if you have a passionate interest in having your own experiential sessions. (You may even read the rest of the book, but mainly to confirm that there is indeed a glow of enthusiasm in you.) If you have that glow of passionate interest after you read these introductory chapters, you are ready to learn how to have your own sessions, perhaps to make experiential sessions a part of the rest of your life.

A proper introduction can include hearing or seeing someone else having a session. You can listen to audiotapes of my own experiential sessions and then ask yourself if having such sessions is interesting to you. These tapes are useful to help you learn how to have your own sessions, but the first question is whether there is a passionate interest in you. Listen to these tapes and see.

You can attend an introductory workshop. In a genuinely introductory workshop, you might see a teacher working with a person from the group. Most teachers simply start with the first few steps in the session, showing the person what to do and how to do it, and they stop if the person is not ready or, as is common, is not able to do it reasonably well. In an introductory workshop, the teacher does not usually try to push a person through a whole session. Sometimes—rarely—a person has a natural talent for going through a session, or most of the way through a session, and the teacher will continue working with the person. The teacher and the person may—very rarely—go through an entire session. Almost always, the teacher stops when the person is ready to stop or simply not skilled enough to be able to move through the immediate sub-step. You do not need to attend an introductory workshop, but a proper introduction can include watching another person go through a session or a part of a session.

A proper introduction does not involve a therapist doing an entire demonstration session with a client or volunteer. An experiential teacher-therapist will probably invite people in a workshop to see what it is actually like to undergo the opening steps of a session. The teacher-therapist coaches a person from the group at the workshop in the initial sub-steps, or however far the person is ready and able to go. However, it is rare that the demonstration session will go through an entire experiential session.

In contrast, it is common for most therapists of other types of therapies to give a workshop by doing a whole demonstration session with a client or a volunteer from the workshop. Often, workshop participants see a videotape of an entire session of the therapy.

In an experiential workshop, the introductory workshop does not include a videotape of the experiential teacher-therapist going through an entire session with a student or another person. Nor does the workshop include the experiential teacher-therapist doing a demonstration session with a person from the workshop.

You may hear an audiotape of a person going through an experiential session, but the person is skilled enough to go through his or her own session. When the experiential teacher-therapist works with a person, the teacher-therapist is not "doing therapy" on a client. Instead, the teacher-therapist shows the person what to do and how to do it, and the person does it if he or she is ready, willing, and reasonably able. If not, the session stops. Since the main purpose of an introductory workshop is to determine if the person has a genuine enthusiasm for having a session, it seems more helpful for people in the workshop to listen to or watch a skilled practitioner going through his or her own experiential session, rather than watching a therapist do a demonstration therapy session with a client or volunteer.

A proper introduction can include what happens inside of you as you begin to go through an experiential session. I know it sounds backward, but one good way to see if you have a passionate interest in having experiential sessions is to have experiential sessions. Read Chapter 5 and try to carry out the first sub-step, and then the next, and the next. Keep going as far as you can, even if you get only partway into the first step. Or, have an experiential teacher guide you through part of an experiential session.

It is quite likely that something will happen inside of you when you actually lean back and close your eyes, when you spend 30 seconds or so bellowing as loud as you can, when you look for and find a scene of strong feeling, or when you go even further into the session. Something will happen, like the tension in your stomach going away, there is a rising sense of excitement, you can hardly believe you remembered that time from so long ago, or you feel surprisingly alive as you loudly grunt like a virile animal.

Be willing to see what it is like to begin to have an experiential session. Volunteer in a workshop. Ask a teacher to take you through a session as far as you are ready and able to go. Listen to tapes of sessions, read Chapter 5, and then try it out for yourself. By giving yourself a proper trial, you give yourself a proper introduction. You are seeing for yourself whether experiential sessions are for you, whether there is a spark of enthusiasm in you for having your own sessions.

After a proper introduction, if you have a passionate interest, then you are ready to have your own sessions. When I give classes or workshops, the first several classes or the initial workshop is to provide the students with a proper introduction. If some of the people do have a solid interest, a glow of passion, then I want very much to work with them to show them how to have their own experiential sessions. I respect that glow of passionate excitement about having your own experiential sessions. I regard it as essential.

If you go through a proper introduction but that glow of excitement is not there, then you may as well stop—at least for now. Six months or two years from now you may give yourself another proper introduction and find that the enthusiasm is there. Or, maybe not. When it is there, you are ready to have your own experiential sessions.

WHEN DO YOU HAVE AN EXPERIENTIAL SESSION?

Here are some guidelines for when, how frequently, and for how long you might have your own experiential sessions.

Have a session when you have had a strong feeling. Have a session within a few days or so of a strong feeling occurring in you. Look for a feeling that stands out as particularly strong for you. The scene may have been dramatic or mundane; it may seem to account for the strong feeling or have little or nothing to do with why this feeling was so strong in you. The feeling may have been visible to others or completely private. The feeling may have been quiet, not conspicuous, not showing on the outside—saturating, but internal.

The strong feeling may have been good, pleasant, exciting, happy. But, more commonly, you have a session when the strong feeling is painful, agonizing, awful.

Of course, the scene or situation can be one that occurs in your actual life, your waking life. However, I almost feel compelled to have a session when the strong feeling occurs in a dream. Scenes of strong feeling from your real world are precious. Scenes of strong feeling from dreams are, I believe, even more precious (Mahrer, 1989b).

Have sessions at least every few weeks. I seem to have settled into a routine of having sessions about every two weeks or less. If I wait longer than two weeks, I find that I pay two penalties. One is that I begin to hear a voice nagging at me, scolding me: "Have a session! You'd better have a session! You think you can get away without having

56

a session?" The other penalty is that I usually start unraveling, coming unglued. Old painful scenes and feelings gradually begin to trouble me again. The net result is that I find it is helpful for me to have a session at least every two weeks or less.

Have sessions for the rest of your life. Some things you do on an "as-needed" basis. You go to a hospital emergency ward when you are hurt or very sick.. You call the person who repairs washers and dryers when your appliances need to be fixed. Other things are "maintenance tasks" that you probably will keep doing for the rest of your life. If you pray every day or go to church every week, you may do those things for the rest of your life. If you take a bath or shower every day, you may continue doing so for the rest of your life.

Experiential sessions are for your entire life. They should be part of the ritual of your life, whenever they are needed (or at least every two weeks or less), from now on.

If there is no "juice" for a session, don't have one. It is Wednesday evening. You have scheduled a session for this evening. You go into the room, lie back in the chair, and close your eyes. After a few minutes or so, you realize that you are not especially excited about having a session. There is no juice for having a session. But you keep on. Five or ten minutes later, you know that you are still flat. Enthusiasm is low, too low for a session. I find that the best thing to do in such situations is to stop. Don't go through the motions of having a session when there is no juice for one.

For me, this happens perhaps once a year. It is rare, but it happens.

HAVING EXPERIENTIAL SESSIONS IS FOR ALMOST EVERYONE, NOT JUST PEOPLE WITH SPECIAL QUALITIES AND ABILITIES

It is easy to believe that you need special qualities and abilities in order to have experiential sessions, or for the sessions to be any good. That belief just does not hold. In general, almost anyone can have experiential sessions. Nevertheless, there are some helpful guidelines here.

You do not need the qualities and abilities that you probably think you need. When you read about what happens in experiential sessions or when you listen to an experiential session, it is easy to believe that you are not capable of having sessions because you do not have those special qualities and abilities. You worry because you cannot scream or make loud noises, you cannot close your eyes and see things, you cannot remember much of what happened to you when you were a young child, you don't have a great sense of humor, you did not go to college, or you know little to nothing about psychology or psychotherapy.

Your ability to have fine experiential sessions has nothing to do with how long you stayed in school or the grades you earned. It has nothing to do with what you know or do not know about psychology, psychotherapy, or any other field. The person you are in ordinary, daily life has virtually nothing to do with what you can learn to do in your own sessions. You do not need to have a booming voice or to be a screamer in order to have strong feelings in your session. You don't need to have a creative imagination to be able to close your eyes and see things in the session. You can find early scenes, even if you have no memory of the childhood incidents that your brother recounts. You will be able to do things in the session that you almost never do in your daily life. After a number of sessions, you will realize that you can do all sorts of things in your sessions that you do not do when you are crossing streets, eating supper, talking with a close friend.

The readiness and passion may not be here today, but they may be here tomorrow or next year. In order for you to have your own experiential sessions, you must have some genuine readiness, enthusiasm, and passion for experiential sessions. Those feelings may not be here today, but that is not necessarily permanent. You may easily find yourself ready and passionate tomorrow, some weeks or months from now, or even years from now. In the future, you may feel ready and passionate about having your own sessions when you find yourself caught in that same kind of painful situation, when you have a dream that somehow stays with you during the day, when you move to another country and find that the same kinds of painful scenes are still present in your new life, when you meet someone who has their own experiential sessions, or when somehow you just feel ready and passionate about having your own sessions.

If you are a professional psychotherapist, you may find it especially difficult to have your own experiential sessions. Having your own experiential sessions seems to be harder if you are a professional psychotherapist.

At first, it seemed to make sense that a Jungian analyst or social learning therapist would immediately understand that experiential sessions are experiential, not Jungian or social learning. But that wasn't the cause of the difficulty at all. Most professional psychotherapists know that these sessions are not psychotherapy. To begin with, there is no psychotherapist and no patient. No, the conceptual underpinnings had little to do with the difficulty of so many professional psychotherapists with having their own experiential sessions.

The main explanation seems to be that professional psychotherapists love to play the game of psychotherapy, in which they get to play the role of the professional psychotherapist. They did not go through school to learn how to do psychotherapy to themselves, and they are not at all happy about the possibility of losing clients and patients to some method that people can do by themselves.

Accordingly, it is easy to see how professional psychotherapists can view having one's own sessions as a threat. If they love to play the role of professional psychotherapist, they lose the fun of that role when they instead go into a room alone and have their own session. They lose the fun of that role when prospective clients and patients are busy having their own sessions instead of playing the client-therapist game with the professional psychotherapist.

Having your own experiential sessions is for almost everyone, with the exception perhaps of professional psychotherapists who may view having one's own experiential session as depriving them of their cherished role and cherished patients.

Do not have experiential sessions when you are high on drugs or alcohol. It may seem logical that having a session would be helped by being high on drugs or alcohol. That state loosens ordinary controls, which should be a help. However, I find that if you are high on drugs or alcohol, you will have a very hard time having an experiential session. Getting high harms; it doesn't help.

If you are thinking of taking drugs or alcohol to help you have a fine experiential session, don't do it. Getting high will make the session worse, not better. This holds true whether you are a relative novice or a seasoned veteran at getting high.

If being high from drugs is part of your lifestyle, wait until you are free from drugs before you have an experiential session. If you are on prescription drugs because a doctor says you have some illness or psychiatric problem, wait until you are no longer in that state, until getting high from drugs is no longer a part of your world. If you are high on drugs because some professional believes that drugs keep you from being a certain way, keep a supposed condition from worsening, or prevent you from doing something you should not do, wait until you are free of drugs.

When a person is high on drugs, drunk on alcohol, or high for whatever reason, the session tends to just drift around. It is hard to complete even the initial sub-steps of the warm-up and to find a scene of strong feeling. It is most sensible not to have a session when you are high, for whatever reason.

Experiential sessions are fine if you think of yourself, or others think of you, as crazy, psychotic, weird, out of your mind, out of control, or close to being like this. It almost always happens when professional psychotherapists or others in or close to the mental health field hear about experiential sessions, and even when ordinary people hear about sessions: They raise some frightening concerns. If a person is crazy, psychotic, out of their mind, wouldn't experiential sessions make them even worse? Wouldn't an experiential session drive a person off the edge, especially if he or she is already deranged, sick, or has a tendency to be crazy, lunatic, out of their mind?

In general, the answer is that experiential sessions are suitable for you, and you are suitable for experiential sessions, even if you think of yourself, or others think of you, as insane, demented, out of your mind, or crazy. You can go through an experiential session, easily and well, whether or not you think of yourself, or others think of you, this way.

The trouble is that most professional psychotherapists do not use the commonplace terminology of "insane," "demented," "out of one's mind," "crazy," or "weird." They use technical phrases like "paranoid schizophrenia," "borderline state," and "psychotic pathological process." I have no idea what those phrases really mean because I think in terms of an experiential conceptual system; although those phrases have technical meaning in some conceptual systems, they do not in the experiential conceptual system. I have trouble understanding exactly what you mean if you ask about the appropriateness of experiential sessions for someone who is a witch, a warlock, a paranoid schizophrenic, or a borderline. The same applies for someone in danger of a virulent psychotic pathological process. I cannot answer because those terms are meaningless in the context of experiential therapy.

I also tend to think that you are asking about yourself if you question whether experiential sessions are all right for someone who is, for example, very old or legally blind or psychotic. When you ask, "Suppose the person is a paranoid schizophrenic, won't an experiential session worsen and inflame the condition?" I assume this question refers to the questioner, so I have to apologize when the questioner explains that she is the chief psychiatrist of a hospital and, no, she does not consider herself a florid paranoid schizophrenic. Even if the questioner is indeed asking about himself or herself, my answer is the same: Experiential sessions are fine if you think of yourself as insane, deranged, demented, out of your mind, crazy, or weird.

Experiential sessions start with finding scenes of strong feeling. These may consist of scenes in which you are terrified because you were sure there was a monster inside of your brain; you fell apart and lost control when you knew the neighbor's cat was controlling your mind; you felt uncanny dread because your husband was really an alien

63

inside of your husband's body; you opened the refrigerator and saw the face of your dead mother on the second shelf; or you knew that the voice inside of your head was that of the devil.

These are fine scenes of strong feeling, whether or not they include a sense of being out of your mind, deranged, crazy, psychotic. As you will see in Chapter 5, one useful way of finding scenes of strong feeling is to explicitly look for scenes in which there are strong feelings of being crazy, out of your mind, psychotic. Experiential sessions are designed to free you of the awful scenes of painful feeling. If you start with scenes in which the strong feeling is that of being mad, berserk, out of your mind, or falling into such horrible states, the session will free you of such scenes and painful feelings. A session may well accomplish this better than virtually any other way that I know. My experience is that the likelihood of somehow bringing about these painful scenes is rather high in many traditional psychotherapies, but virtually nonexistent in experiential sessions.

You can have experiential sessions even if you are scared that particular sub-steps will drive you out of your mind. If you are even slightly inclined to worry about going crazy, losing control, or going out of your mind, there are particular sub-steps that can justify that feeling of being almost terrified. The session begins with giving up the usual, civilized controls by shrieking and yelling, making thunderous noises, and letting your body have a fit. In the first step, you are supposed to throw yourself into a scene of strong feeling, even one that may be utterly painful. Once you are actually living and being in the scene of strong feeling, you go much further by finding the exact instant when the feeling peaks, and then living and being in this moment of peak feeling. In Steps 2 and 3, you must let go of the ordinary person who you are and throw yourself into being an utterly new and different person, an alien and qualitatively different person. These sub-steps can be frightening. You are entitled to be frightened of losing your mind, going crazy, or becoming deranged.

If you arrive at these sub-steps and you are filled with a terror of losing your mind, even if the feeling is justified, does this mean you are not ready for experiential sessions, or that experiential sessions are not for you? My answer is no, and here are some of the considerations that lead me to that answer.

1. In the first few sessions or so, you may indeed arrive at these particular sub-steps and feel terrified of plunging into sheer lunacy. Feel free to stop, to end the session. You can always go back later. After you go through a number of sessions, most people find that their earlier terror at going through these particular sub-steps is replaced by a kind of giddy enthusiasm. Throwing yourself into these sub-steps becomes exhilarating fun.

2. Going through these particular sub-steps is not quite like standing on the ledge of a tall building and being terrified of what happens if you fall. Falling is falling,

65

whether you are terrified or exhilarated. However, if you are extremely scared, you will have real trouble doing those particular sub-steps well enough to worry about losing your mind. It is a Catch-22 situation: that is, if you are scared, you will be unable to do the sub-step well enough to justify being scared of what might happen if you do the sub-step. You are rescued from losing your mind by your fear of losing your mind. In other words, you can do the sub-step well enough to scare you only if you are not scared of doing the sub-step.

3. If you are inclined to do something that might make you crazy, lose your mind, or keep you in a lunatic state for months or years, having an experiential session is not high on the list. I would recommend instead having lots of sessions with a psychotherapist whose thinking is filled with notions of psychosis, mental illness and disease, and sever psychopathology.

4. There may have been people who went off the deep end, lost their minds, after having their own experiential sessions. However, I do not know of any, not even one. Nevertheless, it may have happened; or it may happen soon. If it does, I will worry.

When you are just starting to have experiential sessions, you feel scared that particular sub-steps will drive you crazy. Honor your fear, and stop. I find that these fears evaporate after you allow some sessions to show you what delightful changes can occur when you go through the sessions, including those particular sub-steps.

Experiential sessions are for people who do not think they need treatment from a psychotherapist for a mental illness, sickness, or disease. For purposes of public relations, marketing, and public consumption, most psychotherapists do not restrict their treatment to people with mental illnesses, sicknesses, and diseases. They much prefer extending their services about as far as the market will allow, saying they are here to relieve suffering, offer help, and do something about "personal problems." Nevertheless, it is hard to cover up what so many patients and psychotherapists know, even without saying it out loud: If you are getting treatment from a "shrink," you probably have some sort of mental illness, sickness, or disease. Your mental illness may be common, mild, and treatable in less than a year, but it is a mental illness nonetheless. There must be something wrong, some kind of mental problem, if she is getting treatment from a psychotherapist, and that holds true whether she is the woman who lives in the next apartment, the head of the psychoanalytic institute, your older sister, a professional psychotherapist, a government official, your Aunt Esther, the president of the country, or you.

This is the mind-set: "There must be something wrong with me! I must have some kind of mental illness, disease, or serious problem. Therefore, I need treatment from a psychotherapist." If this is the way you think, experiential sessions are probably not for you. But there is a different mind-set that goes like this: "I hate having that awful feeling in that awful situation. I wish I could be the whole new person I can be, so I am going to have an experiential session." If this is the way you think, then experiential sessions are for you. Experiential sessions are for people who do not fall into the trap of needing treatment from some psychotherapist for a supposed mental illness, sickness, or disease.

Picture people who can confess and complain that they feel rotten, they have painful feelings in painful situations, and they wish they could become everything they can become. Picture a concerned person who listens, puts an understanding look on her face, cocks her head to the side, and says, "There is something wrong with you; you need treatment from a psychotherapist." Now picture the same person who confessed and complained, saying: "Oh, I see. You think in terms of mental illnesses, diseases, and sicknesses that need treatment from a psychotherapist. That way of thinking is crazy! By the way, what do you do when you feel rotten?" Experiential sessions are for people like this.

Experiential sessions are especially for people who like learning and doing by and for themselves. Picture a child who seems content spending time by herself throwing a basketball through the hoop, doing cartwheels until she gets it right, practicing pieces on the piano, mastering control of a soccer ball, reading a book, riding her bicycle for long distances, repairing a flashlight—learning and doing things by herself. Picture people who like to take care of most things by themselves. These are the people who take personal pleasure in cooking for themselves, creating a sculpture on their own, taking care of their own bodies, or writing short stories. These are people who like learning and doing by and for themselves.

Picture a woman in her 40s who is interested in attending a workshop on how to have experiential sessions, but who does not want to be called on to be demonstrated upon and does not want to ask or answer questions in the group. She is here to see and learn, which she does. She gets and reads this book, gets and listens to cassettes of experiential sessions, and becomes increasingly proficient at having her own sessions.

Picture people who are repelled by the idea of being a client or patient to some professional counselor or psychotherapist. There is something wrong and unpleasant about placing oneself in such a role. These people somehow cannot buy the idea that if you have a personal problem, you see a therapist; if there is something bothering or troubling you, the automatic answer is to see a therapist. That idea has a flaw—it is not right.

Picture people who like to keep psychotherapists at a polite, but safe, distance because they feel therapists are not really professionals, that they essentially prey on human frailty and elevate themselves above their clients and patients. These people think of most psychotherapists as frauds, quacks, pseudo-scientists, and pretenders. These people believe that, because human beings are so human, they will always need people like prostitutes and psychotherapists, but perhaps only the prostitutes offer a genuine service. These people prefer working things out by themselves rather than seeking out a special group that loves dressing themselves in the costume of professional psychotherapists. Experiential sessions are for people who are like this. Experiential sessions are for people who like learning and doing by and for themselves.

Experiential sessions are not especially for people who want to be in the role of patient to a person in the role of psychotherapist. In experiential sessions, you do the work by yourself. There are many people for whom it is far more important to be in the role of patient than to carry out their own sessions. These are the people who feel they gain precious, important feelings and understandings when they are in the role of patient to a special person who is in the role of therapist. They have a wonderful sense of being understood; having someone on their side, being watched over by a powerful person; charming a high-powered person; getting very close to someone they would ordinarily not get very close to; having sexual feelings in the company of an attractive person; being cared for by a concerned person; having someone sensitive to talk to; talking at length about marvelous personal things with a person who is truly interested; having a life manager or someone who coaches you through important life decisions; being deeply understood by an intelligent professional person; or of having the special relationship you wished you had had with your mom or dad.

When you have an experiential session, you miss out on the special feelings of being with a special person. If having these special feelings is so important, find someone to play the role of psychotherapist to your role of patient. Experiential sessions will lack that special something that being a patient to a psychotherapist may provide. If those special feelings are so important to you, experiential sessions are probably not for you. Instead, find a person with whom you can play the role of patient to their role of psychotherapist.

In general, experiential sessions are for almost anyone and everyone. They are not restricted to special people with special qualities and abilities.

IF HAVING YOUR OWN EXPERIENTIAL SESSIONS IS SO WONDERFUL, WHY ISN'T IT POPULAR?

I believe there are some good reasons why having your own experiential sessions is not popular now. Some of these reasons can also explain why having your own experiential sessions may not become popular, even though I do hope that almost everyone will have their own experiential sessions some day in the future.

The idea of having your own sessions and how to do them came about only in the past few years. This is the first book that says: "Here is the way to go through an experiential session. The method has been developed and is ready for use. Now it is time for almost everyone to go ahead and have their own experiential session."

My book on dreams (Mahrer, 1989b) was written for psychotherapists and people who wanted to use dreams in their own self-change. However, the people I had in mind were those who already paid close attention to their dreams. I did not think all sorts of people could use dreams in their own sessions. I did not think big enough.

My earlier book on experiential psychotherapy (Mahrer, 1996) was for psychotherapists, not for almost everyone. Only in the final two paragraphs of that book did I write that almost any person can have his or her own experiential sessions.

In other words, only fairly recently has there been a workable method for becoming the person you can become and freeing yourself of painful feelings and the painful scenes in which they occur. And it was only recently that the idea was born that experiential sessions can be carried out by virtually everyone, not just psychotherapists. Let's give experiential sessions a decade or so to see if they become popular.

There is a given sequence of steps, so there is one correct way of proceeding through a session. First, go through Step 1, then Step 2, then Step 3, and finally Step 4. There is a sequence. If you jump from Step 1 to Step 4, or depart in any way from the four steps, the chances of having a successful session are low.

A teacher can listen to a taped session and tell whether you are proceeding through the session correctly or incorrectly. He or she may say: "If you start a session without the warm-up, without doing some exercise to loosen the usual controls over your feelings, it will probably be hard to have a successful session. You went directly from Step 2 to Step 4. Step 4 might be easier to achieve if you first went through Step 3."

Many people are turned off by the idea of an organized sequence of steps. The idea conjures images of some authoritarian rule that is imposed from outside, a lockstep method that everyone must follow in unison, in ridiculous precision.

Many people prefer a method whereby they first get the general idea of what to do, and then go ahead and do it. Just sit quietly and let your thoughts drift. Don't think about what happens. Don't monitor the flow of thoughts. For these people, it is distasteful to have to follow a stepwise regimen.

Many people take pride in demanding plenty of room for their own personal artistry. They value flexibility and shun rigidity. When they hear there are four steps, and they see that there is one correct way of proceeding through a session, some people feel violated. Their personal freedom is threatened. They react against conformity. They turn away from having to go through the steps, and from there being a correct and an incorrect way of proceeding through a session. It does little or no good to argue that the organization is general and loose; although there are some limits, experiential sessions do not discourage personal artistry and flexibility. Still, I have some doubts about how popular experiential sessions will become because there is a given sequence of steps and a correct way of proceeding through a session.

It takes time to know what to do and how to achieve the goals of each of the steps. It takes time to learn the skills well enough to carry them out well enough to go through a complete session. Chapters 5 through 8 tell you what to do while going through each of the steps. Chapter 9 tells you how to develop enough proficiency to be able to have your own sessions.

I believe that having your own experiential sessions will not become wildly popular because it takes will, effort, and actual time to learn what to do and to become good enough to have your own sessions. That is unfortunate, but realistic.

You face the scary risk of actually becoming a whole new person and living in a whole new personal world. The idea of actually becoming a whole new person can seem so appealing on paper. It is celebrated by so many people who write and speak about the wonders of becoming an optimal person; developing your potential; becoming mature, ideal, and the way a person can be; and growing to your fullest.

. The idea sounds good, but take a careful look at the actual contract. You are facing the scary risk of actually becoming a whole new person. You may well lose your old self. The risk is far more than giving up some behavior that you don't much like anyhow, adopting some new philosophy or outlook, or giving up some way that you think. Are you really prepared to risk losing your very self, the essence, the very core of the special, precious person that you are? You risk going out of existence, dying. You risk no longer being the person who has that certain behavior, that philosophy or outlook, and those thoughts. The risk is akin to losing weight or even losing your arm. You risk losing the very essence of the person you are. Are you willing to risk paying what may be the ultimate price to become the whole new person you are capable of becoming?

For many people, the answer is no. It may be all right to sacrifice a behavior or two, or even a way of thinking, as long as "I" am still around. But I will not sacrifice the very core of the person I am to become some other person. This is what you risk when you turn inside to look at the person you are and the person you might be.

The risk is just as great when you look outside at the special things about your personal world. Few people are willing to risk losing the precious things in their personal worlds. Are you willing to let go of your artistic talents so that you no longer paint, compose, play the violin, or dance? Everything is put out on the table, including your precious baby. Are you willing to give up your wealth, your best friend, your life's work, your patrician looks, your strong body, your lovely hair, that precious singing voice, or your older son?

Having experiential sessions is serious. You risk losing your very self and the precious things about you and your personal world. The risk can be too great. The experiential method will have a hard time becoming truly popular.

Experiential sessions may violate your precious beliefs.
Experiential sessions rest on a bed of beliefs that may clash
with and violate some of your own precious beliefs. This
alone will make it difficult for experiential sessions to
become truly popular.

One of the underlying beliefs in experiential sessions is
that you can actually become a qualitatively new person, that
it is valuable and a lifelong mission to become everything
you can be. Not everyone holds such a belief. Indeed, this
belief can easily clash with more common beliefs, such as:
One should learn how to accept oneself. Or, there can be
changes in oneself, but not radical, qualitative changes.

Experiential sessions proclaim that two main goals can be
achieved in a single session, in each experiential session. This
raises the eyebrows of most people, who believe that it takes
decades of real effort to become a whole new person. It
takes many sessions to be truly free of a painful scene and the
painful feeling in the scene. Accomplishing all of this in a
single session is miraculous—or quackery.

Experiential sessions are built on the belief that all of this
can be done by oneself. For many people, this idea is wildly
inconceivable. Accomplishing such major changes must
require the presence of a person with years of professional
training, a person with special knowledge, a particularly wise
person, a learned person, a doctor, a high priest, or a healer.
I cannot achieve these magnificent changes by myself. I am
an ignorant person, a mechanic, an accountant, or a
supervisor—just an ordinary person.

Experiential sessions are grounded in the belief that painful feelings in painful scenes are eliminated by entering more fully into the very "eye" of the pain. This idea violates most beliefs about how to reduce pain, hurt, and suffering by understanding the problem, or finding a solution to the painful situation, or searching here and there for the causes.

Experiential sessions assume that what is deep inside is precious, valuable, the seed of what you can become. This belief violates so many common beliefs that what lurks deep inside are all sorts of things that are bad, wicked, and monstrous. Things to be avoided and guarded against.

Experiential sessions may not become popular because they rely on beliefs that clash with and violate so many deeply held, precious, cherished, and ingrained beliefs of so many people.

. *Making the experiential method popular calls for someone good at making it popular.* I would like many, many people to have their own sessions. I know that it would help if someone handled the marketing, public relations, and popularizing of having your own sessions. I am not that person. Maybe someone like this will come along and help make it popular.

If you are inclined to have your own experiential sessions, I am excited about talking with you, corresponding with you and learning about what seemed to work or not work so well. I think of you as someone who is also drawn toward having these sessions. It is harder for me to think of you as the public, the consumer, or someone to whom I am trying to sell this concept.

When I have the choice, I prefer working at making experiential sessions better, improving this or that part, trying to solve this or that problem, and making this big or little change. I would much prefer spending a day doing that than I would negotiating with a program chair about how to advertise a workshop so we will attract as large a crowd as possible. I would prefer spending hours with someone who is enthusiastic about having sessions, rather than spending the time talking with someone about how to sell experiential sessions in South America. Making these sessions more popular is important, but making them better is even more important to me.

I do think of experiential sessions as magical, wondrous, and designed and developed well enough to accomplish their goals. I envision a fair number of people all over the world having their own experiential sessions. But I also can see some good reasons why there will be limits on the popularity of experiential sessions. I hope it will become as popular as possible and that good people will make experiential sessions better and better, and more and more usable by more and more people.

I WANT EVERYONE TO HAVE EXPERIENTIAL SESSIONS.
IF YOU DO NOT, IF YOU DECLINE OR RAISE OBJECTIONS,
I HAVE AT LEAST THREE REACTIONS

I can picture you reading this book, participating in a workshop, or talking with me face to face. I want you to have your own experiential sessions. I want everyone to have their own experiential sessions. But suppose that you do not. Suppose that you have read enough to decide not to have your own sessions. Suppose that we are in a workshop, and I ask for a volunteer to come up front so I can show you how to begin a session, but you decline. Suppose that a month from now, and a year from now, you still have not had any experiential sessions.

Or suppose that you raise objections. You do not like starting a session by yelling, letting yourself go, kicking, and shrieking. There are lots of ways to become a better person. What makes me think this works? Aren't people going through change all the time? Wouldn't a person get worse? Where is the research to show it is effective? I wouldn't want to end up hurting people, being wild and crazy, or being violent. I know what is deep inside of me. Deep down, everyone is basically alike. I will change when I am ready to change; it can't be forced. The method sounds powerful, so it must be dangerous for some people. Suppose what is deep inside of me is something I don't like? Most psychotherapies have similar goals and methods, so what is so different?

If you are not especially drawn toward having experiential sessions, or you simply decline or raise some questions, concerns, and objections, I have at least three reactions.

1. *I can respect and understand your decision not to have experiential sessions.* I can honestly respect your decision. I acknowledge that many people will decline, and only a

small proportion of people will truly want to have sessions. I honor you and your decision. Of course, it is up to you. I am offering you something I value, inviting you to see if it is appealing to you. If some people say yes, I feel good. I know that having your own sessions works if you are genuinely drawn toward the idea, and if knowing what happens in the sessions is attractive to you. I am that mature. I often feel this way, and it seems right and good.

2. *I can happily fight with you.* At times, with the right people, if you let me, and if I feel solid, grounded, and comfortable with you, I can get so upset, frustrated, annoyed, and angry, that I will fight with you. You are merely raising issues and concerns to ensure that you do not undergo truly deep-seated change. You will never become the person you can become. You are ensuring that the painful scenes in your world will always be there. All your objections and questions are merely decoys and excuses aimed to avoid real, wonderful, deep-seated changes. Whatever matters you raise, I will argue and fight with them. If you have a better way of achieving these two magnificent goals, tell me what it is. I dare you. I challenge you. I am right, and you are wrong. Your reaction to me may be that I am obnoxious. If this is what a person is like who has experiential sessions, you certainly do not want to have them. You think of me as aggressive, a know-it-all. If I want people to have experiential sessions, this is not the way to present the

material. I am bad, strong-willed, disgusting, not respectful, and not empathic. Who do I think I am? I am much too extreme. I should stop criticizing you, yelling at you, and putting you down. Experiential sessions cannot be that good.

3. *I can be happily excited about finding and appreciating your own way of thinking, which makes it sensible for you to say no.* There are times when I am drawn toward grasping, understanding, clarifying, and studying whatever way of thinking lies behind your decision, questions, and objections. What I write is provocative, different, and out of the ordinary. Can you and I come to know and appreciate the good reasons, thoughts, and ideas that make it logical for you to say no, to raise your sound questions and objections? If we take our time, we can learn a lot about your own personal way of thinking. Your decision, issues, and questions are honorable and come from deep-seated notions and ideas. Now I can see what these notions and ideas are. I do see. I respect and appreciate your way of thinking.

You are honestly scared by the idea of becoming a whole new person, the person you are capable of becoming, especially in a single session. "Who knows what I would be like?" If I work with you to try to uncover your beliefs here, it can be exciting for me. I say to you: "The picture I get is that you are afraid that you might do something awful or become some awful person, right? No?" You say: "I have a real temper, and when I get drunk . . . well, I don't drink anymore because I used to get violent. I'd yell and start fights. I'm scared that I'd just get into fights." This is your fear. I can appreciate such a fear. So you already have a picture of what you might become, a person who loses his or her temper and gets into fights, and that is awful. Sure, that makes sense. My picture is different. I see you as finding something so deep inside you that it is a surprise. It is something new. You probably don't know now what you might find, and when you do find it and see what it is, then you can decide whether you do or don't want to be like that. But I see what you mean. Does my picture make a difference, or are you still scared that you will become a person who gets mad and gets into fights? What do you think?

These are the three reactions I have when someone does not want to have experiential sessions, when they say no, or when they bring up worries, fears, questions, and objections.

4

There Is A Curious Relationship Between The Field Of Psychotherapy And Having Experiential Sessions

Having your own experiential sessions may be among the more ambitious members of the "self-change family." However, the entire family has a curious relationship with the large family of psychotherapies. Ever since the family of psychotherapies came about, in the past hundred years or so, the two families have lived almost on top of one another, yet each almost completely ignores the presence of the other. They do business together, yet each pretends the other is not around. Coexisting with the field of psychotherapy are millions of people having their own sessions of meditation and contemplation, taking steps to lessen some personal pain or to attain a loftier plateau, and doing self-change activities, whether formal or informal. The two families are all over each other, but they barely talk to each other.

At the same time, it is almost as if the field of psychotherapy senses its own mortality in the presence of so many people taking part in so many kinds of self-change programs. It is as if there is a quiet war between the field of psychotherapy and the ancient, thriving field of self-change. Psychotherapy fears it will lose the war and isn't quite sure whether to ignore the enemy, make friends with the enemy, join forces, try to assimilate the enemy, or declare an out-and-out war. The relationship is certainly a curious one.

For Freud, Jung, And Others, Creating Their Own Psychotherapies Was Inspired By And Helped Their Quest For Personal Self-Change

It is probably no accident that most of the greatest theories of human beings, our theories of personality, and our psychotherapies, were created by people who were passionate about knowing themselves and undergoing their own self-change. Sigmund Freud, Carl Jung, and others were passionate about studying themselves, knowing who they were, understanding what made them tick, and probing into their deepest insides. They were their own precious patients, even as they were developing their own grand theories and psychotherapies. Their laboratories were themselves. Much of the passion in their developing psychoanalytic and analytic theories came from their intensely personal quest to know themselves and address their own personal anguishes and pains, impulses and desires, growth and development.

Freud and Jung were convinced about the unconscious, unconscious phenomena, and unconscious impulses, not by statistical analysis of research findings, but by finding these things in themselves. It is not hard to make a case that their self-analyses and self-changes both fueled and benefited their wonderful theories and psychotherapies. I believe much the same case can be made for most of our grand theories and psychotherapies, and the people who created them. The conceptual mission was inspired by and helped in answering such simple personal questions as "Who am I? How did I get to be the person I am? How can I be different? What can I be?" There is a curious relationship between the fields of psychotherapy and self-change.

IF PSYCHOTHERAPISTS TRUST THESE METHODS FOR THEMSELVES, WHY NOT USE THEM WITH THEIR PATIENTS? IF PSYCHOTHERAPISTS TRUST THESE METHODS WITH THEIR PATIENTS, WHY NOT USE THEM WITH THEMSELVES?

Picture that I am with some colleagues, either a few or even a large audience of professional psychotherapists, and I sincerely ask them some questions. The first is, "What do you generally do when things get really tough for you, when you have that same awful feeling, when you feel miserable and rotten, when you feel yourself coming apart, when you know you are in an awful situation, when you are having trouble coping, when you feel at loose ends, when you are racked with worry, or when you are truly unhappy?" The second question is, "What do you generally do to try to become a better person, a more wholesome person, more mature and adjusted, better put together, a more ideal person, closer to the kind of person you can be, a little more of an optimal person?"

Most psychotherapists have no answer, nothing that comes to mind right away, nothing they do regularly, nothing they truly trust. But some do. They say that they take long walks by themselves, spend five or ten minutes concentrating on their breathing, or keep a log of their dreams. Some sit still, half-close their eyes, let thoughts, images, and feelings come without censoring them, and attain a state of being that is essentially free from thoughts, images, and feelings. Some study their dreams to find themes, answers to questions, or information about themselves.

Some pray, either in a special place where they live or in a church. Some spend a day or so in a special place where they can be alone, a place that has special meaning, such as where their parents are buried, the house where they spent their childhood, or the bank of a river. Some indulge themselves by doing something they dearly love, such as reorganizing their collection of coins, repairing their special sports car, spending the day shopping, taking a long time to prepare a gourmet meal, or going for a long ride on a motorcycle.

Some count on doing something artistically creative, such as painting, sculpting, or composing music. Some get high on drugs, play a guitar, close their eyes and let images flow by, read the Bible, write poetry, or fly an airplane. Some go on retreats where they spend several days alone, far away from their ordinary lives.

Some rely on talking things over with a close friend, a grandmother, an older sister, or an old, wise person. What makes this so special is putting themselves in the unusual role of the concerned one, the one who needs to talk things over, the one who tells about himself or herself. What makes this so special is being with someone who is wise, who listens with intense interest, who lets you be the little child, the proud achiever, the prized jewel, the thoroughly frustrated one, the unappreciated baby, or the frightened child.

I respect that some psychotherapists do these things; they rely on, count on, and trust these things. Now I can ask my question: "If you trust using these methods for yourself, why not use these methods with your patients?"

Typically, there is a pause. Ordinarily, they have not thought about this. Maybe this is a trick question. What is he really after? There is usually a scramble for some kind of answer. One answer is that there is no comparison. Their patients are sick, have a pathological condition, need treatment, have a personality disorder, or suffer from psychological-psychiatric problems. (This answer could use some propping up if it is even slightly inspected.)

A second answer is a form of stalling. "But how could I do it, even if I wanted to?" I suggest that psychotherapists could find out what methods their patients have available, and then show them how better to use them. Or psychotherapists could show their patients how to select an appropriate method from those that they use. Show patients how to take long walks, meditate, study their own dreams, do guided imagery, use prayer, be alone in a special place, take time out to indulge themselves, do something creative, and go on a personal retreat. After all, psychotherapists in general rely on these methods; maybe they are appropriate for their patients.

A third answer is that their patients' problems need high-level therapeutic methods. This is a variation on the theme that patients have serious pathological problems, whereas therapists do not. However, this answer loses much of its steam when you look at specific instances. For example, if a psychotherapist relies on certain things to do when she has persistent fights with her husband or feels unhappily lost and alone, why shouldn't a patient do those things when he or she has persistent fights with his or her spouse or feels unhappily lost and alone? Can the psychotherapist explain? Typically, the psychotherapist cannot explain this dilemma.

A fourth answer is given by many psychotherapists who rely on talking things over with a special, other person. These psychotherapists typically do a little defensive mumbling about the client-therapist relationship and the helping alliance. However, the conversation usually comes to an embarrassing impasse when the questioner suggests, for example, that the therapist's aunt is not a professional psychotherapist, yet he seeks her out when he feels awful, and it feels so helpful when his aunt allows him to just be a mixed-up little boy every so often. Perhaps his patients could talk to his aunt, or find someone else with whom they might also be allowed to be a mixed-up little kid every so often. Perhaps patients can find better people to talk things over with than turning to professional psychotherapists. That is when we usually run into an embarrassing impasse.

The question still sits there, essentially unanswered: If psychotherapists trust these methods for themselves, why not use them with their patients? It makes simple sense that psychotherapists would be inclined to use these methods with their patients. We are still waiting for a good answer to this question.

Let's turn to the second question: "If psychotherapists trust these methods with their patients, why not use them with themselves?"

Imagine asking these same professional psychotherapists to identify the methods they trust, rely on, and commonly use with their patients. They describe such methods as reliving the birth trauma; interpreting the transference neurosis; attacking irrational cognitions; adopting the psychoanalytic, feminist, Adlerian, or social-learning philosophical outlook; using the two-chair method; gaining insight between present pathological behavior and key childhood relationships; finishing out traumatic events; learning anger management or assertiveness skills; or replacing problematic thoughts with healthy thoughts.

Now comes the question: "If you trust these methods with your patients, why not use them with yourself?" Or, perhaps the question can be better put in these words: "If you trust these methods with your patients, why do you use completely different methods with yourself?" Here is where we usually run into the same sort of embarrassed silence, inadequate answers, effective diversions, and creative counterattacks.

It seems sensible to me that psychotherapists would rely on and use much the same methods with their patients as with themselves, but that is not generally the case. Again, there is a most curious relationship between the field of psychotherapy and that of self-change, of doing things with, for, and by oneself.

TO MOST PSYCHOTHERAPISTS, HAVING EXPERIENTIAL SESSIONS HAS NOTHING TO DO WITH PSYCHOTHERAPY

If you sit in with a group of professional psychotherapists who are learning how to have their own experiential sessions, you might well think that they are all experiential psychotherapists who want to learn how to have their own experiential sessions by and for themselves. You would probably be surprised to learn that the group is made up of behavioral, Gestalt, social-learning, cognitive, Adlerian, Jungian, solution-focused, constructivist, and psychoanalytic therapists—among others.

To most of these professional psychotherapists, what they are learning has almost nothing to do with psychotherapy. They may as well be learning how nutrition can help people who exercise, how to use contemplation to eliminate headaches, or how reading can be enriched by cultivating a flow of mental imagery. To most of these professionals, there is as little conflict between having one's own experiential sessions and doing psychotherapy as there is between having one's own experiential sessions and being a Lutheran or a political conservative or a lover of classical music or a vegetarian. To most of these professional psychotherapists, experiential sessions have little or nothing to do with psychotherapy.

Most psychotherapists have no regular program of becoming the person they can become, and being free of scenes of bad feeling. Experiential sessions are to be carried out on a somewhat regular basis, perhaps once a week or once or twice a month or so. Furthermore, experiential sessions serve a purpose. Explicit goals are to be achieved in an experiential session. Imagine that we ask a fair number of psychotherapists, "Do you do something on a fairly regular basis, say once a day or once a week, to keep your gums healthy?" Now imagine us asking, "Do you do something on a fairly regular basis, say once a week or once or twice a month, to help you become the kind of person you can become, and to free yourself of painful scenes of bad feeling?"

Most psychotherapists would say no. I have found so many who answer negatively that I have wondered what that meant. Maybe these psychotherapists are in much better shape than I am, are far closer to becoming who they can become than I am, and have far fewer painful situations than

91

I do. I am a mess; my colleagues are the way I should be. Maybe the two goals that experiential sessions are meant to achieve have little or no meaning to most professional psychotherapists. The goals may be as far from the goals of most psychotherapies as those of achieving perfect pitch, having teeth with no cavities, or achieving a state of oneness with God or one of meditative bliss.

Or, maybe it simply means that, for most psychotherapists, having one's own experiential sessions is so far outside the realm of psychotherapy that it has little or nothing to do with psychotherapy.

THERE ARE MAJOR DIFFERENCES BETWEEN HAVING YOUR OWN EXPERIENTIAL SESSIONS AND BEING A PATIENT WHO GETS TREATMENT FROM MOST PROFESSIONAL PSYCHOTHERAPISTS

In seeking to protect their "turf," professional psychotherapists can easily equate people having their own experiential sessions with trying to be their own psychotherapists. Then comes the argument: "These are untrained people! If they want psychotherapy, they should go to a trained professional psychotherapist." In this section, I build a case that having your own experiential sessions has little or nothing to do with being a patient who gets treatment from most professional psychotherapists.

Most psychotherapists actively oppose and reject the aims and goals of having your own experiential sessions. Most psychotherapists have a knee-jerk reaction to hearing about the aims and goals of experiential sessions. They immediately put their hands over their ears or eyes. They gasp and chortle, cough and stutter, wheeze and snort. It is as if they are hearing the intolerable. They are almost galvanized into opposing and rejecting what they hear.

The goals of the session for each person are to undergo a deep-seated transformation; to undergo a radical qualitative change; to become the person they are capable of becoming; to discover an inner, deeper potentiality for experiencing that is to become an integral part of the whole new person; and to enable the person to be free of the painful scene of painful feeling so that the painful scene is no longer a part of the new person's new world.

Most psychotherapists are not reasonably tolerant of the aims and goals of an experiential session. Instead, they will oppose and reject these goals, either directly or indirectly, with or without justifying arguments, coolly and rationally, or with plenty of huffing and puffing.

Having your own experiential sessions is not the same as getting therapy from a professional therapist. Here is one big difference:

The desire to have your own experiential sessions must be present in you; conversely, most psychotherapists want you to be a client treated by a psychotherapist. People who have their own experiential sessions have a spark of enthusiasm for having their own sessions. They want to. It is important to them. They make the effort to listen to tapes, attend workshops, read and talk with others about experiential sessions. There is some passion.

The field of psychotherapy does not say: "Go, have your own experiential sessions. Become your own practitioner of self-change. You do not need to become a client of a psychotherapist." Instead, virtually the entire field of psychotherapy encourages you to become a client who is treated by a psychotherapist. Books and journals on psychotherapy tell you to be a client of a psychotherapist. The mental health professions tell you to be a client of a psychotherapist. Newspapers, movies, television, magazines, short stories, and plays tell you to be a client of a psychotherapist. Training programs for psychiatrists and psychologists, as well as lots of other groups, tell you to become a client and a patient of a psychotherapist. Hospitals, clinics, agencies, programs, and private practitioners tell you to be a client of a psychotherapist.

In rather stark contrast, you are the only one who can say, "No, I want to have my own experiential sessions."

Instead of trying to achieve the aims and goals of experiential sessions, most psychotherapists are here to treat your mental illness and pathological problem. In an experiential session, you move toward becoming the person you are capable of becoming and free yourself of a painful situation. Most psychotherapists are after almost completely different aims and goals. They are here to cure you of your mental illness, your mental disease, or your pathological mental problem. You will then be "less sick," better adjusted, more normal, and less pathological. Your mental illness and disease will be treated. You will have normal sexual urges. Your thoughts will be less abnormal. Your behavior will be less pathological. Whatever is wrong with you, whatever your mental condition, will be alleviated, treated, put in remission, and maybe cured.

Most psychotherapists look for your diagnostic condition via the symptoms of your psychopathology, abnormality, maladjustment, mental illness and disease, or pathological problem. Then they set out to do something, whether it's to treat it, to apply interventions, or to work on it with psychotherapy. There really is a world of difference between the aims and goals of experiential sessions and those of most psychotherapists.

Experiential sessions are for just about everyone; psychotherapy is for people who need treatment for their mental illnesses and pathological problems. Are you inclined to become more of the kind of person you are capable of becoming? Are you ready to free yourself of a painful scene of painful feeling in your personal world? If so, then experiential sessions are for you. This means that most people can have their own experiential sessions if they are so inclined.

In rather sharp contrast, psychotherapy is for people who have something wrong with them, that is, a pathological problem, mental illness, or disease. The label that you put on yourself, or that is assigned to you by the family, the neighbors, the people at work, the social workers, the physicians or counselors, the friends, the psychiatrists or psychologists says that you need psychotherapeutic treatment.

You are an abuser, or have a bipolar disorder. You have emotional lability, need anger management, are mentally disadvantaged, lack communication skills, have agoraphobia, lack impulse control, are alcoholic, lack gender identity, have a poor self-image, are hyposexual, lack assertiveness, have identity diffusion, have delusional thinking, are a victim of emotional abuse, are suffering from post-traumatic stress, or are fixated at the anal stage.

Experiential sessions are for virtually anyone and everyone, including people who think of themselves as having mental illnesses and pathological problems, including all those people who label other people as having mental illnesses and pathological problems, and including psychotherapists who treat people's mental illnesses and pathological problems.

Experiential sessions are for you throughout your whole life; psychotherapy is for when you need treatment. If you seek therapy from a psychotherapist, it is usually when things are so bad that you decide that you need some help, or someone else pushes you into seeking treatment. You go to a psychotherapist when you need treatment, just as you go to a hospital when you are hurt, or you call a roofer to fix a leak. Treatment is finished when the problem is fixed—that's the idea.

In contrast, you can begin having your own experiential sessions whenever the spirit moves you. You may begin in adolescence or earlier, when you are a young adult, when you are quite old—almost any time. You begin when you are ready to become the person you are capable of becoming. You begin when you are motivated to be free of that painful situation that is so much a part of your personal world. Once you begin, you may have as many sessions as you wish, continually and regularly, or in batches. You may have sessions on and off for the rest of your life. Experiential sessions are always there for you to have, forever and ever, and at any time.

Each experiential session offers its own payoff; when psychotherapy is finished, someone else determines if the whole program of treatment was successful or not. In most psychotherapies, a phase of diagnostic assessment and evaluation precedes treatment to determine what mental illness or pathological problem to treat. Generally, the diagnosed mental illness or pathological problem remains the continuing focus of treatment. When treatment is finished, someone does a post-treatment assessment and evaluation to determine if treatment was successful or not. The determination is based on the whole program of treatment in regard to the initially diagnosed mental illness or pathological problem.

In contrast, each experiential session starts with selecting a scene of strong feeling. You are quite free to start with any scene of strong feeling; it may be similar to a scene you began with in a recent session, or it may be a relatively new scene of strong feeling.

Each experiential session offers you the opportunity to discover a deeper potentiality for experiencing, and to become a qualitatively new person, with that deeper potentiality for experiencing as a whole new, integrative part of the whole new person. If the opening scene of strong feeling was a painful scene with a painful feeling, this very session gives you a golden opportunity to be free of that painful scene and painful feeling.

The success or failure of each experiential session is determined in and after each session. Each session offers its own payoff changes, which can be—and usually are—quite different from the session before and the sessions to come.

Initial psychotherapy sessions aim to diagnose your mental condition; initial experiential sessions have the same aims and purposes as do all other experiential sessions. Before psychotherapy starts, or in the first few sessions, the psychotherapist does some things that are almost never repeated in later sessions. The psychotherapist tries to identify your mental condition, your mental illness or disease, your pathological problem, what is wrong with you. To do this, the psychotherapist tries to elicit all sorts of information that might help, such as information about things you did in and out of school; the way you answer personal questions; topics you seem to shy away from; how you got along with spouses, siblings, and kids your age; unusual things about you; and special habits of yours. The first sessions are special because they are used to determine what is wrong and how to treat it.

Each experiential session has the same two aims and goals and goes through the same four steps. In other words, the initial experiential sessions are generally similar to all subsequent sessions. In psychotherapy, initial sessions are generally quite different from later treatment sessions. In experiential sessions, all the sessions are cut from the same cloth; you do the same things in the initial sessions as in all other experiential sessions.

In psychotherapy, your attention is mainly focused on the therapist; in experiential sessions, your attention is mainly focused on you and the important things in your personal world. In psychotherapy, your attention is mainly directed toward the therapist. When you talk, you talk to the therapist. When the therapist talks, you pay attention to the therapist and what he or she is saying. Throughout the entire session, your attention is almost always mainly directed toward the therapist.

In experiential sessions, your attention is mainly focused on whatever is front and center for you at the moment. You are attending to the ongoing bodily sensations, that important scene or situation, that meaningful person, the cancer inside you, the way your friend looks at you, that look on your father's face, the letter, the feel of the warm bath water, or the sense of caring as you hold the baby. Your attention is mainly focused on the things in and of you, the things in and of your personal world.

In psychotherapy, you fulfill the role of patient, and the therapist fulfills the role of therapist; in experiential sessions, there are no such roles. In psychotherapy, the patient almost inevitably fulfills some sort of role. The role may come from the patient, it may be imposed by the therapist, or it may be worked out by the patient and therapist together. But the patient almost always fulfills some sort of role, usually in relationship to a role that the therapist fulfills. Sometimes, the role is pleasant and appealing, and sometimes it is rather painful, but there is almost always some role.

In your own way, you may be saying to the therapist: "I am frail and delicate. Will you acknowledge this and be gentle and kind with me, please?" or "I know I appear hard and tough and sure of myself, but can you find the softness and gentleness in me?" or "I am searching for someone who is truly interested in me, in the little details of my life and me; can you be that person for me?" or "I am here to defy you, to win, to never be the way you will try to get me to be; do we have a deal?" or "I am so lonely; will you be the one person I can talk personally to, because I have no one else?" or "I know I am nasty and abrasive, but I need someone with whom I can be this way and it is all right; will you do this for me?" or "I am looking for an attractive, older man to be with and to talk about sexual things with; I figure that finding a therapist is better than searching the Internet or going to singles bars." or "I love having someone try to cheer me up and make me feel better; will you do this for me?" or "I am looking for someone who is on my side, who can defend me and be my buddy; can you do this for me?"

Therapists typically fulfill their own roles, and it is important that the therapist role and patient role complement one another well. If the roles do not fit, you will usually leave the psychotherapist after a session or so. If the roles "click," the relationship is a good one and will last for a while.

Fortunately or unfortunately, you do not have such opportunities to fulfill roles when you have experiential sessions. If it is important for you to have someone on your side, to take your part in things, to defend you, this may be apparent in the scenes of strong feeling that you start a session with. However, there will be no therapist to fulfill the complementary role for you, to fail to provide that role for you, or to put pressure on you to fulfill a role that he or she finds important for you to fulfill.

In experiential sessions, you do the work; in psychotherapy, the therapist carries out and applies the treatment. In experiential sessions, you are the one who learns what to do and how to do it. A teacher may show you how or go over your tapes with you to help you learn and get better, but in the actual session, you do the work.

In almost every part of every session of every type of psychotherapy, it is the psychotherapist who carries out the treatment. It is the psychotherapist who has the plan for the session, has the training in how to apply the treatment, knows what methods to use, and applies the methods. The psychotherapist is the one in charge, no matter what treatment method the therapist applies. The patient is the subject, the recipient, of the methods that the therapist selects and uses on that patient.

In experiential sessions, you are the one who learns how to find a scene of strong feeling. If you do it well, you take the credit. If you do not do it well, you take the responsibility. In psychotherapy, it is the therapist who gives the interpretation and looks for and attacks the irrational cognition. If it is done well, the therapist is applauded. If the therapist does a poor job, the therapist is blamed. Someone has to do the work. In experiential sessions, that person is you. In psychotherapy, it is the therapist.

The picture I hope to portray is that there are major differences between having your own experiential sessions and being a patient who receives treatment from a professional psychotherapist. In this picture, there are virtually no substantial similarities between having your own experiential sessions and being a patient treated by most psychotherapists.

In Psychotherapy, There Is A Client And A Psychotherapist; In Experiential Sessions, You Are The "Practitioner" And The Other Person Is Your "Teacher"

The words "client," or "patient," and "psychotherapist," or "counselor," never seemed to fit what I did, whether I had experiential sessions by myself or I worked with another person. Those words evoked images of someone called a psychotherapist or counselor who provided services or applied treatment to the recipient, who was called a client or patient. The therapist treats the client. The therapist applies the interventions. The therapist does things to and for the patient.

When I became familiar with meditation, the word "practitioner" was sometimes used to refer to the person. That word seemed to fit, and I have adopted that word. For me, the person who has experiential sessions is the practitioner. The person who carries out the practice is the practitioner. When you have your own experiential sessions, you are the practitioner.

What word seems to fit the person who teaches you how to have your own experiential sessions, how to become a practitioner? I like the word "teacher." When my work is to help you have your own sessions, I am your teacher, not your psychotherapist. I am your teacher when I am with a group of students and tell them about experiential sessions, when I study tapes of your experiential sessions and help you do them better, and when I teach you to go through a session so that you can go through a session by yourself.

However, that leaves one situation for which I am not satisfied with the words to use. This is the situation when I am teaching a person to go through a session, my job being to show the person what to do for each step and sub-step, but the person is not really there to learn and eventually have experiential sessions on his or her own. I am still the teacher, but the person is not a student. I am almost being a psychotherapist, except that my role is mainly that of a teacher who shows and invites the person to do the work—if the person is ready and willing. In that situation, I do not know what proper words to use. The best I can do, so far, is to offer myself as the experiential teacher who shows you how to proceed through a session, and you are the person who carries out the work, provided that you are quite ready and willing. We are not therapist and client, but I do not know what words to use.

IN EXPERIENTIAL SESSIONS WITH AN EXPERIENTIAL TEACHER,
THE TEACHER KNOWS AND SAYS WHAT TO DO NEXT;
IN YOUR OWN EXPERIENTIAL SESSIONS,
YOU KNOW AND SAY WHAT TO DO NEXT

Imagine that you are learning how to have your own experiential session. You read this book. You may have listened to tapes of a teacher having her or his own sessions. You may have tried out the initial sub-steps of a session. Then you ask a teacher to go through a session with you. You know that the teacher will take most of the responsibility for knowing and saying what to do next, in proceeding through each sub-step. You also know that the teacher will accompany you as far as you are ready and willing to go in the session.

In a session with an experiential teacher, the teacher will know and say what to do next. Gradually, you learn what to do next. Gradually, you take over saying what to do next. At first, the instructions are known and spoken by the teacher. Later on, the instructions are known and spoken by you. You become the one who knows what to do and how to do it. You become the one who voices the instructions. Here are just a few of the instructions. When these words are voiced by the teacher, you are having an experiential session with the teacher. When these words are voiced by you, you are having your own experiential session.

> *First do the warm-up . . . Look for earlier times when you had that same feeling, maybe much stronger . . . It's a dream, so go to the other place in the dream where there was a rising up of feeling . . . There has to be a real commitment to doing this, really feeling this way, a real commitment . . . Freeze this scene; hold it still; freeze it. Louder! With much more feeling! There are some other ways of accepting this deeper potential . . . The next thing is to just wallow in being in, going all the way, with no hesitation or restriction at all.*

In a session with an experiential teacher, it is the teacher who speaks with the voice of the method. The teacher is the one who says these words. Thereafter, you are the one who speaks with the voice of the method. You are the one who takes over and says these words. When you know what to do and say, the teacher is replaced. The teacher is gone, replaced by you.

HERE IS A CASE THAT HAVING YOUR OWN EXPERIENTIAL SESSIONS GIVES YOU PRECIOUS ADVANTAGES OVER BEING A CLIENT OF A PSYCHOTHERAPIST

I am talking to people who are having their own experiential sessions, to people who are clients of almost any type of psychotherapist, and people who are neither, but may some day be one or the other. The case I want to make is that having your own experiential sessions does indeed give you some precious advantages over being a client to a psychotherapist.

If you want to discover the potentialities that are deep inside you, an experiential session can probably do it; a psychotherapist almost certainly cannot do it. You may not even believe in the notion of deeper things inside you, deeper possibilities, deeper potentialities, deeper ways of being. I find it so very useful to think of the deeper possibilities for experiencing that are hidden inside me. If you do, and if you are curious to know what these possibilities are, if you want to know the person you can become and what that person can be like, how can you find out? You can turn to having an experiential session because experiential sessions were created and designed to do just that, to discover the possibilities that lie deep within you. To be more specific, the explicit goal of the first step is to discover the deeper potential for experiencing. That is its job.

There are a number of reasons why sessions with most psychotherapists will not lead to discovering deeper possibilities inside you. One reason is that most psychotherapists do not put much value on possibilities and potentialities that lie hidden deep inside of you, beyond your own consciousness and awareness. Psychoanalytic psychotherapists usually do believe in unconscious material, but most psychotherapists do not.

A second reason is that those psychotherapists who do believe in inner, deeper possibilities and potentialities do not consider them valuable, precious, the nucleus of the whole new person you can become. In stark contrast, most psychotherapists consider inner, deeper material as bad, something to be sealed off, kept down, guarded against, maintaining proper controls over, something you should have insight and understanding of, but only to ensure that it is buried. They consider what is inside to be psychopathological, animal instinctive material, the root of your mental illness, material that is traumatic material that deserves to be hidden and forgotten, or drives and needs that are uncivilized, antisocial, dangerous.

Another reason is that most psychotherapists have plenty of other things to do. Instead of helping you discover inner, deeper possibilities, most therapists are hard at work getting you to feel good with the therapist; to change the way you think about yourself and others; to show your feelings and emotions; to accept the therapist's notions, ideas, and interpretations; to talk about what you are reluctant to talk about; to see things the way the therapist sees things; and to act and behave in different ways than you do.

Finally, and in the light of these other reasons, most psychotherapists simply lack the necessary skills to discover the deeper possibilities and potentialities that lie deep inside of you. There are methods and techniques for accomplishing this, but most psychotherapists do not have these skills.

If you are drawn toward seeing, knowing, and discovering the inner possibilities and potentialities that lie deep within you, an experiential session can probably do the job. Most psychotherapists almost certainly cannot do the job.

An experiential session can enable you to become a qualitatively new person; psychotherapy sessions do not do this. Are you drawn toward going through a session that can take you through an amazing shift into becoming a whole new person? Do you want to become the entirely new person who you are capable of becoming? Are you ready to let that deeper potentiality inside of you become an integral new part of the whole new you? If you are ready and willing to become a radically new person, that is precisely what experiential sessions were designed to offer you. Every time you enter an experiential session, you are getting yourself ready to go through these changes.

An ordinary session of psychotherapy will not do this. With virtually no exceptions, psychotherapy sessions will not accomplish these changes. Study a thousand sessions, or study a million. Of course, there may be a rare exception, but the above changes will not occur in a session of psychotherapy. Psychotherapeutic sessions were not designed to accomplish these extraordinary goals. They have plenty of other things to accomplish. Nevertheless, an experiential session has the advantage over a psychotherapeutic session because the experiential session is designed to open you up to becoming the whole new person you are capable of becoming.

An experiential session can enable you to be free of the painful feeling in a painful scene or situation; psychotherapy sessions do not do this. The painful feeling is a sense of being unwanted, out of place, not belonging. The painful scene or situation is being at your North American husband's family home, celebrating a holiday that you did not celebrate in Iran, where you grew up, and no one is talking to you as if you were a real person. By the end of the experiential session, that painful scene or situation is no longer in your personal world. It is drained of its painful feeling. You are no longer a person for whom it is painfully important to have such painful scenes in your personal world.

An experiential session frees you of this painful scene or situation and of the painful feeling in that scene. Only the rarest of psychotherapy sessions would claim to be able to accomplish this goal. There are at least two reasons for this.

One reason is that psychotherapy ordinarily stays away from one-session cures; instead, psychotherapy thinks in terms of a whole program of treatment. Such a goal might be accomplished, perhaps, by the end of treatment, but not by the end of one session of psychotherapy.

Second, almost all psychotherapies have a different mind-set. Ordinarily, sessions are to treat mental illnesses, diseases, disorders, and pathological problems. Occasionally, treatment may stir up a painful feeling in a painful scene or situation, but only occasionally. It is rare that a psychotherapeutic session would explicitly focus on freeing a person of an explicit scene of painful feeling. Almost without exception, psychotherapy sessions stop short of identifying an explicit scene of painful feeling because they are looking for problems and indications of problems instead. Psychotherapists would be far more inclined to stop short of an explicit scene of strong painful feeling when they have found enough material to label the person as, for example, having problems of rejection, lack of cultural identity, marital or relationship issues, feelings of not belonging, or cultural conflict.

If you want to be free of the painful feeling in an explicit painful scene or situation, that is the explicit goal of an experiential session. It is almost certainly not the aim of most single sessions of most psychotherapies.

Having your own experiential sessions frees you of being encased in a psychotherapist's personal values, judgments, and prejudices, and being pressured to be the way the psychotherapist thinks you should be. Most psychotherapists will not nod their heads in candid agreement with this section because it is indeed a serious indictment against virtually all psychotherapists. On the other hand, this book is for people who are in the position to have their own sessions or put themselves under the treatment or care of a psychotherapist. I am not trying to convince psychotherapists to look at themselves the way I do.

When you are a client or patient who has sessions with a professional psychotherapist, you are, most likely, focused on the things that concern you. You are thinking about what just happened, the awful feelings in you, how concerned and worried you are, the troubles that are all around, and the thing that scares you, worries you, makes you feel bad.

What you are probably *not* thinking about is the fact that you are extremely vulnerable. You are the willing or unwilling target and victim of your psychotherapist's value system; personal judgments about you; and prejudices that are alive and vibrant when your therapist is with you. In ways that are subtle and not so subtle, your psychotherapist exerts massive and continuing pressure for you to be and become the way his or her values, judgments, and prejudices lead you to be and become.

Psychotherapists are virtually unrivaled as the most professional con artists, salespeople, and missionaries in the world. Making matters worse, they are dealing with stakes that are far higher than your money, possessions, group belongingness. The stakes are you, the person you are and can become. Beware the personal helpers, the psychotherapists.

Almost without their explicitly knowing, just about every psychotherapist arrives at his or her own notion of what is wrong with you, what needs changing, what is sick or disordered about you, who and what kind of person you are, and what there is about you, your relationships, or your current world that needs fixing. Then (again, almost without their explicitly knowing), your psychotherapist forms some picture of how you should be, what there should be more of or less of in you and your personal life, ways in which you should be different, and things about you that should be more like this or that. Sometimes, the way you should be has to do with your world. For example, you should not live with a person like that, or you should not spend your days doing this or that. Sometimes, the way you should be has to do with you. You should be more this way or that way. You should be more tolerant, more assertive, more expressive, less self-centered, or less vulnerable. Finally, most psychotherapists are exceedingly persistent, undeviating, and either subtle or overtly powerful in using all their tools to get you to be the way they think you should be.

Picture a workshop of approximately 50 psychotherapists from the community, together with trainees and staff members of a hospital. The group heard about 15 minutes of the beginning of a taped experiential session in which a woman was looking around for a scene of strong feeling. When the tape shut off, she was talking about a recent argument she had had with the woman she was living with, an argument about whether or not to have a Christmas tree for the coming holiday season. I asked the group to write down some notes about what the problem might be, what the goals of therapy might be, and what a therapist might do to begin progress toward the therapeutic goals.

What was so impressive was not only how quickly most therapists arrived at their opinions of what was wrong and what needed to be done to meet the therapeutic goals, but also how certain the psychotherapists were. One therapist said: "I would start exploring her relationship with her father. I think she has to deal with her issues with men to resolve her problem of confused sexual identity." Other therapists had different notions about the woman's life, the way she was, how she should be, what was wrong with her, and how to get her to change in the ways the therapists wanted her to change.

At this point, a young trainee stood up and addressed the group. She was bothered that the person on the tape was simply looking for a scene of strong feeling in having her own session. She was not a patient in psychotherapy. The trainee was appalled at the way the group was talking about the woman behind her back, in much the same way her aunts and uncles would gossip about people in the small town where she grew up. The trainee said she was ashamed of being a psychiatric resident and of being so intrusive, so prejudiced, and pushy.

Even if you get little from your own experiential sessions, at least you are free of most psychotherapists' personal values, judgments, and prejudices; you are not pressured to be the way the psychotherapist wants you to be.

Having your own experiential sessions frees you from whatever role the psychotherapist puts you in to complement the psychotherapist's own personal role. Most psychotherapists like to think of themselves as professionals who help people, relieve troubled and anguished patients, treat problems, and do good. I have a somewhat different mind-set in which being a psychotherapist to a client or patient is a useful way of playing out an important personal role for the psychotherapist. The psychotherapist's personal role is all-important, and in order for him or her to fulfill that role, it is critical for the client or patient to fulfill a particular complementary role that the psychotherapist works hard to get the client or patient to play.

For Dr. Koslowski, it is important to be in the role of your best friend, the one you can trust, the one you can confide in and tell everything to. His patients should play the role of loners who need a best friend, people who have never found that special other person to whom they can tell all, who value a true confidante.

For Dr. Wong, it is important to play the role of the person who is on your side, sees your side of things, is here to defend you against them, and has enough power to do things. She needs patients who are up against it, embattled, attacked by others, and have no strong person to be on their side.

Dr. Lawton loves the role of being the model of mental health, the ideal person, the elevated one, and the example of what an optimal person can be like. He is perfection. He needs clients who are looking for a hero, someone to be like, look up to, almost worship and admire—a god on earth.

Dr. Perez is a rock, someone who is the voice of reality. She assumes the role of the grounded one, the solid one, the unflappable one, the one with both feet planted firmly on the ground. In order for her to enjoy this role, she needs clients who are mixed-up and at loose ends, who need someone firm to depend on, who crave a mooring, solid ground, a rock of Gibraltar.

For Dr. Castonguay, the important role is that of the one whose word is important; what he has to say makes a difference and should be listened to. In his role, he says little, but he takes things in. Then, he makes a pronouncement, which should be taken as highly important. In order to play this role, he needs patients over whom he has power, patients who elevate him, think of him as wise and authoritative, and wait for and hang on his every word.

Dr. Williams plays the role of the one who is so close, who is virtually one with you; she shares everything, up to a point, until danger lurks. She is seductive in subtle ways, with promises of the delights of absolute closeness, oneness, and sharing. In order to fulfill her role, she needs patients who are secretly looking for that spiritual other, that one person who is soul mate.

For Dr. James, the important role to play is that of the rescuer, the savior, the one who prevents the awful fate and makes the horrible situation normal again. He needs patients whose lives have suddenly fallen apart, who themselves have fallen apart, who are in a terrible crisis where all hope is lost.

When you step into the psychotherapist's world, you will almost certainly be outfitted and auditioned for a role that complements the role the psychotherapist wants to fulfill. In the psychotherapist's role, he or she will have important personal feelings and experiencings. This is what psychotherapy is all about, as far as the experiential perspective is concerned. But in order for the psychotherapist to have these important personal feelings and experiencings, you must provide the appropriate context. You must fulfill the complementary role. All this almost always takes place underground, covertly, without fanfare. You will probably not even know the exact role you have been cast into.

Sometimes, the role you are being asked to play is pleasant, maybe even valuable and cherished for you. In that case, two adults are fulfilling complementary role relationships with mutual consent and with both gaining pleasure from their mutual relationships. However, it is more common that the role you are asked to play is not your role and is not such a pleasant one, but one that calls for you to be suffering, hurting, and in pain. It is not a role of your choosing.

When you have your own experiential sessions, you are free from being forced into a complementary role. You are free of playing a role that includes being sick, pathological, having something wrong with you, hurting, and being in awful straits, broken, abnormal, and painfully needy. You are free to accomplish what an experiential session can accomplish, instead of playing out some kind of unhappy role that the psychotherapist unwittingly forces upon you so that he or she can gain the important feelings and experiencings that are provided by the psychotherapist's own role.

Yes, I do believe that having your own experiential sessions can give you some precious advantages over being a client to a psychotherapist.

THE RISE OF ONE'S OWN SESSIONS MEANS THE FALL OF PROFESSIONAL PSYCHOTHERAPY—THE WAR IS ON!

On the one side are professional psychotherapists of all kinds and stripes. On the other side are people having their own experiential sessions, doing meditation, and doing all sorts of things, by themselves, to feel better, less bad, more ideal. There is a war, a real war. In an important sense, professional psychotherapy is fighting for its very life.

The tradition of having your own sessions is far older than that of professional psychotherapy. Professional psychotherapy means that some institution, some granting body, awards a person a degree, certificate, or diploma, and that person is called a professional psychotherapist. In medicine, this started in the late 1800s. In psychology, this started in the early 1900s. Of course, the roots and history can be traced to much earlier periods, but professional psychotherapy truly began only in the late 1800s and early 1900s.

Experiential sessions arose in the very late 1900s, so it would be difficult to make the case that they have a long tradition. However, other ways of having one's own sessions have existed for much longer than professional psychotherapy. The war that professional psychotherapy is fighting is with a collection of enemies that have been around for and have developed over hundreds of years.

People were carrying out the methods of meditation for centuries before professional psychotherapists had their first conference. Books and treatises about how to make sense of one's own dreams have been around for several thousands of years, almost as soon as tablets and papyrus were available. Thousands of years before psychotherapists held professional meetings, people were having their own sessions of personal prayer to achieve a relationship with deities. Long before professional psychotherapists started getting paid for their services, people were taking all kinds of drugs to feel better, to relieve stress and suffering, and to achieve valued and elevated states of being. Many centuries before there were associations of professional psychotherapists, people were going on personal retreats, and spending hours, days, and weeks by themselves.

Professional psychotherapy is fighting a tradition whose methods are ancient and are continuously developing.

Professional psychotherapy is engaged in a war to take over and proclaim exclusive ownership rights over ancient practices and methods. Many of the practices and methods used by professional psychotherapists were being used long before such a thing as professional psychotherapy ever existed. These practices and methods include letting go of one's own thoughts; passively watching the flow of one's own images, thoughts, and memories; finding themes in a series of dreams; interpreting the meaning of one's dreams; using dreams to foresee the future; using methods of achieving higher and elevated states; using all manner of drugs; taking time out and away from situations of personal stress; trying to "get inside" whatever person or thing plagues or frightens you; using methods to open up and let out what is inside you; taking on and adopting better ways of thinking and better outlooks, attitudes, and philosophies; exposing yourself to fear little by little; backing away from doing the bad thing little by little; and rewarding yourself for doing something good and punishing yourself for doing something bad.

When professional psychotherapy originated, it adopted these methods, which people had already been using for a few thousand years. But then professional psychotherapy did a bad thing: It tried to take over exclusive ownership of these time-tested ancient practices and methods. It pasted its own technical labels on these practices and methods. It got laws passed to ensure that only professional people could be designated as capable of using these practices and methods, and designated itself as the authority on how to correctly employ these ancient practices and methods. It taught these practices and methods to its students, wrote articles and books about these practices and methods, encased them in its ethics and codes, and supervised trainees in the use of these practices and methods.

Consider that, for a few thousand years, people have been using practices and methods to feed themselves when they are hungry. Along come professional chefs who declare exclusive ownership of all those practices and methods. If you are hungry, you must go to a professional chef. It is unprofessional, unethical, and illegal for you to use those ancient practices and methods by and for yourself. The same applies to psychotherapy. Instead of you using these practices and methods for yourself, go to a professional psychotherapist, who will use those practices and methods on you.

As self-change programs continue to grow and develop, as this movement keeps getting bigger and better, and as professional psychotherapy keeps trying to accumulate and proclaim exclusive ownership rights over the practices and methods of self-change, a real war is being fought. Professional psychotherapy insists that it has exclusive rights over these practices and methods. Such a declaration virtually begs the self-change movement to object. My own position is that those practices and methods are generally part of the public marketplace, and no group has exclusive ownership rights. Professional psychotherapy is indeed engaged in a war—largely of its own making.

Professional psychotherapy is not pleased that you are using the practices and methods of having your own experiential sessions. Those practices and methods belong to professional psychotherapy. Professional psychotherapy is at war, even if it looks like a quiet war.

The big business industry of professional psychotherapy is at war with you having your own sessions. If enough people have their own experiential sessions, do meditation, and conduct their own sessions of any kind, it will be the veritable end of the big business of professional psychotherapy. Therefore, the industry is at war with you having your own sessions.

Psychotherapy is a huge business, a massive industry. Many people are directly and indirectly invested in your using its services. When you dare to have your own sessions, the whole industry faces the spectre of its collapse. There is a war.

On the one side, picture a woman who goes into a quiet room and has her own experiential session, or a man who sits in a quiet room and meditates. Now picture the big business industry of professional psychotherapy. There are important meetings between insurance company representatives and committees of psychiatrists and psychologists, negotiating the amount of money insurance companies will pay for a session of psychotherapy. Myriads of accountants, managed care clerks and supervisors, and psychotherapists attend such meetings, along with lawyers and their secretaries, volunteers, public relations people, administrators, bureaucrats, statisticians, lobbyists, and staff of psychotherapy associations and university departments— enough men and women to populate a small country. All these people are important parts of the big industry of professional psychotherapy. Money is involved, lots and lots of money. All the money comes from people having sessions with professional psychotherapists; each session costs money.

Every time a person has an experiential session, a meditative session, or any kind of self-change session, a professional psychotherapist's income drops. The mental health worker's income drops. The hospital, clinic, or agency administrator's income drops. The support staff's income drops. If enough people have their own sessions, the incomes of all these people evaporate. These people have plenty of reason to fight the war.

This big industry will not tolerate that individuals go into their own quiet room to have experiential sessions or to meditate. Oh, no. It is a war. People must get treatment from professional psychotherapists who charge money and keep the wheels of professional psychotherapy turning. The huge industry of professional psychotherapy is at war with those individuals. If the industry wins the war, each woman and man will not be allowed to have her or his personal sessions of meditation or experiential sessions. Instead, treatment from a professional psychotherapist is needed. If the industry loses the war, people will be having experiential sessions and sessions of meditation instead of sessions with professional psychotherapists. The war is on.

Professional psychotherapists are at war to be the ones who impose their values and judgments onto you. Consider that a rather large group is listening to an audiotape of a woman having her own experiential session. The group is made up of people who work in accounting, teachers in public schools, secretaries and support staff, computer technicians, physicians and nurses, nuns and priests, taxi and truck drivers, a sprinkling of other workers, and a fair portion of professional psychotherapists. After the audiotape is played, there are many comments from the audience. Most of the comments address the steps and methods of carrying out the experiential session, but other kinds of comments include statements like these:

"She needs to take into account how others might feel, like her parents. She is just living off the money of her lesbian lover; shouldn't she be more independent? She has to rethink her lifestyle; maybe lesbianism is not the right choice for her. She's never had a stable relationship in her life; her lesbianism is a false search for the long-term relationship she never had. She ought to figure out what she wants in life, before she commits to a lesbian lifestyle."

These comments almost exclusively come from the professional psychotherapists. It is almost as if professional psychotherapists spew their value systems and judgments. If a member of the audience talks about how the person should and needs to be, imposes their values and judgments onto the person, the judge usually is a professional psychotherapist.

When people have their own sessions, many professional psychotherapists are incensed. They are deprived of their precious opportunity to impose their own personal value judgments: This is the way you should be. This is what you should do. This is what you should change. Here is how you fare on my personal list of what I approve and disapprove of. I know what is best for you. I have to watch that you lead the good life. You are to abide by my moral standards, my value judgments. I have to guide your decisions. I decide that your weight is your problem, and that you should lose weight. I decide that the way you are with your husband is not good and should be more like this or that.

Some professional psychotherapists are candid about imposing their value judgments on patients. Other professional psychotherapists are less candid and more covert. They mask their value judgments under the innocent claim that they get their directions of change from the patient, never from the professional psychotherapist's own personal system of value judgments. Oh, no. Many professional psychotherapists hide their personal value judgments under diagnostic labels and psychopathological problem names. "She has a gender identity problem, a denial of her identification with her mother, and a borderline condition." In other words, the professional psychotherapist imposes his or her judgment that the patient should treat her mother better and stop this lesbian nonsense, and then she'll be less of a weirdo.

A person who has experiential sessions, or meditates, or undergoes his or her own self-change program is a threat. That person is the enemy. If that person wins, professional psychotherapists are deprived of their self-imposed role as the one who gets to impose personal value judgments onto another person. It is indeed a war, even if that person is unaware of being in a war.

Psychotherapists are invested in warning that bad things can happen if you try to have a session by yourself, without a psychotherapist. When I talk about having experiential sessions, a few people will commonly raise objections such as these: "But suppose the person is a borderline psychotic. Wouldn't a session be dangerous? What about someone who is fragile and could just fall apart? Suppose the person has a weak ego. Wouldn't a session be dangerous? What about a person who is psychotic? Wouldn't having a session make his condition worse?"

Usually, questions like these are posed by professional psychotherapists. However, since I so strongly support people having their own sessions, I try to shift my thinking to the framework of most psychotherapists. "Are you a psychotherapist?" Typically the question asker is indeed a professional psychotherapist. Sometimes I like to play a little. "What you say makes good sense to me. If you really are a borderline psychotic, are fragile and could easily fall apart, have a weak ego, or are psychotic, perhaps you do have a basis for worrying about what would happen if you have an experiential session. By the way, how did you find out that you were that way?"

If I try to understand the professional psychotherapist's framework, the much-preferred picture is for people to have their own sessions only under the watchful eye and protection of a professional psychotherapist. Consult your professional psychotherapist before and during your own sessions. Better yet, don't have experiential sessions, because they replace being a patient of a professional psychotherapist. All it takes is a little stripping away of the professional jargon and it becomes clear that there is indeed a war between professional psychotherapists and the unsuspecting people who have their own self-change sessions.

Often, the objections of professional psychotherapists are covert, arcane, and inconspicuous. When listening to a person having a session or hearing about a person having an experiential session, professional psychotherapists will occasionally make pronouncements about what the person is like, pronouncements that carry the warning label: Bad things can happen if you try to have a session by yourself, without a professional psychotherapist. The professional psychotherapist will pronounce: "She is overly attached to her mother; she needs to be more autonomous . . . She is engaging in projective identification . . . She is avoiding the real issue of her lack of empowerment in her relationships with men."

I am inclined to ask the psychotherapist, "How can she be saved from being so attached to her mother, from using projective identifications, and from avoiding the real issue?" We almost always return to the same underlying framework that led to the psychotherapist's pronouncements in the first place, namely, that bad things can happen if you try to have sessions by yourself; everyone needs the help of a professional psychotherapist.

The professional psychotherapist has a lot of trouble imagining a person having an experiential session alone. "What about the therapist-client relationship? Research has shown that the relationship is important for psychotherapeutic change." My answer is usually that, if you think in terms of psychotherapy, it probably makes good sense to have both a therapist and a client who talk to each other. If we consider the goals of an experiential session, however, a person by himself or herself can usually accomplish these as well as or much better than with almost any psychotherapist.

It is rather striking that the objections coming from many professional psychotherapists tend to disappear when the picture shifts from a person being a patient under a therapist to the psychotherapist having his or her own experiential session. It is so hard for many professional psychotherapists to conceive of having their own sessions. It is so hard for many professional psychotherapists to conceive of a context other than that of administering treatment to a patient.

Professional psychotherapy uses its hired research guns to fight the enemy. Professional psychotherapy hires its own researchers to fight the war against the self-change movement. Professional psychotherapy trains its own researchers and pays their salaries. Their researchers work in institutions that are owned and operated by professional psychotherapy, and aided by grants from agencies that essentially work for and with professional psychotherapy rather than for and with the self-change movement.

Their researchers usually practice professional psychotherapy and teach and conduct their research in places that teach and practice professional psychotherapy. Their researchers hold office in, chair committees in, and serve as active members of professional psychotherapy organizations and associations.

When their researchers speak, write articles and books, and deliver speeches and talks, they wear the robes of elevated and unbiased fairness. They are the voices of truth, of scientific pronouncements. The trouble is that all of this is a lie. It is not true. With rare exception, the researchers are on the side of professional psychotherapy, not the self-change movement.

The job of the hired research guns is to fight the enemy and to subjugate the self-change movement. Their job is to prove that professional psychotherapy is superior to the self-change movement and that self-change methods are inferior. Their job is war. Their job is not to learn and discover more about how personal change works, how the methods can be improved, or what new and better methods can be found. Beware the research guns hired by professional psychotherapy.

The war can show which side is better trained. On one side are professional psychotherapists with special knowledge and training. They have graduate degrees. They are doctors. Many are physicians with specialized training in psychiatry. Many are psychologists with specialized training in psychotherapy. They have diplomas. They have passed state or provincial examinations. They are trained professionals. When they look at their opposition, they see ordinary people without doctorates in psychiatry or clinical psychology, nor graduate degrees in any of the psychotherapy professions. Their opposition is no real opposition. The war is a piece of cake.

However, if we take a closer look, the war just might reveal which side is better trained, and you may not want to bet on the professional psychotherapists. Here are some reasons why the professional psychotherapists just might lose the war.

Who would be the actual competitors? On one side might be a professional psychotherapist who is reasonably competent in carrying out some kind of psychotherapy, perhaps psychodynamic psychotherapy, cognitive psychotherapy, or integrative psychotherapy. Who is on the other side? Suppose that the opposition is a person who is reasonably competent at having experiential sessions. The war is between reasonably competent professional psychotherapists and reasonably competent practitioners of experiential sessions. Are you ready to bet on the winner?

The professional psychotherapists claim that their specialized training took up to seven years or so. But suppose we take a closer look at the actual amount of time that was spent teaching them how to employ the methods used in their sessions with patients. They ask questions to try to find out what is bothering the patient. They listen to what the patient says. They give patients their impressions of what the patients are like. They tell their patients what they believe is best for their patients to think about or do. They tell patients what to do to make things better. They try to get their patients to remember how the problem began. Most of the actual working methods that most professional psychotherapists use took about one hour or less to learn. I am not talking about a supervisor going over sessions conducted by a professional psychotherapist. Rather, I am focusing on precisely how long it took in training for the trainee to get the idea, to be shown how to do the methods. In fact, granting an hour for each method might well be generous.

Now let's look at practitioners of experiential sessions. They learn each of the experiential methods given in the figure in Chapter 2. How long does it take for people to learn each of these methods? For example, how long does it take to learn how to get ready to have a session by putting yourself in a state of readiness for relatively strong feeling? How long does it take to learn about discovering the deeper potential in a moment of strong feeling? When learning consists of reading this book and perhaps listening to a teacher's audiotape, with the teacher explaining it sufficiently, the first method can probably be learned in less than one hour. Learning the second method may take two or three hours. It seems to me that learning the methods takes about the same length of time for most psychotherapists and most practitioners of experiential sessions.

But the story is different when it comes to the length of time it takes to practice the methods sufficiently to achieve a level of competency. Once you get the idea of a particular method, you can practice the skill until you do it well, until

129

you are competent. For example, once you get the idea of throwing free throws in basketball, you have to spend hours and hours practicing to become skilled at throwing free throws. Once you get the idea of playing chords on a piano, you have to spend hours and hours practicing to become reasonably competent. Once you get the idea of the experiential methods, you have to spend hours in dedicated practice to be able to achieve proficiency in using the methods in actual sessions. Virtually none of this occurs for the psychotherapist, who gets the idea of interpretation or looking for an irrational cognition. Psychotherapists rarely spend hours and hours practicing interpretations until they achieve a level of competency.

In terms of sheer hours of practice to acquire competency in skills, the person who has experiential sessions spends a fair amount of time in sheer practice. The psychotherapist spends essentially no time in sheer practice of a skill in order to achieve a level of competency in the skill. Psychotherapists first get the idea of methods and then they use the methods. It is beginning to look as if the psychotherapists may not do so well in the war.

Let us get even closer to the actual war. Professional psychotherapists claim that it takes up to seven years of specialized training for them to do what they do. Suppose that all it really takes is two days! The test is whether or not an audience of professional psychotherapists can differentiate "psychotherapists" who have been trained in two days from those whose training took nearly seven years.

I start with professional actors, two male and two female. First, they watch videotapes of professional psychotherapists with actual patients. Then, they rehearse the role of psychotherapist, with their cohorts playing the role of patients. I go over their roles, explain this and that, and show them what to do. The actors then study the videotapes of professional psychotherapists and patients, and again rehearse their role of psychotherapist with fellow actors as patients. There are six hours of studying videos of professional psychotherapists at work and ten hours of rehearsal and direction by me.

After the two days of training, the four actors join ten professional psychotherapists. Each "therapist" is given patients from a hospital with whom to have videotaped sessions. The videotapes are shown to a large audience of professional psychotherapists. On the first viewing, no one in the audience noticed that some of the videotaped psychotherapists were fakes. The audience was then told that some of the videotaped psychotherapists were actors who had been trained in just two days. The audience sat for a second viewing, after which they were asked to identify the impostors. They couldn't. Interestingly, many in the audience chose some rather well-known and seasoned psychotherapists as fakes. (Some of the laughing was rather forced.) The conclusion was that perhaps actual training to do what psychotherapists do in actual sessions can be done in about two days rather than seven years.

If people with no formal training in psychotherapy cannot be distinguished from professional psychotherapists with up to seven years of formal training, plus years of actual practice, these untrained people could justifiably taunt: "We can do psychotherapy just as well as you, and we have no formal training. Ha, ha, ha!" Can the tables be reversed? Can professional psychotherapists be successful in having their own experiential sessions without any training in having their own experiential sessions?

Here is a test: Picture a group of five professional psychotherapists with four to ten years of postdoctoral experience. They claim that their training and experience means they can easily have their own experiential sessions. All they need is the general idea. We agree that all they require is to be told something about the sessions. They are each given a three-page description of the goals of a session, the four steps in each session, and a little information about achieving each step. Is this sufficient? The professional psychotherapists all agree it is plenty. They are each told to go have their own session and to record it.

The next day we listen to their taped sessions. None of the professional psychotherapists even came close to completing the first of the four steps. They were embarrassingly ineffective. Their years of training and experience as professional psychotherapists were of no help whatsoever in having an experiential session.

The battle is over which side is better trained. Professional psychotherapists dress for battle convinced of the superiority of their training. By the end of the battle, the vaunted training of professional psychotherapists has been reduced to practically nothing. And, when the dust clears, it seems that those who are trained to have their own experiential sessions are better trained than the professional psychotherapists. At the end of the battle, the training program of professional psychotherapists is in tatters. At the end of the war, the surprising conclusion may well be that practitioners of experiential sessions are better trained than professional psychotherapists!

The challenge is that experiential sessions are more sophisticated than sessions with a professional psychotherapist. The field of professional psychotherapy lives the life of the ruling class, certain that it belongs at the top of the heap. Suppose that we play a little by seeing what it is like to look down upon professional psychotherapy as an unsophisticated, lower field. If there is a war, let us see what it is like to win.

An experiential session starts with the way a person is at the beginning of the session, but by the end of the session there is a deep-seated change in the person. There is a radical, qualitative change in who and what the new person is. An experiential session can start with a painful scene or situation that is part of the person's immediate world. By the end of the session, the person is free of that painful scene or situation. It is no longer a part of the person's world.

These are mighty sophisticated goals for a session. They are huge, impressive, high-level, and sophisticated aims. Most sessions with most professional psychotherapists have aims and goals that are less sophisticated. Indeed, essentially no session of any professional psychotherapy has aims and goals that are as impressively high level and sophisticated. Essentially no session of any professional psychotherapy can match these high-level aims and goals.

Experiential sessions are more sophisticated because each session is aimed at achieving these two high-level goals. The challenge is that not every session of other professional psychotherapies is aimed at these two high-level goals.

Let us turn to the careful assessment of each session as successful and effective. Here again, experiential sessions are far more sophisticated than sessions with professional psychotherapists. Few, if any, professional psychotherapies can match experiential sessions in the rigor of criteria for assessing the successfulness and effectiveness of each session. Each experiential session must attain four in-session steps, and the steps must occur in a particular order. Each step is identifiable by observers. The indications of having achieved each step are clear, objective, and systematic. By the end of the session, the two goals should be achieved. Again, the criteria for determining if the two goals were achieved are clear, objective, and systematic.

The challenge is that few, if any, professional psychotherapies can match experiential sessions in the clarity, carefulness, and objectivity of criteria for determining the success and effectiveness of sessions. Experiential sessions are more sophisticated than professional psychotherapies.

In experiential sessions, the unit of study is the individual session. Each session is organized and defined as comprising four steps. This is a mark of sophistication. In comparison, the unit of study in most professional psychotherapies is an entire program of sessions. This unit of study is less systematic, less sophisticated. When you study a whole series of sessions, there is less precision than if you carefully study a single experiential session that proceeds through four identifiable steps. Once again, experiential sessions seem to be more sophisticated than sessions of professional psychotherapies.

The rise of more and more "practitioners" means the fall of "professional psychotherapists" and their "patient-clients." The field of professional psychotherapy is entitled to be at war with the field of self-change if enough professional psychotherapists peer into the future and catch a glimpse of the increasing numbers of people who are having their own sessions. There will be increasing numbers of "practitioners" doing meditation, carrying out their own self-change sessions, and having their own experiential sessions.

Professional psychotherapists have always counted an abundance of people to be their patients and clients. Large numbers of people are designated as "needing" psychotherapy. Suppose the number of potential customers plunges. Suppose most of these people make having their own sessions a regular part of their life. Suppose that having conversations with a professional psychotherapist no longer does what having your own sessions can accomplish.

The picture is that of more and more people having their own sessions. The end of professional psychotherapy will be signaled when more and more psychotherapists also carry out their own sessions. Gradually, the field of psychotherapy will be eroded and replaced with people having their own sessions, especially as they are joined by those who had previously placed themselves in the role of patient or client and psychotherapist or counselor.

There is already a war, although it is mainly a quiet, undeclared war. Experiential sessions can accomplish what the field of professional psychotherapy cannot. Meditation can accomplish what most psychotherapies cannot. Self-change methods are getting better and better. The field of self-change is alive, active, growing, and developing. The field of self-change is not at war with the field of professional psychotherapy, but the field of psychotherapy is at war with the field of self-change. The field of professional psychotherapy senses that the rise of people having their own sessions means the fall of professional psychotherapy. In some real respects, the war is already on.

There may always be some people fulfilling the roles of patient and psychotherapist because of the important personal experiencings provided by those roles. Some day, the number of people having their own sessions will grow and grow until there are far more people having their own sessions than there are psychotherapists and their clients. Still, a fair number of people will probably always perpetuate the roles of psychotherapist and patient because these roles allow people to have important personal experiencings. The roles of psychotherapist and patient are too rich a "dating service" to dwindle away.

There is the lonely older man, and the important experiencing is just having someone he sees once a week who makes him feel that someone cares about him, knows about his worries and joys, and likes him.

There is the lost woman from a small African country. She has no one here in this big, new country, and she misses her family back home. It is so precious to spend an hour a week with a person who is a little bit like her older sister and who gives her a feeling of family.

There is the man who suddenly lost so much—his wife, parents, job, and home. His life has fallen apart. It is so wonderful to be with a doctor who will manage things and help him keep things together. The doctor is solid and stable, like a rock. How reassuring this feels.

Only with her therapist does she have a sense of being well and truly understood, being with someone who knows her so well. She has rarely, if ever, had that feeling. It is so precious.

No one has ever been so fascinated by every detail about him. He feels like a precious jewel, and he revels in the hour of delving into every nuance of what he is like, what he thinks, and what has happened to him. These are his finest hours.

She is in her early 20s, but she has never had sex. With her attractive therapist, she has such wonderful sexual feelings. She could never spend such intimate time with a handsome doctor. Here is safe sex with a special lover, even though they have done nothing more than shake hands. Just being alone with him is enough.

He finally has someone who is on his side and sees things his way. He has never before felt that someone would always be there to take his side. How wonderful that feels.

She now has the close confidante she has always wanted so desperately. She feels so great when she pours out every thought and idea to this special confidante. She trusts her doctor more than she has trusted anyone in her life. She treasures telling her doctor everything.

He has such a great feeling when he defeats the therapist's every effort to help him feel better, get him out of the doldrums. Every week, the good therapist keeps trying. Each effort is blocked, countered, and fails. It feels so good for the therapist to try, but to be defeated.

There are plenty of therapists who play the complementary roles that are important for another person to gain the special experiencings that result from the role of patient. Just like in a dating service, you must find the right therapist in order to have your important experiencings. And the reverse is also true. People who fulfill the role of psychotherapist can gain precious and important personal experiencings, and it is helpful if the person who plays the role of patient is the right kind of person.

The person who plays the role of therapist can get the special feeling that she is truly a giver, someone who offers something of herself, and goes out of her way to help. He can have such a wonderful feeling of being wise, smart, and knowledgeable. She revels in the sense of being looked up to as the heroine, a mythic one, elevated, the kind of person the patient wants to be. He can be closer and more intimate with some patients, more so than with almost anyone in his real life. What she says is listened to, respected, truly important, and may even make a difference in a patient's life. The most precious moments are when the patients fall in love with him, are so attracted to him, and he knows they cannot have him. She revels in the sense of being so important to the patient, of having the patient attend to almost every sentence she says. He is just an ordinary guy, but here he is, and this well-known community figure needs him, is almost groveling. What a wonderful feeling this is.

Therapists and patients need one another to have the important personal experiencings they gain via the roles of client or patient and psychotherapist or counselor. Their experiencings are so important, and the therapist-patient relationship is so fitting and effective in providing these mutually important experiencings that I believe therapists and their clients will be around for about as long as prostitutes and their clients.

WHAT IS NEXT?

Ever since professional psychotherapy arose in the late 1800s, there seems to have been a curious relationship between the well-organized, politically wise establishment of professional psychotherapy and the ancient, more unstructured field of self-change.

In a sense, they both deal with feeling better, or feeling less bad, about personal concerns, troubles, and states, with how and why one acts, thinks, and behaves the way one does, with overcoming pain and suffering, and with becoming a better person. All of this is so general, yet the two fields probably have these general aims in common.

However, when you get closer to the aims and goals of particular psychotherapies and self-change approaches, the differences become apparent. The mind-sets, worldviews, and philosophies are so different, for example, when the professional psychotherapist uses a cognitive therapy to treat depression, and when a person sits quietly in a meditative state. The precise aims and goals of an experiential session are worlds away from the aims and goals of the professional psychotherapist who is trying to get the young woman who argued with her lover about the Christmas tree to give up her relationship with the older woman.

Almost definitely, the big difference is the presence or absence of the professional psychotherapist. The field of medicine might still exist without physicians. There would still be medical aims and goals, methods and techniques. People might administer to themselves, apply salves, use equipment, run tests, and so on. But once you remove the professional psychotherapist, virtually the whole field of psychotherapy washes away. Its aims and goals come from and justify the psychotherapist. Its methods and techniques require the psychotherapist. Everything about the relationship, the helping alliance, and almost all the tools and techniques emanate from the presence of the psychotherapist. Without the psychotherapist, there is essentially nothing left of the field of psychotherapy.

There is a war, but the war is declared and fought by the professional psychotherapist. The enemy is the ancient history and growing presence of the person who has his or her own sessions of some form of self-change. The person who meditates is the enemy. The person who has his or her own experiential sessions is the enemy. This enemy may well be the advanced guard of improved self-change methods that will eventually replace most of the professional psychotherapists.

What is next? I foresee the eventual demise of the field of professional psychotherapy and its replacement with better and better self-change approaches. I believe that having your own experiential sessions will become better and better, and these sessions, along with other emerging self-change approaches, will replace what we now know as the field of professional psychotherapists.

p. 142
blank

5

STEP 1. DISCOVER THE DEEPER POTENTIAL FOR EXPERIENCING

Chapters 5 through 8 are the working manual for how to go through Steps 1, 2, 3, and 4, respectively. The emphasis is on what you actually do and how you do it.

Use the figure (the two-page figure in Chapter 2) as a summary-guide in going through Chapters 5 through 8.

Some of the major subheads in these chapters are in capital letters, and others are in italics. The headings in capital letters concern what you actually do. The main headings in italic type give you guidelines for what you actually do and how you actually do it.

The purpose of this chapter is to show you how to do the first step of the session. When you have completed Step 1, you have discovered a possibility for experiencing that is deeper inside of you, a potentiality that has been hidden deeper inside of you: a deeper potential for experiencing. The session begins with you putting yourself into a state of readiness for relatively strong feelings. Then you are shown how to find a scene of strong feeling, how to fully live and be in that scene of strong feeling, and how to identify the precise instant at which the feeling reaches its peak. When you are living and being in this dilated, frozen instant of peak feeling, the chapter shows you how to discover the deeper potential for experiencing. At that point, you have completed the first step.

RECLINE IN A CHAIR OR ON A BED, CLOSE YOUR EYES, AND KEEP THEM CLOSED THROUGHOUT THE SESSION

Find a room that is reasonably soundproof so that you do not hear sounds from outside the room and people outside the room cannot hear you. Make sure that there will be no interruptions for at least two hours and that you can be in the room for at least a few hours.

Lie back in a large, comfortable chair, with your feet on a footrest. Or, lie on a bed or a comfortable pad.

Close your eyes, and keep them closed throughout the entire session. If it helps, put something over your eyes so that you cannot see.

The light in the room should be low.

Step 1. Discover the Deeper Potential for Experiencing

PUT YOURSELF IN A STATE OF STRONG FEELING

There are a number of ways to put yourself in a state of strong feeling, of intensely powerful feeling. You can take 15 to 30 very deep breaths and blast out the exhalations. Each time you inhale and forcefully exhale, make exceedingly loud noises of any kind. You may growl, snarl, screech, bellow, howl. Make exceedingly loud noises each time you inhale and exhale.

Another method is simply to make noises as loud as you can. Just remove all your usual self-control and let the powerful noises rip. Groan and moan with absolutely no constraint. Make guttural sounds. Roar. Hiss. What comes out of you are fierce screams, blasts of violent hatred and sheer rage, unrestrained lust, absolute ecstasy, extreme shock or horror, unbounded surprise and disbelief, orgiastic shrieks, incredible awe and wonder: every kind of imaginable feeling.

Another way to put yourself in a state of strong feeling is to start with the feelings that are already in you and make them absolutely powerful. If you are already tense, anxious, and scared, belt out the feelings so that they are beyond intense. If you are pleased and proud, crackling with pleasure, open up the lid and let that pleasure explode. If you are mad, furious, then crank up the fury until it is unbounded. If you are in the grip of heavy uselessness, giving up all hope, in complete despair, then totally give in to those feelings. If you are dripping with craziness, lunacy, out of your mind, feed that feeling.

Combine these methods with unrestrained movements of your body. Let your whole body tighten, clench, and then wholly relax. Kick hard with your legs and feet. Clench and unclench your fists. Jerk your whole body this way and that way. Twist and untwist your body. Pound your chest. Throw your head from side to side. Get your body into a state of absolute strong feeling.

Some people have told me that they are helped to get into a state of strong feeling by listening to audiotapes of such loud noises as tornadoes, hurricanes, earthquakes, explosions, crashes and smashes, and thunder, or by hearing the sounds of one person or thousands of people shrieking, yelling, screaming in joy or terror, ecstasy or agony. Although I have listened to a few of these audiotapes, I have not used them in my own sessions.

Whatever you do that works for you, keep it up for about a minute or so. Keep it up until your body reverberates all by itself, has its own strong sensations quite aside from you. That is, your heart is simply pounding, your arms and legs are shaking and trembling all by themselves, your whole body seems to be rising up or twisting or swirling all by itself, your tongue is so thick it cannot do its usual work, there is a leathery coating over your face, you feel waves of heat or cold or electricity, and your muscles are quivering.

Keep it up until you no longer have a sense of knowing what is happening, of being watchfully aware of what you are doing, of having private thoughts about what is going on.

Step 1. Discover the Deeper Potential for Experiencing

Keep up this exercise of putting yourself into a state of readiness for strong feeling until you no longer have this usual sense of self-awareness, of observing and watching yourself, of self-consciousness, of I-ness. You no longer have private thoughts like,:"I wonder if she can hear me . . . Hey, that sounds like I'm having an orgasm . . . I'm doing this pretty well!"

Keep it up until no one can recognize that it is you. It is no longer your voice. You sound like a completely different person who is yelling, hissing, groaning, laughing, making those ridiculous sounds. Your voice is far louder and high-pitched than it usually is. Your voice is unrecognizable. So are you. It is hard to tell if you are female or male, young or old; even your close friends would not be able to recognize the person who is making all those weird noises.

Let Go of the Controls You Usually Have Over Your Feelings

If I tell most people, "Say it again, much louder, and with much more feeling!" many will soon hit a barrier. Their neck muscles are tight. Most people tightly contract their chest, neck, throat, and voice. They maintain a tight control over their feelings, and they will not let go of that control. They have worked hard to have just the right voice quality, and they are going to keep that tight control no matter what.

You must let go of that control. When you do, your voice quality will be quite different. Your voice will no longer be that of the person who is constantly controlling the voice, who is always using the muscles in the chest, neck,

147

throat, face, and mouth to produce that familiar voice. Keep letting go of your second-to-second controls so that your voice is louder, much more filled with feeling; it is an open passageway for feelings.

It Is Probably Not Enough if Your Voice and Body
Are Quiet Outside and You Try to Have Strong Feelings
"Inside Your Head."

The reason for starting by putting yourself in a state of strong feeling is for you to be able to go through the steps and sub-steps of a session. If you do not start by putting yourself in a state of strong feeling, letting go of the usual controls, then you will likely have trouble going through the session.

Some people say that they can get into a state of strong feeling by having a strong feeling inside their head, even though they keep their body still and their voice quiet. They may even sit quietly, with no movement and no sound. They say that, although they may be relatively quiet outside, inside they are filled with absolute ecstasy or agony or some other powerful feeling. They say that they can get into a meditative state of sorts, a state in which they allow a strong feeling to fill their body inside, without showing outside. They say that when they are dreaming they can be undergoing powerful feeling without screaming or yelping, and without their body thrashing or undergoing powerful movements.

When I listen to their sessions, I occasionally find them to be just fine. More often, however, I find that their sessions are quite poor, and they do not go through the steps well. The clincher, for me, is that when these people begin with the way I believe is useful, that is, to give up the usual controls and to get into a state of strong feeling, then they do just fine in proceeding through the session.

BE IN THE STATE OF RELATIVELY STRONG FEELING THROUGHOUT THE WHOLE SESSION.

For a minute or so, you have put yourself in a state of exceedingly strong feeling. This state is extreme. If you do this well, you will be in a state of relatively strong feeling throughout the whole session, a state that is less than this opening state of exceedingly powerful feeling, but one that is more than your usual state of controlled, ordinary feeling.

Throughout the rest of the session, remain in a state where your feelings are pumped up, your voice is unnaturally loud and filled with feeling, and there are bodily-felt sensations over at least a part of your body.

Throughout the rest of the session, keep talking unusually loud and with relatively strong feeling. Make sure there are no silences, no periods of even three to five seconds of silence. Say words or make noises and sounds, but keep up the patter. Instead of a silence, say: "Yes. Yes. Crack. Oh. (Smack your lips. Make puffing sounds.) Baby tree. Wind. Crackers. I see Mommy's face. She smoked all the time. Ah. Wow. I am not moving in with Sam. No way. His son is the barrier between us. Pooh. That kid. Maybe it's for the best. For now."

I have heard sessions where the person does a fine job of putting himself or herself in a state of strong feeling, but after a minute or so, the person returns to the usual state of highly controlled, ordinary, normal, dead talk, with a tightly controlled, normal voice. That is wrong. Instead, stay in a continuous state of relatively strong feeling throughout the rest of the session.

FIND A SCENE OF STRONG FEELING

As shown in the figure in Chapter 2, once you put yourself into a state of strong feeling, you need to find a scene of strong feeling. Look for some scene, some time, some situation when the feeling in you was powerful, filled your whole body. The feeling may have been a good one: sheer pleasure, joy, exuberance, ecstasy. Usually, however, the feeling is horrible, painful, bad.

The scene of strong feeling may have just happened. It may be a recent scene that has implications for the future, like being told that you have less than a year to live, or that the brother you haven't seen in 20 years will be visiting you in a few weeks. The scene of strong feeling may be from relatively recently, like within the past few weeks or months. It may have occurred a few years ago. It is often one that happened many years ago, when you were just a child, or maybe even during your infancy. Whenever it happened, the feeling is extremely powerful.

The scene of strong feeling may have happened in your real life, or it may be from a dream. Dreams are a rich source of scenes of strong feeling. Indeed, when looking for the kinds of experiencings that are deep inside you, scenes of strong feeling from dreams can be more helpful than what happens in your actual life. Here is where I hope you might read my book on how to use your own dreams (Mahrer, 1989b).

When looking for a scene of strong feeling, you must be honest with yourself. Sometimes that is hard to do. When you were seven years old, you were the one who played with the little pistol and aimed it at the thing moving in the bushes. You were almost out of your mind with terror when you were told that your uncle lost his eye; someone had shot him in the eye when he was weeding in the bushes. After that, you convinced yourself that you were up in your room at the time and that some mysterious stranger's stray bullet was the cause. Be honest with yourself. You are a respected lawyer, and yet you steal nail clippers from a store every week like clockwork. Although you have been doing this for years and years, and you are almost beside yourself with terror each time you steal, you want to omit these from your scenes of strong feeling.

The scene may be one in which your strong feeling is conspicuously public or one that is undetectably private. In one, anyone nearby can see the tears streaming down your wrenched face. In another, the police officer is oblivious to the pounding panic inside you when she stops your car to let you know that your taillights are not working. You are so cooperative and appreciative, all the while knowing there is a small bag of cocaine in your coat pocket.

151

Usually, each new session starts with a different scene of strong feeling. Occasionally, the scene of strong feeling is similar to the one you started with last session, or perhaps a few sessions ago. Sometimes several sessions in a row start with almost the same scene of strong feeling. For example, the last few sessions started with scenes in which you are torn apart by the overwhelming sense of weakness and fatigue from the cancer that has spread all through your body. In the last session, you started with a scene of complete fatigue over your entire body when you awoke in the morning. In the present session, you started with the scene of being unable to get up out of the chair; the feeling was that same heavy tiredness, of being eaten away by the cancer. Ordinarily, though, each session starts with its own, unique scene of strong feeling.

Probably the Best Starting Place Is a Recent Scene of Powerful Feeling or a Dream

One of the best places to start is with a scene that happened in the past day or so, a scene in which the feeling was so powerful and compelling that the powerful feeling is still beating inside. Your whole world collapsed yesterday when your nine-year-old son found you masturbating on the bed. Your best friend's sister told you that Sarah cut her wrists and killed herself this morning. Last night your husband lied to you about money, and you went crazy, running around the apartment in a frenzy, shrieking. Yesterday you and your friend were having coffee at a table outside the coffeehouse in Zurich on your first trip to Switzerland, and you were gripped with this sense of awe of having been here before and of knowing every detail of what happened next: the waiter asking about your ring, your friend giving you the gift of the collection of Nordic poetry, and the young lady at the table to your left removing a harmonica from her pocket and playing a languorous melody. When there is a recent scene that filled you with powerful feeling, this is the place to start.

If you have had a dream in the past few days or so, use the dream if it had two scenes of even relatively strong feeling. A dream with two scenes of relatively strong feeling is much more useful than a dream with just one scene of feeling, even if the feeling is powerful. The scenes and feelings need not be dramatically different, but there should be two places where there is a rising up of some feeling or feelings.

In one dream, you are driving the car up a hill, and you notice that the car is losing power, slowing down. The feeling is one of helplessness, fear, being scared. Then, the car starts sliding down the hill slowly. You turn your head, look back, and see a huge lake not far behind you. Now you are really terrified that you and the car will end up in the lake. Use this dream, even though the scenes are rather similar and so are the feelings.

In another dream, you are filled with silliness and giddiness as you float high in the air above the rolling countryside. You know you can go up or down, forward or backward, just by moving your arms. This is sheer fun. Then, you are a little girl in a classroom, and the mean teacher is punishing you by ordering you to sing in front of the class. You are standing in front of the class, looking down at the floor, and feeling so awful, so ridiculed, so laughed at by the class, especially the two girls in the front who are smirking about your plight. In this dream, the two scenes are quite different, as are the two feelings.

Later on in this chapter, I will show you how to use the two scenes of relatively strong feeling in the dream. The main point is that fine starting places of strong feeling include a recent dream or a recent scene of very strong feeling in your waking, daily life.

Record a Dream in Which There Are Two Places Where There Is a Rising Up of Feeling

Keep a tape recorder or pen and paper next to your bed. Have everything within easy reach so that you can record dreams almost effortlessly, without having to get out of bed. As you are awakening and remembering the dream, record it right away.

Pay special attention to recording any dreams in which there are two places where there is a rising up of feeling. Record this dream even if the feeling is not powerful in either place. The feeling may even be somewhat similar in both places. Usually there is a rising up of feeling in one episode, and then another episode.

When you record the dream, make sure to pay special attention to recording as much detail as you can in the two places where there is a rising up of feeling. Tell the details of what is happening in the scene when the feeling rises up. Describe as much as you can about the feeling itself. Your recording need not be orderly, starting at the beginning and proceeding through the story of the dream. Do not first review the dream as it may have occurred in the unfolding of the story. Instead, record what you remember as you remember it. Record in bits and pieces.

ASK YOURSELF THESE QUESTIONS TO FIND A SCENE OF STRONG FEELING, AND THEN FIND A SCENE IN WHICH THAT FEELING WAS EVEN STRONGER

When you begin the session, you may already be filled with a recent scene of strong feeling or a dream. It is already the compelling center of attention. If not, then learn to ask yourself the questions at the end of this section.

Say the questions out loud. Remember, throughout the session you are to remain in the continuous state of relatively strong feeling. If you use two or three questions in one session, use a different set of questions in the next session. The idea is that you learn to find scenes of strong feeling by using all of the questions over five to ten sessions. If you notice that you are using the same one or two questions session after session, then deliberately start by using some different questions.

When you say the question out loud, say it again and again until some scene of strong feeling comes to mind. Take whatever comes to mind; do not censor any scenes of strong feeling. If the question has to do with something that truly bothers you, worries you, and makes you feel awful, and you see a scene from childhood in which you screamed at your father that you hated him, you can use that scene even though it is not something that bothers you, worries you, and makes you feel awful today. If the question has to do with some horrible feeling, and the scene that comes to mind is a sheer wonderful feeling, you can use that scene. Take and use the first or second scene that comes to mind when you ask a question. No matter what the reason, do not censor any scenes of strong feeling.

Most questions are followed by another question to guide you toward finding a time when that feeling was much stronger. The aim is to find a scene in which the feeling was most powerful, most intense. Here is an example, starting with the first question on the list: "When was it that the feeling in me was so strong, so powerful, so full, and it was so painful, so hurtful, so awful? It may have lasted only a moment or so, or much longer. When did it happen? What were the circumstances?" The scene that comes to mind is when you arrived at your apartment door to see the painted words: "We don't want you here. Go back to China where you belong." The horrible feeling is that of being invaded, raped, hated. But when you ask the next question, "Was there some other time, maybe earlier in my life, when that feeling was even more dramatic, more powerful, more intense, filled me even more?" you remember when you were a child and your father beat you mercilessly. He had never before struck you. He banished you from home, sent you to live far away with your grandmother, and never spoke to you from that time on.

Or, you begin by asking yourself the third question: "What is the thing that bothers me the most, that worries me so much, that makes me feel so awful?" Your answer is that when your wife wants to have sex, you always say no. You are negative. You always say no to everything. "When was it that I felt this powerful feeling? What were the circumstances? What was happening?" Your answer is just a few days ago, when your wife was so friendly and happy and asked about going on a vacation. You never go on vacations. You told her you didn't think you had time to go. Bam. That's when it happened. "Go back in my life. What times come to mind when I think of early times when I had that feeling so fully, so filling me? What scenes do I see?" You remember that horrible time when you said no, you were so negative, you wouldn't do it. You were a little boy, standing outside the closed bathroom door. Your grandfather was inside, on the toilet, pleading for you to get your mother. You were filled with the feeling of no, I won't do it. You just stood there. The next thing you remember is your mother shoving you aside, rushing into the bathroom. Your grandfather had collapsed on the floor, and he was taken to the hospital.

Some of the questions are not followed by another question that invites you to look for some other time, usually earlier, when that feeling was even stronger. The seventh question is: "In the past week or so, what dream did I have in which there was some feeling, either good or bad?" When you find a dream to work with, stay with the dream. Do not move from the dream feeling to an earlier time when the feeling was stronger.

Here are the questions to say aloud in order to find a scene of strong feeling. Know them well enough to be able to select a few at a time. If it helps, in the early sessions, open your eyes, look at the list, and then close your eyes and say a few questions out loud until you find a scene of strong feeling. When was it that the feeling in me was so strong, so powerful, so full, and it was so painful, so hurtful, so awful? It may have lasted only a moment or so, or much longer. When did it happen? What were the circumstances?

1. Was there some other time, maybe earlier in my life, when that feeling was even more dramatic, more powerful, more intense, filled me even more?

2. What is the feeling I have that is so powerful, so strong, so full, and is so painful, so awful?

   When is a recent time when I had this painful, powerful feeling?

   Go back in my life. In my whole life, when was it that I felt this even more?

3. What is the thing that bothers me the most, that worries me so much, that makes me feel so awful?

Step 1. Discover the Deeper Potential for Experiencing

When was it that I felt this powerful feeling? What were
the circumstances? What was happening?

Go back in my life. What times come to mind when I
think of early times when I had that feeling so fully, so
filling me? What scenes do I see?

4. What scene or time seems to be on my mind right now,
when I just let myself pay attention, a time when I feel so
bad, worried, troubled?

Now go back. In my whole life, when did I have this
feeling so fully, powerfully, intensely?

5. In my life today, during the past five or ten years or so,
when did I have one of the worst, most powerful feelings?
So powerful, so terrible, so intense, so dramatic?

Go back. In my whole life, when I let myself have that same
horrible feeling, what scenes and times come to mind?

When I was a child, when did I have one of the worst,
most powerful feelings? So powerful, so terrible, so
intense, so dramatic?

6. In my life today, during the past five or ten years or so,
when did I have a powerful feeling of going crazy, falling
apart, losing my mind?

Go back. In my whole life, when did I have that powerful feeling of going crazy, falling apart, losing my mind?

When I was a child, when did I have a powerful feeling of going crazy, falling apart, losing my mind?

7. In the past week or so, what dream did I have in which there was some feeling, either good or bad?

8. What dream did I seem to have over and over again, almost the same dream?

9. What is the kind of bad feeling I have had as far back as I can remember? The feeling that is a part of who I am, the thing that has been wrong with me since I was just a child?

When did I seem to have that feeling intensely, fully, powerfully? What scenes come to mind?

10. Lately, recently, what kind of nice change seems to be happening in the way I am, in how I feel, in something about me, in the way I am with people and the way people are with me? It may be a subtle, little change or a bigger one. What is this change?

When did I notice this change, when it was kind of strong?

11. Lately, recently, when did I have a strong feeling that was really wonderful, exciting, happy, full of pleasure?

In my whole life, when did I have that same great feeling so powerfully, so intensely?

12. When I was a child, when did I have a strong feeling that was really wonderful, exciting, happy, full of pleasure?

You need not use the exact words in each question. Read the question and then put it in your own words. Say the question out loud, over and over again, until you get a scene of strong feeling. Then, search for the time, the scene, when that feeling was even stronger, perhaps the most saturatingly intense time that you had that feeling. You have succeeded in finding a scene of strong feeling.

Read or Listen to the Entire Recorded Dream, and Then
Identify Two Scenes of Heightened Feeling in the Dream

If you start with a dream, you usually have a tape recording of your recollection of the dream, or it is written on a sheet of paper. Start by listening to or reading the whole dream. Then, pick out the two places where the heightened feeling occurred: these are the two scenes of strong feeling. Use these two scenes even if the feeling is not powerful, as long as it is heightened. For example, in the first scene, when the feeling is heightened, you are looking for the staircase down to the first floor. You are in a warehouse, and the floor is way up above ground level. There is a hidden staircase, and you are looking for it. The feeling is exciting, like a game, a competition, but friendly, with about eight or ten others also looking for the staircase. Later, in another part of the dream, a huge bear comes up to your doorway, even though there is no door. The scene of strong feeling occurs when the bear goes away and comes back with a door, puts it in place, stands outside the door, and yells, "Open the door!" You feel like laughing. This is funny. The bear is funny. You are lighthearted and happy. These are the two scenes of heightened feeling.

Stay with these two scenes. You do not need to look for other times in your life when you had the feeling more intensely. The dream scene will do nicely.

In the Most Basic Scenes, the Strong Feeling Is in Your Parent, and the Scene Is from Your Parent's Life, from a Year or So Before You Were Conceived to Three to Five Years after You Were Born

When you go back in your life to find a time when the feeling was even stronger, every so often you might try to find that feeling in your parents rather than in yourself. Just suppose that the feeling was happening in your mother or your father, not in you. Pay special attention to the period from approximately one year before you were conceived to three to five years after you were born.

Suppose that the strong feeling is that of being invaded, raped, hated. You shift your focus to that period in your parents' lives and suddenly you see a scene: "My God! Before I was born, my mother was almost raped by a friend of my father, and my mother was blamed for the whole thing. My father's family hated her from then on. They thought of her as a prostitute! She was pregnant with me when it happened. She was the one who felt invaded, raped, hated!"

Or, you look for an earlier time when you had that terrible feeling even stronger, the feeling of saying no, being negative, refusing to do it. This time, you shift the focus from yourself to your mother or father. The time frame is the period from one year or so before you were conceived to three to five years after you were born. "That's when the big family fight happened! Dad's whole family came. I barely remember. I was about two. Later I found out. Dad and Mom lived in this little town in the mountains in Colorado and ran this little store. But his family was rich. My grandfather was dying, and the whole family came from Boston. They tried to force Dad to come back and help run the business there. They were really wealthy, and they pressured Dad. But Dad and Mom said no. That was the huge fight. We never went back to Boston, ever, and they never talked. Dad and Mom said no; they wouldn't give in. They told me about it when I was older, because I wondered why Dad never talked about his family and they never came to visit. Dad's not a defiant guy, but he must have done a big thing then!"

In the experiential way of making sense of your basic nature, of understanding how and where your basic potentials for experiencing come from, a great deal of importance lies in the scenes of strong feelings in your mother's and father's lives during this primitive period of your life. This is the "soup" out of which the very basis of you arose. Some of these scenes may have occurred in relationship to you as an infant, but many did not. Every so often, try going back to those primitive scenes in the lives of your mother and father.

Just Finding the Strong Feeling Is Not Enough;
You Must Find the Scene in Which the Strong Feeling Occurs

The second question in the list invites you to locate the strong feeling, specifically one that is painful: "What is the feeling I have that is so powerful, so strong, so full, and is so painful, so awful?" Once you identify the strong feeling, the next question asks you to find the scene, or the context, in which this strong feeling occurred: "When is a recent time when I had this painful, powerful feeling?" First find the strong feeling, and then find the scene in which it occurred.

It is easy and common to be able to find the strong feeling. You can start by finding the strong feeling of being dismally depressed and gloomy, fallen apart, torn to pieces, fragmented, enraged, furious, or overcome with sheer, undiluted craving and lust. The trouble is that it is so easy and common to dance around the strong feeling without ever finding the scene in which it occurs. The strong feeling is compelling. It can entice you to tell more about it, think about it, remember the things you have done about it, ponder endlessly what accounted for it, and even experience it right now. Instead, your job is to find the situational context, that is, the scene in which the strong feeling occurs.

"I know I have such a temper. I get so scared when I start to get mad. I can feel it. I get scared that, once I blow, I don't know what I'll do! Like I'm almost going to explode." This fellow rolled around in this feeling until he asked himself when and where this feeling happened. He answered: "Hilde tells me to repair the window. Not the first time. Oh, no! She stands right in front of me and tells me again, with that look on her face. It drives me crazy! Over and over. She's after me! Yes, I will do it. But she has to stop torturing me! I just can't stand that!" You can first find the general feeling, but then you must find the scene in which it occurs.

It is easy to roll around in depression. "What's the use? I'm alone. Who would care if I died? Sam is gone. I've got nothing in my life. Every day is the same. I sit around, scared about nothing, dead. I am dead. I never used to think about death. Now I do." It is much harder to find a specific time when this feeling is strong. Wallowing in the bad feeling seems to be inconsistent with the effort it takes to find the scene when the feeling was stronger. "My God, I have to find when I felt this way. Ah, yes, yesterday, no more milk. I felt so low, and started drinking, in the morning. I'm drinking and I don't care any more. I'm so disgusted with myself. I'm a drunk! It's morning, and I'm already drinking. What the hell is happening to me?"

There is a relatively common state of nonspecific, bad feelings, a mixture of feelings that are not of one identifiable

165

kind. It is a state of feeling low, depressed, hopeless, tense, edgy, withdrawn, glum, slowed down, inactive, scared, and somewhat agitated. Look for a scene. It is almost essential to find a scene; otherwise, you can wallow in this general state of nonspecific, bad feelings for days, weeks, or much longer.

How can you find a scene? Look for a scene that has two features. First, it is a scene that occurred before you were enveloped in this state of bad feeling. Usually, the scene happened recently, probably in the day or so before the feeling filled you. Second, it is a scene in which you did little or nothing; you did not act or react. It happened, and you just coasted through.

For example, down the hall is the neighbor whom you hate. He is your enemy. You open the door to go down the hall to get the elevator, and, as you take a step out into the hall, you see him waiting for the elevator. This is the recent scene of strong feeling. In this scene, you stood frozen by your door, turned to lock the door, and deliberately waited there until your neighbor was gone. That is the scene. Here is another example: You are looking for a recent scene in which you did nothing, you almost froze. You recollect a scene yesterday when the fellow you slept with, the fellow you liked so much, asked to use the phone. As you make coffee, you hear him on the phone, and you know he is talking to his old girlfriend. "I'll be right over." He hangs up, mutters that he has to go, and stands there, as if waiting for you to do something. You smile and nod, holding both cups. "Give me a call tonight?" He leaves. Scenes such as these, which happened recently, scenes in which you almost froze and did nothing, are very common.

Just knowing the strong feeling is not enough. You must find the appropriate scene around the strong feeling.

If the Feeling Is Nagging, But Not Strong ,
Search Carefully for Subtle Times When There Is
a Momentary Burst of the Strong Feeling

Sometimes, the feeling that is front and center is one that seems almost always to be present. It is a kind of mood you are in much of the time, like "background noise." It is almost always there, ready to fill you. Yet the feeling seems never to be very strong. It is more mild or somewhat moderate, but unpleasant, unhappy, and bothersome. It does not seem necessarily tied to any particular scene or time. Instead, it seems to be something you carry around or feel much of the time.

It is a mild or moderate general feeling of being low, depressed, gloomy; of being a loser, second rate, not good enough; of being tense, worried, fretful, ready for an awful thing to happen; of being alone, always by yourself, never really close with anyone; of being out of place, not belonging, not a part of things; of being suspicious, watchful, distrustful; of being guilty, the bad one, at fault, accused; of being critical, resentful, negative; of being vulnerable, defenseless, open to attack; of being mixed-up, unsure, confused; of being not quite normal, something is basically wrong with you, something is fundamentally missing, twisted, or crazy; of being annoyed, angry, and mad.

Make a real effort to look for subtle times when that feeling is actually strong. Ordinarily, these are times that are not dramatic; they are tiny, inconspicuous. They quickly come and go, and are over in a flash. They seem almost unrelated to the feeling. The surge of stronger feeling happens for just a brief instant and then it is gone. These times are quickly and easily forgotten. But for a brief instant, the feeling was strong.

Make an effort to search for these brief moments. If it helps, spend a day or so keeping a diary in which you log these subtle little scenes. It happens when you pass by three coworkers in the corridor, and none of them even glances at you. It happens when you unpack the groceries and three of the eggs are broken, and the contents are running all over the container. It happens when you get home and there are no telephone messages or e-mails. The brief spurt of strong feeling happens when you notice a little blood in your urine, or when the waiter has that look when he hears the way you talk, or when the fellow at work makes that snide remark about your memo, or when your husband seems so animated and excited when he says hello to the woman on the street. It happens when you are in the kitchen of your friend and her daughter, and they look at each other in a warm bond of love.

These scenes often happen when you do not do what your insides want you to do. Instead of doing something, you did nothing. It happens in a flash, but from then on you have that low-grade feeling of being tense and tight, or pulled-in and depressed, or annoyed and irritated. The feeling stays with you across most situations. Your friend is telling you about another friend, and she says: "Gail is fun to be with. Of course, she can be sneaky sometimes, you know, like you can be, and . . ." Pow! The strong feeling explodes inside, but you do nothing. For the next day or so you have that mild, nagging feeling of being tense and tight, or pulled-in and depressed, or annoyed and irritated. It is as if your insides are grumpy or scolding you because you did nothing, you just let the hurtful moment pass.

When you look hard, you can find subtle times when the feeling is strong in you, but it comes and goes in a flash. The scene is not a dramatic one; someone who is with you would probably never know that, for a brief moment, you were experiencing a strong feeling. These are the scenes you look for. Otherwise, you are left with a low-grade feeling that seems to be always there, a little more or a little less, all the time, everywhere and unrelated to any particular situation.

Do Not Give In To The Exceedingly Clever Ploys That Keep You From Discovering Your Deeper Potential For Experiencing

Experiential sessions use a rare and precious way of discovering a deeper potential for experiencing. It starts by finding a scene of powerful feeling. That is almost unheard of. The next step is to live and be in the scene of strong feeling. That is almost never done. Then, you find the exact instant when the feeling peaks. That is unheard of. Finally, you access the deeper potential for experiencing when you are in the exact moment of peak feeling. That almost never happens outside of experiential work.

169

What almost always happens is that you do some exceedingly clever things that are marvelously effective at keeping you from ever discovering your deeper potential for experiencing. These ploys are used virtually all the time by virtually everyone. They are found in almost every session of a professional psychotherapist, and they are found outside professional sessions when ordinary people do extraordinary things to make sure they never discover a deeper potential for experiencing.

Talking About Problems, Having Bad Feelings, and Telling Stories Are Ways of Keeping You from Finding a Scene of Strong Feeling

You will have a very hard time finding a scene of strong feeling when you spend your time talking about problems, or generally complaining about things, feeling mildly negatively or sad, or telling stories about yourself, your life, or the thing you are worried about. In fact, these reactions almost ensure that you do <I>not<P> ever get to an explicit scene of strong feeling.

Instead of finding a scene and getting at a strong feeling, you "talk about" something called "problems." You talk about the fights you two have had and how different things were the first months you lived together. You talk about the way you can't really trust her because she uses you. You talk about how heavy you are; how, now that you are older, your weight is starting to make a big difference. You talk about your problem of lacking self-confidence. All these things are problems, and you can spend years and years just talking about them.

Step 1. Discover the Deeper Potential for Experiencing

Right now, either by themselves or with someone else—a friend, a good listener, or a professional psychotherapist—millions of people are probably doing a good job of talking about problems. They can do this for 20 minutes or 20 years, but they will be no closer to finding an explicit scene of strong feeling. Indeed, they will likely be farther away, more insulated from a scene of strong feeling and their deeper potential for experiencing.

A related ploy, another one that is so easy, so common, and so effective in keeping you from finding a scene of strong feeling, is to try to make sense of, to understand, to create an explanation for, the problem that you talked about. Once you have defined the problem, such as the two of you having fights, then you can spend a career inventing ways of understanding the fights, making sense of the fights, identifying what caused the fights, and explaining the fights. You can find endless answers that are cultural, dietary, sociological, psychological, and neurophysiological. There are plenty of intrapsychic factors, situational factors, mental illness factors, childhood history factors, and religious factors. As you go round and round about the endless supply of understandings and explanations, you have managed to sidestep finding an explicit scene of strong feeling.

Instead of talking about problems and living in a world of explanations and understandings of the problem, you can wallow in a general state of negativity and sadness. Simply be in a state of mild, generalized unhappiness, self-pity, loneliness, tension, failure, guilt, gloominess, uselessness, rejection, irritation, and annoyance. Find your own general state of bad feeling and dip into it for half an hour or so. Complain about yourself, your life, your situation, other people, and life in general. Almost everyone knows how to do this and is pretty good at it. It is easy. It is also a highly effective way of ensuring that you never find an explicit scene of strong feeling.

You will avoid finding a scene of strong feeling if you tell stories about whatever is on your mind, whatever concerns or worries you. You can tell stories about how your childhood friend Pierre wanted to ride the freight cars, how that was a dream he always talked about. Tell how that influenced you so much that you took up a life of riding freight cars when you were grown up, and that is how you met the old fellow whose daughter you fell in love with, and on and on. Or, start with the thing on your mind, whether to stay in England or return to Iran, and then tell long stories about becoming a dentist in Iran, and how you have always had trouble making even little decisions.

Your job is to find a scene of strong feeling. Keep this as your aim and ask questions that help you find this type of scene. Do not move into distractions and interesting topics. Find a scene of strong feeling.

The Rush to Name the "Problem" Is An Exceedingly Clever Way of Keeping You from Discovering the Deeper Potential for Experiencing

Beware of the rush to name the "problem." Whether you are alone, with a companion, or with a professional psychotherapist, you spend a few minutes almost every day rushing to name the problem, to give it some meaning, to give it a name, a description, a label.

If you have a dream, fall down the stairs, have a big argument, feel exhilarated, get nudged, forget something, or do almost anything that might qualify as a scene of strong feeling, you will rush to name the problem, and that is an effective way of sealing off the deeper potential for experiencing. You will seal off the deeper potential for experiencing by rushing in to explain that you have a problem with authority figures, have trouble communicating with the person you live with, had a dream about death, have a problem with forgetting, have fears of heights, have financial worries, have feelings of loneliness, are compulsive, have a fear of failure, are scared of being in enclosed places, have aggressive impulses, are alcoholic, are overly competitive, have a problem of overeating, have trouble falling asleep, have a great sense of humor, hear voices, or are too shy.

The trouble with rushing in to name the problem is that, although you are probably correct and your label, your thumbnail description, is probably a good one, it deflects you from ever going on to look for and discover the deeper potential for experiencing. You are indeed shy. That is indeed a sexual dream. You do indeed have a fear of heights. However, calling it that is an exceedingly effective way of making sure that you never go on to discover the deeper potential for experiencing.

Labeling a problem, describing some worry or trouble, serves to keep you from the exciting search for the deeper potential for experiencing. You are right. The trouble is that you are also irrelevant. You are accurate, but you are also fooling yourself.

Do not just talk about problems. Do not just label or describe problems. Doing these things can be great fun and is exceedingly common. They fuel what most people do most of the time. They fuel an entire field of psychotherapy and counseling. They also ensure that you never discover the deeper potential for experiencing. Instead, stay on track to find a scene of strong feeling. Once you find the scene, there are things to do so that you can discover the deeper potential for experiencing.

Fully Live And Be In The Scene Of Strong Feeling

Once you find it, you are to live and be in this scene of strong feeling. It is to be alive and real. It is to be as if the scene is actually happening right now, as if you are literally living the scene. Whether the scene happened a day ago or when you were a child, it is to be as if you went back and are living in that scene or as if the scene is happening right now.

Fully living and being in the scene means that all of you is living and being in the scene. Your sense of identity, of who and what you are, is living and being in the scene of strong feeling. There is no part that is held back, that knows you are not really living and being in the scene, that thinks:

"I'm doing pretty well, remembering what happened . . . I was scared of even being in the elevator with that guy and whatever he had in that package, but I don't feel scared now, not even a little." Your sense of identity, of I-ness, is living and being in the scene; it is not held back, removed, having thoughts about what is going on.

You and your body are living and being in the scene. If, in the scene of strong feeling, you are pressed back against the wall of the elevator, your body should be in that position. If the scene is from when you were a child, kneeling on the floor, stroking the cat, then you are literally to be a child, with the child's body, kneeling on the floor.

The aim is for you to literally and actually be living and being in the elevator, your back pressed against the elevator wall. You see out of the eyes of the person who is pressed against the elevator wall. You are not remembering the scene; you are living and being in the scene. You are not seeing the little girl kneeling on the floor, stroking the cat. Instead, you are inside the skin of the little girl, looking out through her eyes, seeing what she is seeing.

The aim is for you to live and be in the alive, real scene of strong feeling. This is your goal, your intent. You enter into this scene so that it is alive and real, immediate and present. Once you find a scene of strong feeling, it is as if you can say out loud, "Now I am going to fully live and be in this scene of strong feeling." While you are doing the work, it is as if some small part of you is still saying, "Keep going until you are fully living and being in this scene of strong feeling."

FREEZE THE SCENE AND DESCRIBE MORE ABOUT THE SCENE
OUTSIDE AND WHAT YOU ARE THINKING AND FEELING INSIDE

Ordinarily, the scene of strong feeling lasted from a few seconds to a minute or so. Things happen and things move on. Keep the scene still. Freeze it. Slow it down, and play it in slow motion. You slow the scene down so you can study it, see it carefully, and see all its parts.

Do not be in a rush, even if the actual scene rushed by in an instant. You are a little girl kneeling on the floor, stroking the cat, and the noise of yelling is booming in your ears. When you heard the loud noise of something smashing, your body was jolted. More yelling. When you slow down the scene, you can keep it around to study it. It is still filled with high drama and sound effects, but it is considerably slowed down.

Make an effort to keep the scene the way it is. You are looking down at the cat. See the cat. Hear the sounds. Do not let the scene get hazy and unclear. Do not let it dissipate. Do not let the scene fade away.

Describe what is happening in the scene. The more you describe it, the more you are living and being in the scene. Each part of the scene that you describe pulls you more and more into living and being in the scene.

Describe what is happening in the present tense. It is happening now, right now. You are seeing it from inside the skin of the little girl kneeling on the floor. "I am in the dining room, on the floor, a wood floor. My hand is on Daisy. I am touching you. You are still. And they are yelling. They're in the kitchen. No one else is here . . ."

176

Step 1. Discover the Deeper Potential for Experiencing

Some parts of the scene may not fill in: "What am I wearing? What time of day is it? I can't tell . . . " Other parts may fill in when you concentrate and focus your attention: "What are they yelling about? I hear Mom. She's crying and sounds so mad. Yes! It's about Dad's drinking. She's saying she's had it with his being drunk. Did something happen? I can't tell. And what broke? Something broke, like against the wall. A loud noise. I am so scared . . . I don't know what it is."

Describe what is happening inside. Tell what you are feeling and thinking. Take your time. Feelings are filling you. What are they like? What are the sensations in your body? Are there thoughts racing through your head? What are they? Just take your time.

With the scene frozen, as you are describing what is happening inside and outside, use your voice to express your feeling. Pump up the feeling level. Talk loudly. Talk with strong feeling, even unnaturally strong feeling. Experience sensations in your face and chest and all over your body. Whatever feeling you have in this scene, have it with real strength. If a teacher were with you, the teacher might be saying: "Louder! With more feeling!" By yourself, be your own teacher or coach. Train yourself or the voice inside you to say: "Louder! With more feeling!" Here you are, a little girl, scared, frightened to death, hammered by your parents' screaming. Be scared. Let your body be scared. Be very scared. Let your voice be full of loud fear.

Keep talking, with no pauses, no moments of silence. Not even for just a few seconds. With your attention focused, keep making noises, keep saying words: "Something broke, like against the wall. A loud noise. I am so scared. I don't know what it is. I don't know, I don't know. Loud noise . . . Wall . . . Something smashed. Not a dish. Something broke, like a loud smash against the wall. I don't know what it is. I don't know. I hear the voices, each one yelling. Loud . . . Loud . . . Loud . . ." Describe with no pauses, no silences.

Actually Live and Be in the Scene; Do Not Give In to Those Very Clever Ploys to Pull You Out

Your job is to stay inside this alive and real scene. Stay living and being in this scene. You are you, a little girl, stroking your cat, on the floor, pounded by the screaming voices of your mother and father, feeling the feelings and having the thoughts of the little girl that you are.

There are clever things that will do their best to pull you out of this scene. Fight them. Don't let them pull you out of the scene.

You may be pulled or sucked into wallowing in the mere feeling, and then you are out of the scene. No longer a little girl on the floor, with the pounding of the noise from your mother and father, now you are just having the feeling of nondescript fear, drifting on a cloud of fear and fright. Avoid this ploy. Stay living and being in the scene. Do not let yourself be pulled out of the scene into drifting along with the mere strong feeling.

Do not let yourself be pulled out of this scene and into another scene, even if the other scene is related. Suddenly, instead of being here on the floor, stroking your cat, you are in high school, playing on the volleyball team. Or, you suddenly see Tom, the boy who lived next door when you were a little girl, and Tom is giving you a candy bar, which you want but somehow think you should not accept. Sliding into another scene can distract you from your goal. Do your best to stay in the scene of strong feeling.

Do not let yourself be pulled out of the scene by having thoughts about what is happening. For example, instead of being the little girl with the cat and the screaming parents, you are out of the scene, thinking: "No wonder I talk with such a low voice and so softly. No screaming. At least Mom was tough. Hell, she didn't take any shit from Dad. I wonder if he was scared of her? The trouble is, I never did anything. I was so good. I don't think I even mentioned it to them." No matter how accurate or seemingly important your thoughts are, they pull you right out of the scene. Avoid letting yourself be yanked out of the scene by any thoughts.

Do not let unusual and dramatic bodily sensations pull you out of the scene. If they start to happen, ride them out while doing your best to remain in the scene. You may start to become dizzy, your calf muscles may start to cramp, you may feel that your whole body is tilting, or you are sure your nose is bleeding. Do not pull out of the scene and open your eyes, for example, to see if your nose really is bleeding. Do your best to stay living and being in the scene.

Discover The Peak Moment Of Strong Feeling In The Scene Of Strong Feeling

What you do now can be described rather simply. As you are living and being in the scene of strong feeling, look for when the feeling is strongest, when it reaches its peak. Discover what is happening in the moment when the feeling is strongest. You have slowed down the scene of strong feeling. You have frozen it. Now that the scene is set, search about within it. Try to find the actual fraction of a second, the actual moment, when the feeling is strongest, when it peaks. At precisely what instant is the feeling strongest?

Freeze the scene as the little girl on the floor, pounded by the noise from your screaming parents in the next room, and filled with the awful feeling. In this scene, probe for when the feeling is most powerful, all the while living and being in the frozen scene. Train yourself to search for the moment of strong feeling while still living and being in the scene, filled with the strong feeling.

It Is Exceedingly Rare to Discover the Actual Moment of Strong Feeling

Prior to training yourself to do so, you have probably never spent even as little as five minutes searching inside a scene of strong feeling to find the actual instant when the feeling was strongest. Across your whole life, you have probably had hundreds or thousands of scenes of strong feeling, but you have almost certainly not searched for and found the actual instant of strong feeling in those scenes.

Step 1. Discover the Deeper Potential for Experiencing

Going beyond the scene of strong feeling to try to discover the actual instant of strong feeling doesn't happen when you think about the scene of strong feeling after it happens, or when you talk about it with a friend, a counselor, or a psychotherapist. You talk about the scene. You think about the scene. Whether the feeling is awful or delightful, you almost always just stop with thinking or talking about the scene. You do not delve inside the scene to try to find the instant when the feeling peaks. Even if you think about or talk about the scene for hours and hours, over years and years, you will likely not search for and discover the precise instant of peak feeling.

There are many reasons why you rarely probe inside a scene of strong feeling to find the instant when the feeling is strongest. If you dare to find that instant, you are entering the territory of the deeper potential, which can be difficult and painful. It can feel safer to stay far away from what is deeper, because you never really know what will happen when you enter the world of the deeper potentials.

It is also hard work to find the exact moment of strong feeling. You are sure it was during the telephone conversation with Mary; there is no question. So you search around in what you said and what she said. Then, with some work, you find that the peak of strong feeling only occurred after you hung up, with the images and pictures that came into your mind as soon as you hung up.

Instead of finding the actual moment when the feeling peaks, it can be much easier to drift around on the feeling and watch the scene of strong feeling. You are frozen with horror as you see flashes of the black car, the twitching hand, the slow-moving police car, the blood on the pavement, the barking dog, or the commanding voice ordering you to step back. There are swirls of flashing images, and you are saturated by the anxiety, the terror, the frozen horror. It is understandable that you are caught up in the full feeling of the scene. This alone is almost enough to keep you from searching for the precise moment when the feeling reached its peak.

In general, the bad feeling is an effective means of keeping you from ever finding the exact moment of peak feeling. If you are trying to find the precise moment of strong feeling, one of the things that stands in your way is the feeling itself. The bad feeling welcomes you, seduces you, and you end up engulfed in it instead of proceeding to find the exact moment of peak feeling. No wonder it is so rare to find the actual instant of peak strong feeling.

Another interference is that we tend to label the scene, to put it in some category, to understand the scene, to make some sense of it. All of this keeps you from taking the next step of looking for the precise moment of strong feeling. Instead, you explain that the scene was traumatic, it was a scene of high stress, the accident you witnessed reminded you of the terrible car accident you were in when you were a child, you did nothing because you were in a state of shock, you are not emergency minded, or what you witnessed was a scene of primitive violence. The easy rush to label, to make sense of the scene, effectively ensures that you do not even begin to look for when the instant of peak feeling occurred.

When I am living and being in the scene of strong feeling, one part of me is searching for the precise instant when the feeling was strongest. Another part is trying its best to make sense of the scene, to rush in with a label that explains it: "The little girl is being abused. Her parents are out of control. She is leaving the world of reality because it is too stressful." This rush to label the scene, to make sense of it, will effectively stop you from finding the precise instant of peak feeling. Watch out for the rush to label, to make truth pronouncements, and to understand because these keep you from finding the moment of peak feeling.

It is also difficult to find the moment of strong feeling because you have little or no experience doing it. You have no practice and no training. You do not know what it is like to live and be in a scene of strong feeling, and to go even further by searching for the instant of peak feeling. If you stay in the scene, it is so easy to be caught up in the feeling and not even think about the instant when the feeling peaks. What would make you look for a moment when the feeling is strongest? Probably nothing would. Throughout your whole life, there were probably few, if any, times when you had any reason to search for exactly when the feeling peaked. You are not good at doing this search because you have probably rarely done it.

An Exception Is That It Is Comparatively Easier to Discover the Precise Instant of Strong Feeling in a Dream

I am not sure why, but it seems to be much easier to locate and identify the moment of strong feeling in a dream than in a scene of strong feeling from your real life. This is one of the reasons why I prefer to work on a dream rather than on a scene of strong feeling from real life. If the scene from real life is very compelling and insistent, I work on it. Otherwise, I prefer working on a dream, and the ease in finding the actual moment of peak feeling in a dream is one reason.

In a dream, the moment of peak feeling is usually portrayed, that is, it is "hung" out in front of you so that you can see it, with little effort. In scenes from real life, it generally takes a great deal of hard work to find the moment of powerful feeling.

The Moment of Strong Feeling Is the Precious Window into Your Hidden, Inner, Deeper World.

If you are interested in or passionate about knowing your hidden inner world, the world of what you are truly like, deep down inside, start with a moment of peak feeling. This instant is the precious window into the hidden world inside you, the world of which you are essentially unaware, the world of the deeper potentialities for experiencing.

In the moment of peak feeling, you and what is deeper inside you are within close touch. In this moment, you and the deeper potential for experiencing are closer than under any other circumstances. I know of no better way of touching and being touched by your insides.

Why is this? How can you picture this special state of peak feeling? Imagine that, when the moment of strong feeling occurs, your deeper insides intrude into you, puncture the wall between you and your deeper insides, implode into you, come close to overrunning you, cracking you apart, entering into the very person you are, spilling into you, eradicating your very existence. This state occurs whether the feeling is ecstatic and thrilling or horrible and terrifying.

To my knowledge, virtually all other ways of trying to know your inner, deeper self only manage to shed some light on the person you already are, the person who is you, the person who is on the surface. These other ways do not allow you to see down inside the deeper, hidden regions beyond you into what is hidden, sealed off, barricaded, into your nether regions, into the truly deeper potentialities for experiencing of which you are not aware, not knowing, not conscious.

The Discovery of the Peak Moment of Strong Feeling Is Almost Always a Surprise

You know the general scene of strong feeling. You know it is when you are the little girl on the floor, stroking your cat, aware of your mother and father screaming in the other room. That scene is familiar. What you almost certainly do not know is the precise instant when the feeling is strongest. Finding this moment, the actual discovery of this exact instant, is almost always a surprise. It is a genuine discovery of something new. It is accompanied by a burst of surprise, of wonder. This sense of surprise is one of the indications that you have succeeded in discovering the instant of strong feeling.

In The Moment Of Strong Feeling, Discover What Is Deeper By Using One Of These Methods Until There Is A Qualitative Shift In Experiencing

Simply living and being in the moment of strong feeling is essential for you to discover what is deeper inside you. But it is not sufficient by itself. You must use one of the following methods to arrive at a point where you are touched by the deeper potential for experiencing. You will undergo it. You will be touched by it. You will sense it. But you will not yet know what it is, its nature, its content, its description.

When You Use the Approrpiate Method, There Will Suddenly Be a Qualitative Shift in Experiencing

It is truly a qualitative shift. This shift occurs all of a sudden, in a flash. That is when you stop. That is when your work is over. That is when you touch or are touched by the deeper potential for experiencing. If the experiencing, in the moment of strong feeling, is good, there will be a qualitative shift to a different state, a different feeling, a different experiencing. If the experiencing in the moment of strong feeling is bad, the qualitative shift will be to a feeling that is not as bad, the experiencing is less painful. This qualitative shift happens suddenly, in a flash. When that qualitative shift happens, you stop. You have discovered the deeper potential for experiencing.

Step 1. Discover the Deeper Potential for Experiencing

The Following Methods Take You into the Unexplored, Hidden, Inner World of Your Deeper Potential for Experiencing

When you find the actual moment of strong feeling, you enter territory that is almost never reached, whether you are thinking about a bothersome event by yourself or whether you and another person (a psychotherapist, for instance) are trying to understand a bothersome event. With these five methods, you are ready to go much further. Each of these methods takes you into the hidden, deeper, inner world, into the unexplored region of your deeper potentials for experiencing. This is almost surely new territory. These methods are the keys to what lies hidden deep within you.

In the Moment of Strong Feeling, the Deeper Potential for Experiencing Is So Close, Right Here, Almost Breathing on You; Just By Using the Right Method, You Can Discover It

When you are in the moment of strong feeling, you and the deeper potential are extremely close to each other. It is like the deeper potential is right here, happening before your very eyes. The trouble is that you cannot see it. You cannot touch it or be touched by it. Nevertheless, it is so close that you could almost sense it if you knew how.

That is the function of the methods. Use the proper method, and the nearby deeper potential for experiencing is revealed. All it takes is the right method. Learn the methods and become skilled in using them.

When you are living and being in the moment of strong feeling, it takes only one of the proper methods to discover it. It does not take careful decoding. It does not take high-level reasoning. It does not take a complicated maneuver or clever twisting of one thing into another. The deeper potential for experiencing is not distant, buried under lots of wrappings, hidden by a mathematical formula. It does not take a genius to find it. It does not take a wise person. You do not need years of scientific or professional training. When you are living and being in the moment of strong feeling, all you need is one of the five methods to discover what is so close by, right next to you. Here are the five methods.

METHOD ONE: FILL IN THE MISSING CRITICAL DETAIL.

Although you have a fairly good notion of the general scene of strong feeling, when you look for the actual moment of peak feeling, you run into some problems. For example, you know the scene is in that small bedroom, that scary room in your grandfather's attic. You know you were so scared. But you can't find the actual instant of peak feeling. Bits and pieces are vague, missing, shadowy. Keep trying to fill in the missing details. Exactly where is all of this happening? Precisely where is it happening in the moment of strong feeling? Are you on the bed? Standing near the door? Where are you? You know your grandfather is here, but how? Is he standing? Where? Is he holding something? What is it? How are you dressed? Is it nighttime? What exact words are being said when the feeling is strongest? Fill in all of the cloudy, vague, and missing details.

Step 1. Discover the Deeper Potential for Experiencing

When you fill in the missing critical detail, something magical will happen. The exact instant of strong feeling will click in, and this is when the qualitative shift occurs. You now are living in the exact moment of strong feeling, and you sense or feel or touch or are touched by the deeper potential for experiencing. As you search for and locate the moment of peak feeling, the details are filled in. Then the last remaining detail is filled in—somewhat like the last piece of a puzzle. Until now you are scared, so scared. Your grandfather is over you, whispering that what he is doing is for you, that you will like this. He is touching you down there. No one should do this to you. And then? Suddenly you know someone else is there, in the doorway. But who is it? Finally, this last missing detail is filled in. It is your grandfather's new lady friend. There she is, smirking! This is the missing critical detail. As it is filled in, the whole instant changes meaning. There is a qualitative shift. Instead of the sense of dread, there is a qualitatively new feeling. You are used! You are a piece of meat! Damn! You are just a passive thing, used by them both! And the sense, the experiencing is now so different.

Use This Method First, Before Turning to Any of the Other Methods

Every time you start with a scene of strong feeling, your goal is to search for and identify the exact instant of peak feeling. When this moment is hard to find, when parts are cloudy, vague, and missing, this first method can bring you into touch with the deeper potential for experiencing by filling in the final, critical missing detail. Always start with this method.

Here Are Some Examples of the First Method

You are driving the exalted leader of a political movement to the airport. She chatters on and on, and, throughout the drive, you are quiet, but seething inside. Then you say, tightly, that you have something to say to her. You start criticizing her. She lets others twist her mind. They tell her stories about you. They are jealous of you and hate you, partly because you have been there so many years, and they are the young newcomers. As you talk, you try hard not to yell, and not to cry. You are so scared of talking to the leader in this way. Finally, you say, "And I am so disappointed in you!" Is this the instant or peak feeling? No. You turn and look at her. Your mind is blank. Vagueness. The pressure is pounding in your face. There must have been a look on her face! What was it? This is the missing critical detail. And then you actually see the look. She is frightened! She is almost helpless! She has a look of a frightened deer. She is so vulnerable! This is the missing critical detail. You found it! And in this instant, something happens in you. There is a qualitative shift. You have an utterly new sense of power over her, of being right, of a sure sense of strength. This is the deeper potential for experiencing.

You remember a scene when you were just a little boy, not even in school yet, sitting at this desk. Your mother is crowding against you, smelling awful, and yelling at you, telling you how bad you are. You feel so awful, yelled at, hated by Mommy. As you work toward finding the exact instant of peak feeling, you fill in some of the details. You have a pencil in your right hand. The sheet has lines, and your mother is getting you to write the alphabet. It is morning, and she is standing on your left, and loud noises are coming from her. There is an explosion. This is the instant. The explosion is her screaming at you and hitting you hard on the head. You did something. She exploded at something. Look down at the sheet. What do you see? Something about the sheet. That is what did it. What could it be? Then, suddenly, you fill in the final critical missing detail. Mommy is yelling at you to write E, and not only do you make the E backward, but you also know it is wrong, and you know it will drive her crazy. That is the instant of peak feeling. By filling in the final, critical missing detail, you undergo the qualitative shift. For a flash, you are touched by a newfound sense of showing her, getting back at her, driving her out of her mind, fighting back, being a wicked little devil. Ha, ha, ha! This is the deeper potential for experiencing.

You know that you felt so low, gloomy, and depressed after the telephone conversation with Tom. You called him because you hadn't heard from him in months. Tom is your older brother. He used to be your buddy, but he hasn't been for months now. The conversation did it. You search for the instant during the conversation when the feeling was strongest. You search. The conversation has turned to mush in your memory. You cannot tell when the feeling peaked.

Then, with careful effort, you hear him say the critical words: "You know the way you live. I talked it over with Mom and Dad." That did it! Suddenly, in a flash, you have an image of the three of them talking about you. The image fills you with rage. And the qualitative shift happens when you hear a voice inside, yelling at you: "You idiot! Say something! Don't just be quiet! You are enraged, so be enraged! What the hell is wrong with you, you wimp?" This yelling at yourself, berating yourself, criticizing yourself, being enraged at yourself is the deeper potential in you.

The scene of strong feeling is in the kitchen, last night. You and your wife are hashing over the same old problems between you, and you are both pleading with Agnes to take your side. Agnes is your wife's best friend, and you respect her. You like her. In the scene, you are feeling rotten, cornered, misunderstood, and disliked. You thought that the exact instant of strong feeling would be when Agnes said, "My God, your marriage really is on the rocks!" but that was not the moment. It was something after that. What was it? Then you find it, the missing critical detail. The moment of peak feeling is when Agnes looks at you and says, "You're ready for an affair." Bam! That is it! Here is the qualitative shift. In you there is a newfound sense of sheer freedom, nice, warm liberation, being rid of it all, doing what you want. It is peaceful, friendly, caressing. This is the deeper potential for experiencing.

You remember the scene well. You are about 14; Susan is older, around 16 or so. The feeling is just wonderful. Susan is on top of you. She is driving you crazy by tightening and loosening her vaginal muscles around your penis. How wonderful it feels! You start searching for the actual moment when the feeling is strongest. The first lurch comes when you realize that you and Susan are having sex in your mother's bedroom, not in your bedroom. The next lurch is when you see the glossy picture of your mother on the wall. Your mother is a country singer who works at the local bar, and the picture is sexy, very sexy. The actual instant of peak feeling is found when the final missing detail is added. The pinnacle of feeling is when you have climaxed; your eyes look on the eyes of the sexy woman in the photo, and there is suddenly a whole new feeling: "I am your man! I can give you the fucking of your life! I am the man for you, Momma! Oh, yes!"

The scene of strong feeling happened yesterday. You walk down the corridor at work. Three coworkers are standing there, chatting. You are ready to say hello, but they don't look up. They stop talking until you pass by. You feel so bad, and so hurt. That is the scene, but what is the actual instant of intense feeling? When you freeze the scene, the moment starts to come into focus when your coworkers shut down and become quiet. The next detail is that you sense they all dislike you, immensely. Dislike you. How? What? What do they dislike about you? The missing critical detail comes, and with it is a qualitative shift. They dislike your hautiness, your superiority. You think you are so good, better than they are. That is it! You feel it. For an instant there is a sense of being superior, haughty, better than. Yes!

The scene happened only a few days ago, at your brother's place. You are crying now, watching your brother's son, Jeffrey. He is slow. Something is wrong with him. You feel so sorry for him when, at the table, your brother grabs the drink from Jeffrey. How sad. How sorry you feel for the poor boy. What is the exact instant? Is it when your brother grabs the drink away? You search further. Something is missing. Then, suddenly, the critical missing detail is filled in. You see the look of fear on Jeffrey's face. Fear. Utter fear. This is when the qualitative shift happens. Suddenly, there is something new inside you: a coldness, a sense of hardness, an icy uncaring. This is the deeper potential for experiencing. You are feeling it. You have no idea what it is, but you are touched by it.

The scene of strong feeling is when you were on the phone with Mother. The feeling is tight seething, hurt, broiling anger. She did it to you again. "Do you have any good news for me?" Damn it! She always does that to me! Am I pregnant yet? But that is not the exact instant. You stay in the fixed scene and search. It is not when Mother waits, pauses. The damned pressure. Mother is quiet. She has you. The qualitative shift happens when you fill in the critical missing detail. Mother pauses, and for the first time, you do too! There! One second. Two seconds. Ha! You outwait Mother! Yes! You don't tumble! No way! When the critical missing detail is filled in, there is this sense of confrontation, me versus her, one-on-one. This is the deeper potential for experiencing.

The scene of strong feeling was when the wife of your best friend called you at the office. You are still in shock. Sam killed himself. You grew up with him, but you hadn't had contact with him in years. You met his wife only once, at the wedding. Here she is, telling you that Sam is dead. When is the exact instant of peak feeling? You slowly go over her words. You are surprised when the critical words come. In all that she said, the critical words were, "Kip, he' s gone." With those words, the tears well up, and the newfound feeling is that of being a baby, safely tucked in the arms of this soft, caring woman, cared for, cared about. Here is the deeper potential for experiencing.

Use This Method if a Critical Detail Is Missing
from the Moment of Peak Feeling;
Otherwise, Turn to the Following Methods.

To experience a qualitative shift, you must find the moment of strong feeling. If critical parts of the scene of strong feeling are missing, filling them in is the first method you should use. Using this method first is almost natural.

On the other hand, there are times when you search for and find the actual moment of peak feeling, and there is no missing critical part. You find the moment of strong feeling, but there is no qualitative shift. When this happens, and this is relatively common, then turn to the following methods.

METHOD TWO: INTENSIFY THE EXPERIENCING

Live and be in the scene of strong feeling, and deliberately intensify the experiencing. Deliberately make the experiencing stronger, more powerful, louder, more saturated, filling more and more of your body. Keep it up, more and more, further and further. Let the feeling or the experiencing become out of hand, out of control. Forget about reality constraints. Just make the feeling and experiencing more and more intense, wilder and wilder, with no controls at all. You are living and being in the instant of strong feeling, and the intensity is out of all bounds.

When you do this, more and more intensely, with fewer and fewer reality constraints, suddenly there will be a qualitative shift. The feeling or experiencing shifts. Something qualitatively new is apparent. In a flash. Stop. What you are now undergoing, what you touch or are touched by, is the deeper potential for experiencing. You have discovered it.

This Method Is Useful with Any Feeling and in Any Moment of Strong Feeling

There are no special circumstances that dictate when to use this method. You can use this method with any feeling, any experiencing. This method is useful when the feeling or experiencing is good or bad. It doesn't matter what is happening in the moment of strong feeling.

Here Are Some Examples of the Second Method

The scene of strong feeling is when your father walks into the dining room. You are studying the manuscript of the novel your friend asked you to read before doing the final draft. You are already tense because it is tax time, and you know your father expects you to do everything for him. You bail him out of everything. He depends on you so much that you feel utterly used. There is no appreciation, just expectations that you will take care of everything. He slowly puts in front of you a whole pile of tax-related material, saying nothing. Even without looking, you know he has that same helpless, pleading look on his face. He is standing up. You are sitting, not looking at him. Suddenly, you hear tight words aimed at him: "What do you want?" That is the moment of peak feeling. You are angry, pressured, furious at the way he uses you and the way you accede. But you do not yet feel a qualitative shift. Using the second method, you pour out your feelings, all the way, louder and louder, getting increasingly angry, giving in to the pressure, blasting out the fury mixed with hurt and guilt. On and on you go, opening up the feeling more and more. You hate him. Never a word of appreciation. Never! With increasing power you go on and on until there is a qualitative shift. Suddenly, you are crying, sobbing. With this qualitative shift, you have a flash of a whole new experiencing, that of being close to him, having no barriers with him, being one with him, a newfound sense of intimacy and oneness with him. This is so new. It is the deeper potential for experiencing.

In the moment of strong feeling, Bob is holding the memo you sent around. He has circled point 7.2 and asks if it means that the committee he chaired is now gone, merged into the new committee that you created. You look directly into his eyes and nod. "You got it. Any problems?" He says no. That is the instant of strong feeling. The feeling is that of sheer power, strength, being the boss. You deliberately pump up that great feeling. Living and being in this frozen instant, you revel in this great feeling. You belt it out louder and fuller, more and more intensely. You scream: "My will is iron! I am the boss!" You hiss this out with greater and greater intensity. Then the qualitative change happens. You are babbling, speaking nonsense, talking in tongues. Utter chaos. You are screeching with silly laughter as you descend into utter babbling nonsense, wholesale disorganization, complete shambles. It is delightful. You are touched by and touching the deeper potential for experiencing.

The scene of strong feeling is when you are about 15 years old. You and your father and mother are in the kitchen, and they are drunk, yelling at each other. Dad has Mother by the shoulders, pinned against the wall. She is calling him crazy and saying she will kill him, and he is hitting her over the head. As usual, in these physical drunken brawls, you are terrified, disgusted, full of panic, withdrawn, and pulled in from both of them. But something happens this time. You jump out of the chair, run up to them, grab your burly father by his left shoulder, and scream: "Let her go! Let her go!" The moment of strong feeling is that instant when your father turns, and the two of you are eye to eye. Keep saying those words, louder and louder, with increasing fear and fright, hate and disgust. Intensify the experiencing. As you pump up the feeling, louder and louder, more and more intensely, the qualitative shift suddenly occurs. In a flash, your voice drops, and something new pours out: "That is enough, you fucker. That is enough." There is a quiet, newfound sense of being older, wiser, rising above things, handling things, being the grown-up in the family. This is a whole new quality, something you have never felt before. It is the deeper potential for experiencing.

The scene of strong feeling is when the older man walks along the corridor toward his apartment. The attractive woman opens her door a bit and then shuts it. He continues down the corridor, enters his apartment, sits in a chair, and has that same awful feeling of uselessness, aloneness, depression, and gloominess. What's the use? The precise moment when the feeling is strongest is when he sees the attractive woman glance at him and close the door. That is when the feeling peaks. Stay in this instant. Intensify the feeling. Feel more useless, alone, depressed, and gloomy. It gets more and more saturated, more intense, gloomier, more agonizingly depressed. Then the qualitative shift happens. A whole new voice comes forth, lower, chilling, hardened: "I could kill you, you bitch." The feeling is a sense of utter hatred, sheer rage, cold fury. This is the deeper potential.

The young woman has a similar feeling of quiet heaviness, depression, death, hopelessness, gloominess, unhappiness. The actual moment of intense feeling is when she is in her mother's living room. She has lived in her mother's home for the past three years, taking care of her aged, frail mother. She loves her mother, and they talk a lot at night after work. Her mother has just said that she had

talked for almost two hours with an old friend that day. Then
she asks: "Are you all right? You look pale." Somehow, this is
when the heavy depression becomes much stronger. She
allows the depression to intensify and wallows more and more
in the heaviness and gloom. "I might as well be dead! What's
the use of living? (Tears, full and warm tears. Then sobbing.)
I should die. I should die. There's no use any more . . .
(Hard crying.) Oh, God . . ." Then the qualitative shift
occurs. Suddenly, she sees her and her mother talking. She is
above and far away from the house, yet sees herself and her
mother talking. The feeling has shifted. It is peaceful. No, the
feeling is light. In this shift, she has a sense of being literally
removed, watching from afar, free, liberated, on her own,
floating, light. It is weird, it is strange, and it feels so good!
This is the deeper potential for experiencing.

Use the Spontaneous Outburst That Happens
When the Feeling Is Intensified

As the feeling is intensified, there often is a spontaneous
outburst. Almost always, that outburst seems to be outside
the moment of strong feeling, outside the context of the
moment. It is as if you leave the scene, and then the
outburst happens. The trick to finding the deeper potential
for experiencing is to put that spontaneous outburst right
back into the moment of strong feeling and open yourself to
whatever touches you.

For example, the moment of strong feeling is when your
mother tells you, face-to-face in the restaurant: "Come over

to my place next Sunday. You'll meet Greg." Greg is the latest of Mother's unending string of men. Right after hearing these words, you are flushed, and you pause. The feeling is one of biting your tongue. As you hold the moment and intensify the feeling, you belt out worry for her, annoyance at her, irritation at years and years of loser men whom she drags up and who use and then dump her. Then, the spontaneous outburst comes: "He'll probably have dumped her by then!" And the guilty giggle. The feelings shift dramatically. Here is the qualitative shift. What would happen if you were back in the moment of strong feeling, and your mother has just said: "Come over to my place next Sunday. You'll meet Greg." This time, you blurt out: "Next Sunday? Ma, he'll probably have dumped you by then!" What do you now experience? It is a sense of shocking her, being brutally honest, being aggressively open, telling it like it is. The spontaneous outburst feels delicious. It opens up the deeper potential.

The scene of strong feeling is being a little girl in a classroom. The teacher ridicules her as she orders the little girl to stand in front of the class and sing out loud. The moment of strong feeling is when she feels tears welling up; she feels hated and ridiculed. The feeling is that of painful hurt, being picked on, being the victim. Intensify the feeling. She wallows in the stronger and stronger feeling and is now sobbing about being the helpless victim. She intensifies the feeling more and more until there is a sudden outburst: "What a crazy idea!" With that outburst, the whole feeling changes. Here is the dramatic shift, the qualitative shift. The feeling is light and airy, and the old, bad feeling is gone. Saying this right here in the moment of strong feeling gives her the sense of being a spitfire, not being the victim, standing up to the mean teacher. It feels great. This is the deeper potential for experiencing.

The moment of strong feeling is watching the supervisor walk away after telling your friend that she was not appointed to the board. You are shocked, angry, and appalled at the way the supervisor told your friend. You freeze the moment and intensify the painful feeling. The words and feelings are louder and louder, wilder and wilder: "How can he do that? How could he ever be a supervisor? That bastard!" And then the switch happens, the qualitative switch, in the form of a spontaneous outburst: "But he sure has a great ass!" And with that outburst, back in the frozen moment of strong feeling, there is a new experiencing. It is a sense of ridiculing him, playing with him, making fun of him, being open and shocking. This is the deeper potential for experiencing.

The moment of strong feeling is when you are sitting in your father's car, before you say good-bye. Your feeling is that of distance, trying to be nice, but feeling pulled-in and withdrawn. You have never forgiven him for leaving when you were just a little boy. He comes for visits now. In the car, he quietly puts his hand on your shoulder; you let it be, but it feels as if you have moved away from your shoulder. You seem nice on the surface, but inside you feel removed, cold. That is the instant. As you let that feeling intensify, you withdraw more and more, increasing your distance from him. You are saying: "No, old man. I will be civil, but never will I let you hurt me again. Never! Never" On and on you go, with more and more intense feeling. And then, suddenly, the qualitative shift occurs. Tears pour out. You are out of the moment, and the outburst comes with warm tears: "I wish I had a daddy." And you sob. Put this in the actual frozen moment. Your father puts his hand on your shoulder, and you turn to him, full face, with tears pouring out: "I wish I had a daddy." The experiencing is true warmth, closeness, no barriers, expressing your love. This is the deeper potential for experiencing.

In the moment of strong feeling, let the feeling intensify. Push it forward. Make it more and more intense, increasingly powerful. Let it get completely out of hand, wholly uncontrolled, more and more powerful. There will be a qualitative shift, perhaps in the form of a spontaneous outburst, or perhaps from the more heightened and deepened feeling. When that qualitative shift happens, you touch or are touched by the deeper potential for experiencing.

METHOD THREE:
PENETRATE THE HEART OF THE AWFUL FEELING.

This method starts with an awful feeling. As you are living and being in the moment of strong feeling, let yourself sink further and further inside it. Immerse yourself in the awful feeling. As it fills you more and more, give in to its awfulness, the terror, the agony. Let the terrible feeling become as terrible as it can get. Plunge into the worst possibilities. Face and enter into the heart of the evil, the core of the agonizing feeling. With all the power of the awful feeling, scream out the questions: "What is so awful about that? How and why is it so terrible? What is the worst possible thing that can happen? Why is that so awful? WHY IS THAT SO AWFUL?"

Keep plunging into the very heart of the terrible feeling until the qualitative shift occurs. It will occur when the feeling is excruciatingly powerful, wholly saturating, and when you reach the very core, the heart, of the horrible feeling. In this qualitative shift, the bad feeling is gone. In its place is a lighter feeling, a qualitatively different feeling. It is here that you touch or are touched by the deeper potential for experiencing. You have arrived. Congratulations!

Use This Method When the Bad Feeling
Is Especially Gripping and Acute.

Use this method when the dream is a nightmare, and the feeling is so gripping, acute, and awful that you suddenly wake out of the dream. You can also use this method when the feeling from real life is very bad, highly gripping, and intense.

Here Are Some Examples of the Third Method

In the moment of strong feeling, you are holding the wheelchair. Your grandmother is frail, sickly, and leaning to the side of the wheelchair. You are waiting for the traffic light to change as you grip the wheelchair at the top of the hill. You hear your name called: "Susan!" As you turn to the left and behind, for a split second you lose your grip on the wheelchair. Here is the moment of peak feeling. You are gripped by panic. Both hands let go of the wheelchair, but only for a split second. Here is the frozen moment. As you are seized by momentary terror, you scream out the awful feeling and plunge toward the heart of it: "What am I so scared of? I'm so scared! Of what? I'm like a kid. Irresponsible! No one can trust me! I can't be trusted with anything! So what would happen? WHAT WOULD BE SO AWFUL?" In a flash, the qualitative shift occurs. The panic is suddenly gone, and there is a devilish giggle. "She'd end up in traffic—DOWN THE HILL!" With this qualitative shift, you are touching and touched by the deeper potential for experiencing, a giddy sense of watching her sail down the hill into traffic, of being deliciously wicked and mischievous. "Hee, hee, hee, serves the old bitch right! Ha!"

The scene of bad feeling is at night, in bed. You and Sandra don't have those big fights any more. Just distance. You say you want sex, but it comes out as a petulant whine. Sandra sucks you off and tells you that she doesn't want anymore penetration. She tells you how boring the marriage is, and the instant of strong feeling is when she seems to really mean it: "You are dull. Living with you is dull!" Clunk. Plunge inside the awful feeling. You are filled with fear, rejection, failure, blame. You are churning with the awful feeling. Your head sways from left to right as you groan. What is so awful? Why is this so terrible? What could happen? What are you terrified will happen? "She'll leave me! I'LL BE ALONE!" Here it is! And the feeling dramatically shifts. It is airy, light, pleasant, even happy. "Yeah . . . I'd be by myself. You bet!" You have touched a deeper potential for experiencing, a sense of being free, liberated, independent, doing what you want, freedom.

You have a reputation as a theorist in the field of theoretical physics, especially in regard to the origin of the universe. You daydream that, someday, you will be awarded the Nobel Prize. However, the scene is fraught with fear after you give a lecture at a meeting of your colleagues. To begin with, very few people attended your lecture, and the important people in your field were not present. Your lecture presented the latest version of your theory. The comments after your talk were polite, but the actual moment of strongest feeling was when you and four of your friends had drinks after your talk. Three of them left. You felt so discouraged. You managed to ask your buddy what his impressions were, and he gave you that look. He paused as if to gain his courage. Before he actually said anything, you were frozen with terror, looking him straight in his distant, cold eyes, terrified of what he might say.

Freeze this instant. Just what is it that you are terrified he might say? Find the thing he might say, the thing you are panic-stricken to hear. When you live in this instant and find that catastrophic possibility, your sense of panic and terror will shift to something qualitatively different. So what is the thing you are so terrified he might say? The panic remains as you try out a few possibilities: "No one agrees with you. Your research is not well done. Your conclusions were not justified. You aren't aware of other studies." Finally, you arrive at the peak awfulness: Your friend looks at you eye to eye and says: "Steven, there is something seriously wrong with you. You should be institutionalized . . . for your own good." Clunk! Here is an immediate shift. The terror and panic are gone. You are at the bedrock. This is it. Your craziness, your dementia, is present; it is out in the open. You know this state of being out of your mind. There is a sense of calmness, of acknowledging something, of literally being out of your mind, of being in a different world, of seeing things in ways no one else sees them, of being totally weird, and altogether different. For a few seconds, you are literally in this state, all of you, and the panic and terror are gone. You are filled with the deeper potential for experiencing a sense of utter madness, being out of your mind, being crazy. However, your friend continues, "You try so hard to be fair to the dominant theories, even though it's obvious that you have utter disdain for all of them." The instant of peak feeling is between the look on your friend's face and the actual words he says. It is in the pause between the look and the words that you discover the deeper potential for experiencing by clarifying what you were so panic-stricken and terrified about, that is, the words he might have said.

The scene of strong feeling is when the secretary stands at the door to your office and tells you that the boss wants to see you. The actual moment of peak feeling is when she accentuates the word "now" in saying, "Mr. Gibbons wants to see you, now." She looks coolly and aloofly in your general direction. As you lower yourself into the well of rotten feelings, you peel off layer after layer of pain: "No respect. Pushed around. The secretaries look down on me. I don't fit in here. I'm not strong; I am weak. I don't demand respect. She knows I'm weak. Oh, God." And then you go deeper. "What is so terrible about this? Why is this so bad? So I am weak. So she looks down on me. Why is this so awful? How is this so terrible?" As you feel worse and worse, the qualitative change happens. The awful feelings wash away and, suddenly, you feel almost silly: "I'm scared of you! I am , I am! I'm a frightened little boy! You scare me!" It is true. Behind the awful feelings, down inside the core of terribleness, is this deeper sense of being the frightened little boy, the uncertain, insecure little boy. This is the deeper potential for experiencing,

The scene of strong feeling happened in a dream. You are on a water bed that has wheels and is rolling along in one-lane traffic. On the water bed with you are two seals, one on either side. You are lying face down, and behind you are three or four joggers. The moment of peak feeling is when you are panic-stricken as these joggers come closer and closer to your outstretched feet. You fix and hold this moment, and undergo the panic. What is so awful? What am

I so terrified of? The panic heightens. "They can actually reach me! All right, so what? What terrible thing could happen? They can actually reach me, so?" The panic becomes stronger and stronger. "They will come up close to me and, and . . . " You try out some horrible possibilities: "They will fuck me in the ass. They will tear my legs apart and kill me. They will laugh at me." This does it! The qualitative shift happens, and the panic evaporates. You belt out in delight: "I am so damned helpless! Go ahead! Do whatever you want! I am just a helpless little wimp! Vulnerable! Anyone can do anything to me!" You are touching and are touched by the deeper potential for experiencing.

METHOD FOUR: BE THE SPECIAL OTHER PERSON OR THING

Describing this method requires that you first describe the circumstances under which you ordinarily use it.

Use This Method When the Other Person or Thing Is the Compelling Main Character in the Scene

There are moments of strong feeling when the other person or thing, not you, is the main character here, the important one. The other person or thing is the active one, the one who is doing the action; you are passive, perhaps even a mere outside observer. Furthermore, your attention is fixed on that other person or thing. It is pulling your attention, is the compelling magnetic focus of your attention. You are not especially aware of or attending to yourself, to your actions, thoughts, or feelings. You are mainly attending to that special other person or thing. Finally, you are so drawn toward that compelling other person or thing that you somehow know what that other person or thing is thinking, intending, feeling what it is like inside. It is as if you are drawn inside the other person or thing, enough to know what it wants, intends, thinks, feels, is.

When these are the conditions of the moment of strong feeling, this method helps you take the next step. Enter into that special other person or thing. Be it. Get inside its skin, inside its head. Move out of being you, in the moment. Follow your focused attention. You are already sensing what the other person or thing is thinking, wanting, feeling, intending. Now you are living and being as this special other person or thing in the moment of strong feeling. When you do this, you will touch and be touched by the deeper potential for experiencing. It will breathe on you. You will sense its presence in you when the qualitative shift occurs.

Here are some examples of the fourth method

The scene of strong feeling is when you awake in the morning. After just a few seconds, you remember that you have cancer. It is going to kill you. It is in both lungs. The depression, panic, and terror now have you in their grip. You lie in bed, staring vacantly. The moment of peak feeling is when you actually see the cancer, and it kills the cells around it. As you freeze and live in this moment, you are compelled by the cancer. "It destroys. It kills. It is not going to be stopped by chemicals. It spreads anywhere it wants. It owns me. It's going to kill me! It doesn't care! It is so cold! It just knows killing! It's like pure evil! It only knows killing, killing!" Go the next step. Be the cancer that you know so well. Your voice drops. You hiss: "I am cold. I am hard. I kill. I destroy. Nothing can reach me. I am cold and removed and I kill. I am a killing machine. I am cold and hard!" In doing so, the bad feelings are gone. In the qualitative shift, you actually sense the deeper potential in you, the experiencing of merciless and relentless evil, utter coldness, killing, and remorselessness.

The scene of strong feeling is in the living room, when your sister's husband so innocently and in such a friendly way asks about your bookstore. It is not doing well, and you made stupid contractual arrangements with your partner. Your brother-in-law is slowly trapping you with innocent questions. The actual moment of peak feeling comes when he zeros in on your business arrangements with your partner. He has that subtly disguised look on his face, and you see the slight elevation of his left eyebrow and the beginnings of a smirk. You feel trapped, pinned, and exposed, but all your attention is magnetically focused on him. He is deadly accurate. He has you. He looks down on you. He has no use for you. He knows you are helpless, and he is going in for the kill. He is going to decimate you. Make the switch. Take the next step, and be him. Be him all the way and see what happens. You become him: "I know the mistakes you have made, little brother-in-law. I am going to take you apart bit by bit. I got you." The former awful feelings are replaced by new experiencings of being in charge, being the controlling one, dominating, taking the opponent apart, being strong and superior. It feels so good! You are touched by your own inner, deeper potential for experiencing.

You have arranged everything for a formal party in the huge garden of the estate. The guests are here, all dressed up. People are mingling. The weather is sunny, but not too warm. The tables are set. In a few minutes you will ask everyone to sit down, and the formal speech will begin, honoring the minister. Everything is fine so far. The scene of strong feeling is when your friend whispers to you: "Caroline, there's trouble. Geeta showed up." Horrors. Geeta is your daughter. You turn and see her about ten feet away, wearing dirty clothes, teetering, drunk as usual, and holding a cigar as if it were a gun. She is yelling, "Hi, Mom!" The instant of peak feeling is when you are frozen, staring at her, rage boiling up and ready to explode. All your attention is on her face. "She is smiling! She is proud of herself! She knows she is driving me crazy! She doesn't care what anyone thinks of her! She is making a fool of me, and she revels in it! She thinks that she got me. She is finally going to embarrass me big time, and she loves it!" Just a few more inches, and you are transported into Geeta's head; you are Geeta. "Okay if I smoke my cigar, Mom? Hey, everybody, look at me! I'm the only one here who doesn't give a damn about sucking up! All of you are so civilized! Worst of all you, Mom!" You are touching and are touched by something deeper in you, an experiencing of ridiculing, rebelling against, and defying convention. You are undergoing it now, and the accompanying feelings are so different from the torn-apart feelings you had in the scene of strong feeling.

In the scene of strong feeling in a dream, you are just inside the flimsy screen door of the shack in the mountains. A few inches outside the door is a huge bear, with blood all over its face, roaring, and beating its chest. In the moment of peak feeling, you are filled with terror as the bear locks its eyes on you. All you are aware of is the violent bear. You are frozen still: "It's got me! It is crazy! It knows it can smash the door down! It's out of its mind! It's so powerful, and knows it can do what it wants! IT'S SO POWERFUL. IT CAN DO WHAT IT WANTS!" Go ahead, be the bear. You are inside the bear's body. You are the bear. "I AM POWERFUL. I CAN DO WHAT I WANT! YES! YES!" The feeling is wonderful. The sense is of being powerful, of doing whatever you want. Yes. And you are undergoing the deeper potential for experiencing right now.

The scene is on the deck of the eighth-floor apartment. You are watching your father and young daughter. They are so close. They love each other. They are sitting in chairs, elbows on the low deck wall, staring intently at the little pieces of toilet paper floating lazily in the light breeze. They have this game of tearing off two little pieces of toilet paper and releasing them, watching them as they float and maybe even land on other buildings. The moment comes when you quietly join them, and watching the two floating wisps of paper compels your attention such that you are almost hypnotized. Everyone is quiet. "Just floating . . . free, so free. Floating, on the air, the breeze . . . just so free . . . floating. Not a care in the world . . ." Go ahead, move into being the floating piece of paper. There. "So light . . . feels so good. Floating . . . it makes me laugh. What's so funny? Floating. Oh, this is fun." You are undergoing a deeper experiencing. You are touching and are touched by the deeper potential for experiencing. What it is may be hard to describe, but don't try now. That comes later. Just enjoy it.

METHOD 5:
REPLACE THE BAD FEELING WITH A GOOD FEELING

Replace the bad feeling with a good feeling, and then be receptive to the new experiencing that touches you. In the actual moment of strong feeling, the feeling is a bad one. You feel scared, lost, rejected, furious, torn apart, or some other bad feeling. Deliberately replace that bad feeling with a good feeling. Whatever is occurring is fun, delightful, enjoyable, feels so good. Work hard at feeling good here, even though the actual moment was filled with genuine awful feelings. Live and be in this moment, acting the artificial good feelings, and the qualitative shift will suddenly happen. There will be a new experiencing in you. The good feelings will be accompanied by a grounding of a whole new experiencing. This is the deeper potential for experiencing.

214

It is as if the bad feeling that you had speaks: "I am not quite sure what the deeper potential for experiencing is, but I do know that I fear it. I must hide it. I must distance it. I must think of it as grotesque, dangerous, monstrous, awful. By feeling so bad, I manage to keep it away, keep it down; I manage to have no idea what the deeper experiencing is."

When you deliberately remove the bad feeling and replace it with a good one, it is as if you are saying: "I also have no idea what the deeper potential for experiencing is. However, if I artificially replace the bad feeling with a good feeling, if I force myself to love what is occurring, to feel good about it, to thoroughly enjoy it, then I can sense, have, undergo what is occurring." And what is occurring is the deeper potential for experiencing.

The bad feeling serves to keep you from knowing the deeper potential for experiencing because it hides and masks the deeper experiencing. It protects you from sensing the deeper experiencing. You are filled with the bad feeling, and that is about all you know. Yet the deeper potential for experiencing is right here, present, so close. The fifth method is to remove that bad feeling by replacing it with a good feeling, any sort of feeling of happiness, enjoyment, and pleasure. When you use this method, the barrier between you and the deeper potential for experiencing is gone, and you can sense, you can know, what the deeper potential for experiencing is. It is revealed, accessed, discoverable.

As with every method, and especially in this method, when you are in the moment of strong feeling, the deeper potential is right here, close, nearby. The trouble is that you don't know how to see it or sense it. The methods allow you to see and sense what is so obvious, so present, even though you cannot see or sense it until you use one of the methods.

Use This Method When the Feeling Is Bad

When the feeling is bad, you can go down inside the feeling itself, deeper and deeper, until you reach the very heart, the core, of the bad feeling. Then the deeper potential is reached. Or, another way is to replace the bad feeling with a good feeling, and then to be open to the deeper experiencing.

Other people often naturally and easily use this method when they watch you working on the moment of strong feeling, or when they hear the audiotape of you working on the moment of strong feeling. In other words, other people use this method when you are the only person in the room who is caught up in the bad feeling and are thereby unable to sense, know, or touch or be touched by the deeper potential for experiencing that everyone else is laughing about because they know.

Here Are Some Examples of the Fifth Method

The scene is in your kitchen. It is around 4:15 in the afternoon, and you are just about to leave to pick up your mother-in-law at the airport. Her plane comes in around 5:30. You need to be there on time. You can't stand her because she looks down on you. You are not good enough for her precious Tom. The last visit ended in your leaving the house when you were so enraged that you almost hit her. But you are a dutiful wife. The phone rings. Tom asks how the two of you are getting along. Your insides start rumbling. "Tom, she's not due in till 5:30." Pause. Tom says, "Check the refrigerator." You turn to the right. In large letters, you had written, "Pick up Elizabeth at 1:30, Flight 622. Friday." Absolute panic. 1:30! You almost pass out, except that Tom is still on the phone, waiting. The moment of strong feeling is the image of the old bitch at the airport waiting for three hours. She is fuming. She is at her wit's end. And you are upstairs having a relaxed bath, and then having a long, gossipy chat with your friend on the phone. Here is the method: Replace the panic with glee. Go ahead. Try. "It is fun to wait here and not pick her up. I love being irresponsible and forgetting so that Elizabeth has to wait, with no one to pick her up." With your eyes trained on Elizabeth at the airport with her expensive luggage, you work hard at having good feelings, and then the switch happens. The artificial good feelings become genuine good feelings as you yell out: "Hey, Elizabeth! Rot there! I don't want to pick you up! I forgot! Ha, Ha, Ha. HAHAHAHAHAHA! And we moved! You don't even know our new address! Oh, this is great! I don't want to pick you up! Take a plane back to Boston! YES!" You are in touch with a deeper potential for experiencing. It is a delightful experiencing of vindictiveness, wonderful revenge, meanness, showing her how pissed off you are, letting her have it.

You are sitting by the side of the road, and the café is off to your right. The bus stopped at this place after three hours of traveling. Everyone had a snack. You took your beer outside and sat, just looking at the barren countryside in this foreign country. You have the beer and the book you are reading. The scene is when you hear a noise, turn around, and see the bus way off down the road. You missed the bus! The instant is the horror that everything is in the bus—your luggage, your itinerary for the meetings in town, the plans you had carefully drawn up for a presentation at the meetings, all your clothes, your camera, everything! And your passport! And all the extra money you brought along! Now you deliberately exchange the feelings of horror with good feelings. At first it is so artificial, until a whole new experiencing touches you, and the feelings become giddy and silly in the qualitative shift. "Oh, what the hell! Let it go! Drop it off! Who needs it! Let go of it! I'm free of it! Here, take it all! Let it all go!" Here is the newfound sense, the deeper potential for experiencing.

The scene of strong feeling happened in the dream. He walks into the house, a lovely home. Once inside, he sees a large atrium that is filled with light. Two families must live in this big home. There is one main entryway. He walks through the atrium and opens the ornate door into the home of one family. It is full of lovely sculptures and paintings. He walks in, increasingly worried and fearful that he shouldn't be here. Then, in the moment of strong feeling, he hears a voice as he picks up an antique jeweled box, admiring it. From upstairs the voice says, "Kathy, is that you?" You are so scared. You might be caught. What could you say? You shouldn't be here at all! Stay in this instant and exchange the awful feeling with wonderful feelings. Be happy here. What you are doing feels delicious. You love this. Suddenly, there is a qualitative shift, and you have an entirely new sense: "I have absolutely no scruples. I go where I want. I respect no boundaries. I wander here and wander there. Hello there! I can sit on your toilet. I wander all over your house. I go everywhere, just follow whatever attracts me. I am the great intruder. Hello, everybody." This is the deeper experiencing. It is newfound.

The scene happened yesterday, and you are still mortified. You feel so guilty. Your daughter won't talk to you. In the scene, your luggage is on the back seat, to the left of where your son-in-law is sitting. It is winter. The car is tiny, and your son-in-law is holding the baby, who is all wrapped up and bouncing on his father's lap. You are trying so hard to be friendly. Your daughter is driving. You are trying to be casual and friendly with your daughter, and your hand is back there, patting the baby's mittened hand. All your attention is on your daughter and the road. The car goes over a bump, and you hear your son-in-law groan. You turn to look at the back seat and see his eyes closed, your hand lightly patting his conspicuously full erection. You are shocked! This is the instant of peak feeling, a feeling of horror. What have I been doing? What will they think of me? What is wrong with me? Your hand is frozen there, on his penis, as if the hand is not even yours.

Now try to replace the awful feelings with feelings of happiness and enjoyment, with nice feelings. "I like doing this. This is so enjoyable. It feels good to pat his penis. I like driving him out of his mind." As you continue, doing your best to have good feelings, a qualitative shift in experiencing will occur. Suddenly, what you have been and are doing takes on a whole different form and shape: "Let's get rid of your wife. I'm sexier than her! I am a vibrant woman. I love sex! Now do meeeee!" The feeling is that of raucous sexuality, full-blown earthiness, vibrant sexuality, open and uninhibited sexuality. Here is the deeper potentiality for experiencing.

The scene of strong feeling is when the elevator door opened, and they all saw you and Daniel. You both got into the elevator on the first floor, pushed the express button for the 17th floor, and immediately grabbed each other. You both were so hot that you were all over each other before the elevator doors shut. Except that the elevator did not proceed leisurely toward the 17th floor. Instead, after about ten seconds, the first floor elevators doors opened, and you heard the gasps. Uh, oh! You turned to your left. There they were—your supervisor, three or four colleagues, and the friend of Daniel's wife! Your blouse was mostly off, and your hand was deep inside Daniel's pants. The instant of peak feeling lasted so long! You two were caught. Everyone is going to talk. You both are in deep trouble. You'll be fired. Departmental ridicule. Divorces all around. Use the method. Happy feelings. This instant is one of good feelings. Be happy. At first it is wholly artificial, and the good feelings are just a thin veneer. And then the qualitative shift occurs: "Hello, everybody. Now, for our next erotic act . . . Everyone take off your clothes. It is group fuck time! Does anyone have any questions? Oh, I feel so hot!" You are now touching and are touched by the deeper potential for experiencing: full frontal sexuality, exhibiting yourself sexually, displaying your wonderful sexuality. And now the feelings are so good.

You are sitting cross-legged on the bed. No one is home. No one saw you at the store, buying a dozen of those special chocolate bars, bags of cherry-filled chocolate candies, and ice cream bars. It is gorge time. Something inside is saying: "Go, go, eat. It is the most exciting time of the week. Go!" The instant of peak feeling is when you have all the goodies on your bed, and you are about to scoop up the first ones to stuff inside your mouth. The wonderful craving is here! Suddenly, the instant peaks when there is a screeching inner voice: "What's wrong with you? You are sick! You are out of your mind! Something is wrong with you!" Use the method right here. Feel good. Replace the awful feeling with enjoying happy feelings. "I am sick. I have a mental illness. I am in therapy for my eating disorder. I love this disorder. I am a nut." The qualitative change happens when something new grabs you from inside: "I am bad! They think I am the good daughter, the smart one, the prizewinner. Ha! No way. I am bad! I have a flaw. I am sick! See! Ha, ha! That shatters everything, right? You don't know me at all!" You touch and are touched by the glorious experiencing of being the bad one, not giving in to them, defying them, not having them know you. It feels good!

These are the five methods to use when you are in the actual moment of strong feeling. When you use the proper method, you will discover the deeper potential for experiencing. The better you become at knowing and being able to use the five methods, the more you will be able to discover the deeper potential for experiencing. Become proficient at the five methods and at using the right one for the right moment of strong feeling. I hope that you read each example carefully and that you are able to discover the deeper potential for experiencing in each example.

When You Work From A Dream, Use Two Scenes of Strong Feeling

One of the reasons I have so much faith in working with dreams in which there are two scenes of strong feeling is that I have so much trust in the deeper potential for experiencing that I discover. I have so much trust because I can get a possibility or two from each scene of strong feeling, and then look for the commonality. Inherent in this procedure is a vision of each scene of strong feeling yielding the same deeper potential for experiencing. In other words, the underlying idea is that the same deeper potential for experiencing underlies both scenes of strong feeling. The model or conceptualization for this is given in my book on dreams (Mahrer, 1989b).

Try to Find Two Potentials for Experiencing in Each Sense of Strong Feeling

In one of the scenes of strong feeling, a woman is a few feet behind you. She moves around in front of you, takes your hand, and leans back, slowly moving her upper body. Your general feeling is that you are intruding, both of you, and you shouldn't be here. You feel used, as though you are just doing the woman's bidding. The moment of strong feeling is when she is leaning back, slowly moving her body, holding your hand, and her eyes lock on your eyes. The feeling in you is one of foreboding; you should not be here in this room. Freeze the moment and use the method of penetrating down into the bad feeling. As you probe into what is so ominous, you arrive at a qualitative shift when you have an exciting experiencing of collusion with someone, of both of you intruding where you shouldn't, of letting another person lead you into bad things, of passively following another. That is one possibility in this moment.

Stay in the same moment of strong feeling. Can you use another method? Suppose that you use the method of being the special other person. In the moment of strong feeling, not only are your eyes locked onto each others', but you are also somehow privy to what she is thinking, intending. She is going to seduce you. You know that. As you actually slide into being her, you have her thoughts, her feelings, her intentions. You literally and physically are this woman. In the qualitative shift, there is a sense of pure sexuality, wicked and tabooed sexuality, full and sensuous sexuality. It is wonderful.

You then go to the other scene of strong feeling. In this scene, there is a party at your boss' home. You and several other people are having fun. Five or six people are with you in your boss' bedroom. Your boss and her husband are in bed, joking with you about being tired and wanting to go to sleep. Everyone is laughing. You are at the foot of the bed, arranging the covers. To your right is another fellow. He has his left hand on your right hand, and you know that he is going to jerk the covers down suddenly. The feeling in you is disquiet, anxiety about what is going to happen. You should move your hand away, but you don't. This is the moment of strong feeling.

The method you start with is the method of replacing the bad feeling with a good feeling, and then waiting to receive the new-felt experiencing. As you replace the disquieting anxiety and worry, you experience the sense of pulling off a prank, of letting the other fellow take the lead, of the wicked little joy of yanking the covers off your boss and her husband, of being the willing partner, of letting the other fellow take the lead, of joining in on the devilish play.

You could use another method to access the deeper potential for experiencing in this second scene. You might, for example, use the method of intensifying the experiencing. You could start with the sense of disquiet and anxiety about what is going to happen if you both yank the covers off the bed. You could intensify that experiencing until a qualitative shift occurs. However, there is something intriguing in the two potentials for experiencing that you

224

accessed in the first scene of strong feeling and the one you accessed from the second scene of strong feeling.

*Look for a Commonality in the Deeper Potentials
for Experiencing That You Get from the
Two Scenes of Strong Feeling*

In the first scene of strong feeling, one of the deeper potentials for experiencing is an exciting sense of collusion with someone, of both of you intruding where you shouldn't, of letting another person lead you into doing bad things. In the second scene of strong feeling the deeper experiencing is of letting the other person take the lead, the joy of doing something wicked, being the willing partner, joining in on the devilish prank. These two share a kind of commonality: letting the other person take the lead, following and colluding with another person in carrying out something wicked, devilish, bad. You get the deeper potential for experiencing by finding the commonality in what you get from the two scenes of strong feeling.

Usually, as in the dream described above, you do not have to get the second deeper potential for experiencing in the second scene of strong feeling. However, it is also typical for the commonality not to be so obvious. You do get two deeper potentials from each scene of strong feeling. Then, study the four of them to find the commonality.

What is so impressive is that you almost always get a commonality. A dream seems to be so special, so precious, especially if it has two scenes of strong feeling. Whether I work on my own dream or with another person on their dream, it is exciting to discover the commonality, and I am so much more confident and trusting in the commonality. That can be taken as the deeper potential for experiencing in you.

Follow the Procedure Carefully in Working with a Dream

Make sure you get two potentials for experiencing from one scene before working on the second scene of strong feeling. Then, it is safest and most reliable to get two potentials for experiencing from the second scene of strong feeling. Just make sure that you follow the procedure.

It can be so easy to start with a dream and make sense of the dream right away, without doing the work, without finding the moments of strong feeling and without achieving deeper potentials for experiencing by using the methods. Avoid these cheap and easy meanings and instead trust the commonality. Trust the commonality, not whatever notions and ideas you initially believe the dream means. Trust the commonality, even more than the other deeper potentials for experiencing that you get by using the methods.

To Discover The Deeper Potential For Experiencing, The Most Unique Elements Are: Finding The Moment Of Peak Feeling, Using The Five Methods, And Attaining The Qualitative Shift

These are the things you do that are probably the most unusual, distinctive, unique, and also the most useful and effective in discovering the deeper potential for experiencing.

Step 1. Discover the Deeper Potential for Experiencing

It is quite unusual, especially in the field of psychotherapy, to find the precise moment of strong feeling, the precise instant when the feeling peaks. You learn to do this in experiential sessions. Not only is finding the moment of strong feeling unusual, it is also critically important. In the moment of strong feeling, you are within breathing distance of the deeper potential for experiencing. Outside of that moment of strong feeling, you are distant, almost sealed off from the deeper potential for experiencing—so much so that you are likely to be unaware of its existence and universes away from its presence.

The five methods I've described are unique and critical in discovering the deeper potential for experiencing. You must know and be proficient in all five methods. They are unique and critical in discovering the deeper potential for experiencing. At the end of each method is the goal: the qualitative shift in experiencing. It is perhaps the third element that is so unique in discovering the deeper potential for experiencing. It is the cap, the final of the three unique elements. Like the other two, it is truly uncommon that you have known what it is like to undergo such a qualitative shift. It happens in the first step of each experiential session, but it rarely happens outside of experiential sessions.

There is a qualitative shift in what you are undergoing. The feeling shifts, changes; the experiencing shifts, changes. It happens rather suddenly, a genuine shift from one to another. This qualitative shift occurs for a flash, a moment, a tiny burst. It may last longer, or it may not.

If you are undergoing a bad feeling in the moment of strong feeling, then there is a qualitative shift in that the feeling is sharply reduced or even goes away. This is a magic, qualitative shift. The pain is diminished, or even gone.

The purpose of the first step is for you to discover the deeper potential for experiencing. You are touching it or are touched by it. It is right here, breathing on you, so very close by. You have discovered the deeper potential for experiencing. Because you are still living and being in the moment of strong feeling, you are not yet able to pull away, to get out of the moment of strong feeling and use words to describe what it is. You are right next to it, but you are not quite able to observe it, describe it, or use words to identify what it is.

You have completed the first step.

6

Step 2.
Welcome, Accept, and
Cherish the Deeper
Potential for Experiencing

At the end of Step 1, you and the deeper potential for experiencing are touching one another. This is a magnificent achievement because you have almost certainly spent your whole life far away from it: keeping it distant without ever knowing what it was, sealing it off, erecting a massive barrier between you. If you ever veered close enough to sense the deeper potential, you likely sensed it in its awful form. It was grotesque, monstrous, twisted, awful. You did not want to know what it was, but you believed it was terrible; it deserved to be kept down, sealed off, barricaded.

The purpose of Step 2 is for you to undergo a massive change. You are to welcome, thoroughly accept, cherish, love, and embrace the deeper potential for experiencing. You are to look upon it with love and affection. You are to bring it close to you. Your feelings about it are to be warm, loving, caring, pleasant, and happy. This is indeed a magnificent change.

This chapter shows you a number of ways to undergo this transformation. The first is to name and describe the deeper potential for experiencing. Try to do this first way for sure. It is perhaps the only way you should use each time. In addition, try to use two or three other ways. However, try to become well versed in all the ways, as you did with the questions in Chapter 5. They all help, even if you use only two or three ways each time you go through Step 2.

WHEN THE DEEPER POTENTIAL FOR EXPERIENCING TOUCHES YOU, SAVOR THE BODILY-FELT SENSATIONS

At the end of Step 1, you and the deeper potential for experiencing are touching one another. You are experiencing the deeper potential for experiencing, or at least you are starting to; you are close enough to feel it. There are sensations going on in your body. For example, you are sitting on the bed, and it is filled with chocolate goodies. It is gorge time, except that there is such a nagging sense of being driven, of having something wrong with you. In the moment of strong feeling, when you touch the deeper potential for experiencing, you are hissing: "I am bad! They think I am the good daughter, the smart one, the prizewinner. Ha! No way. I am bad! I have a flaw. I am sick!

See! Ha, ha! That shatters everything, right? You don't know me at all!" The experiencing is that of being the bad one, not giving in to them, defying them, not letting them know.

Turn to the delicious, bodily-felt sensations. Some wonderful sensations are going on in your body. Go ahead and savor them. Enjoy them. They feel so good. Delight in the electrical tingling all over your face, the muscular strength across your chest, the pleasant lightness in your head.

Quite aside from the inner sense of experiencing, whatever it is, you can savor the accompanying bodily-felt sensations: "My chest . . . peaceful now. I like this. Ooo, I feel sexy, all wet and juicy . . . My feet feel so nice and warm . . . I have this light tingling all over my skin, light, I like this, like I'm floating. My body feels so light, floating. Oh, this is so nice. I've got shivers up and down my back. Hey! Wow! Yes! My stomach feels hard, yes, tight. Wonderful. There's this openness in my chest, open, or like light, airy, free, hard to say, but it feels so nice. My God, I feel strong, my muscles feel strong, all over my arms and chest. I love this."

Take 10 or 20 seconds or more to cruise over your body, noticing the new-felt, bodily-felt sensations. Enjoy them, luxuriate in them for a while. Here is one way to welcome, accept, and cherish the deeper potential for experiencing.

Use This Method First, If It Seems Available

There is no rule that you must use this method first, but the opportunity seems to present itself first. As soon as you discover the deeper potential for experiencing at the end of

Step 1, bodily-felt sensations are evident. They feel good. This state lasts merely 10 to 20 seconds, maybe longer, maybe not. If you can savor these bodily-felt sensations, go ahead and do so.

DESCRIBE THE DEEPER POTENTIAL FOR EXPERIENCING

At the end of Step 1, you were sensing the deeper potential for experiencing, you were actually touching or were touched by it; you may even have been undergoing it. In order to describe it, you have to shift your position and your attention a bit. You have to move away from touching or being touched by it and get into a position of looking at it, observing it, focusing your attention on it.

Describe what the deeper potential is, tell what it is like. When you are working at describing the deeper potential for experiencing, you are attending to it, looking at it, bringing it close enough to see what it is. You are thereby welcoming it, appreciating it, accepting it enough to keep it here with you so that you can describe what it is like. The more carefully you describe it, the longer you take to describe it, the more you are welcoming and appreciating it. This is an important reason for taking time to provide a fair description of what it seems to be.

Another reason to describe it is that all the following methods of welcoming and cherishing the deeper potential for experiencing almost require that you have a description of it. When you move on to Steps 3 and 4, they too require that you have a fair description of the deeper potential for experiencing. If you do not describe it fairly well, if you do not even provide a description or if you give it a one-word label, it can become very difficult to use the other methods in Step 2, and it is almost impossible to successfully go through Steps 3 and 4. Make sure that you give a fairly good description of the deeper potential for experiencing.

It is best to describe it almost as soon as you discover what it is, at the end of Step 1. Up until now, you have probably spent your whole life hiding from it, not knowing it, sealing it off, keeping it down. If you even sensed it, it is likely that you sensed it in its awful form, as monstrous, twisted, and grotesque. At the end of Step 1, things are different. Instead of relating to it as frightening, fearful, hateful, and even terrifying, you are now up close, actually touching it; you are one-on-one with it, you are being touched by it. The Step 1 methods of discovering the deeper potential for experiencing free you of that awful relationship. You are in a position to describe it up close and personal, in its friendly, more appreciative, kinder, truer form and shape. You can see it for what it is, not what it is when you relate to it so negatively, so fearfully, so hatefully.

Describe the deeper potential for experiencing with a number of words and phrases. Your aim is to describe the deeper potential carefully enough to capture its nature and content. Try to find good words and phrases. Usually it takes three or four apt words and phrases to describe it well enough. Sometimes it takes more. These labels almost never work. One-word labels are commonly used in the field of mental health, but they are not enough to capture the quality of the deeper potential. It is not enough, for example, to describe it as anger, affection, competitive, caring, defiant, gentle, removed, sexual, or any other single word, term, label, or category.

Here are some examples of using words and phrases to describe deeper potentials. Notice that some are in the same "neighborhood," but still differ from one another: being used, manipulated, just a passive thing; letting it happen to you, giving in, nonresistant, being moved by it; a sense of power, strength, hardness; cruelty, hurting, doing bad things to; owning, controlling, being in charge of; showing the person, getting back at the person, fighting back; being resolute, never giving in, standing firm; yelling at, being enraged at, pouring out at; being open to, being transparent to, showing it all to; sheer freedom, pleasant liberation, being free of it all; spontaneity, impulsiveness, wildness, no restraint; caressing, caring for, loving; being one with, being intimate with, a sense of bonding with; full vulnerability, openness to, full exposure to; no barriers, no distance, no separation; taking as one's own, complete owning, all mine; exploding, fragmenting, blasting into pieces; joining together with, becoming one with, a full union with; being superior to, reigning over, being better than; being the great one, the God, the one with all the power; a coldness, hardness, sense of uncaring; removal, separation, distance; confrontation, one-on-one, having it out with; gentle, soft, bending with; belongingness, having a home, friendly familiarity; being cared for, nurtured, succored; chaos, total disorganization,

nonsense; absolute silliness, craziness, giddiness, total
whimsy; being weird, bizarre, nutty; letting it go, giving it
up, shedding it off; being the responsible one, the trusted
one, the one who takes care of things; being older, wiser,
experienced; utter hatred, cold fury, sheer rage; destroying it,
smashing it, blasting it apart; removed, unaffected, distant;
being on one's own, independent, autonomous; lightness,
airiness, floating; wicked, nasty, mischievous; dependent on,
clinging to, grasping onto; helpless, passive, vulnerable; being
merciless, unrelenting, remorseless; rebelling against, defying,
never giving in; freedom from barriers, no restrictions, utter
freedom; ripeness, vibrant sexuality, orgiastic; displaying
oneself, exhibiting oneself, showing it all; being drawn
toward, fascinated with, utterly compelled by; being excited,
aroused, stimulated; being pushy, aggressive, taking over;
being the leader, the one in charge, commander.

There is at least one way to determine if your description
is good enough. The description should be accurate enough
and complete enough so that, if two or three fine character
actors used your description, each one would be able to
know what to do and how to act in the scene. They would
portray virtually the same character. They would be having
virtually the same experiencing in the scene.

*When the Session Is Over, Write Down Your Description of the
Deeper Potential for Experiencing*

Your description of the deeper potential for experiencing is
important in order for you to finish Steps 2, 3, and 4.
However, the session is really over when you actually are this

whole new way in your real life after the session. If you are inclined to keep notes of each session, it is helpful to write down your description of the deeper potential for experiencing. If you are inclined, as I am, to keep a running record of the deeper potentials that you have found, have a sheet of paper on which you write down the deeper potential for experiencing arrived at in each session. To help you be clear in doing your post-session homework, to be this new way in the post-session world, it is helpful, after the session, to jot down your description of the deeper potential for experiencing.

Describing the Deeper Potential for Experiencing Is Essential, But Make Sure You Then Also Use Two or Three Other Methods

Describing the deeper potential for experiencing is essential because each of the other methods in this step requires that you first have a good description of the deeper potential. However, just describing the deeper potential for experiencing is not enough in order for you to reach the point where you actually welcome, appreciate, accept, and cherish this deeper potential for experiencing. Make sure that you use at least two or three other Step 2 methods.

Each of the following methods is explicitly aimed at helping you make the wonderful shift to welcoming, appreciating, accepting, and cherishing this deeper potential for experiencing. Even if you seem to like the deeper potential, make sure that you still use two or three of the following methods. If you draw back from the deeper potential, if you do not like it or are bothered by it, make absolutely sure that you still use a number of the following methods.

In the balance of this chapter, the other methods are given in no particular order. You can use any of them in any sequence you want.

TELL HOW AND WHY YOU LOVE AND HATE THIS DEEPER POTENTIAL FOR EXPERIENCING

Tell how and why this potential for experiencing is so wonderful. It is such a fine potential for experiencing, so virtuous and upstanding. Of course you like it. Tell how and why you like it. Or, if the deeper potential for experiencing is bad, and evil, go ahead and tell how and why it is bad and evil. Put into words how and why the potential for experiencing qualifies as bad and evil, as something that ought to be tarred and feathered and run out of town. Or, demonstrate your flexibility by moving from one extreme to the other. Ladies and gentlemen, let me present all the ways in which this little potential for experiencing is laudable, and praiseworthy. Then, I shall take a few steps to my left and explain how this very same potential for experiencing is awful, not to be trusted, deserving of our anger and hatred.

If you are clever, you can think of circumstances and conditions where even a fine potential for experiencing can make for trouble, be inappropriate, or cause problems. And you can think of circumstances and conditions where a perfectly monstrous potential for experiencing can hold its head high and be applauded by the virtuous. Keep a good eye out for these circumstances and conditions.

"All right, so the experiencing is sheer freedom, exhilarating liberation, no constraints, doing what I want. It is good. I like it. It is a nice thing. Valuable. I wish I had it more. If it's a part of me, I want to keep it. Yes I do. Lots of people would like it. I approve of it. I want it. I like it. I don't know what else to say . . . Can it be bad? Maybe. Of course, I have responsibilities. I just can't leave my daughter . . . I could leave my husband, I guess. But I am a lawyer and I have a responsibility to my clients. I can see how being free, liberated, feeling no constraints could get me into trouble at home and at work. But I still think it's a good thing. Sure I value it. It's good.

"You're damned right it's a good thing—defying, standing up for myself, rebelling. Yes! I wish I had that more. I like that thing. Sure it could get out of hand. I can fight against everything. But in its right place, that's a fine quality. I love it. I take pride in it. It could do me good. I don't have much of that. I would pay a lot to get that. If I have it, good. I deserve it, too. I need it. It's a good thing . . ."

Many deeper potentials for experiencing are easy to welcome, to see as good, to appreciate. Think of a deeper potentiality for fondness, loving, intimacy. Think of a deeper potentiality for experiencing a sense of responsibility, being trusted, counted upon. These are generically good things that are easy to feel good about. On the other hand, there are plenty of deeper potentials for experiencing that are questionable, lead to bad things, seem bad themselves, and are hard to welcome and cherish. If you strain, you might find a special circumstance or context or two that can justify the negative deeper potential, but even then you can describe how you do not like the deeper potential for experiencing:

"An experiencing of hatred, rage, fury? I don't like it. I think it's bad. Going around being full of hatred and rage and fury? That's awful! Who could like anything like that? Who could enjoy such a terrible experiencing? I wouldn't. It's bad. It's worse than bad. People like that are bad. I don't like them. How could anyone like being like that?"

The method can include both telling how it is wonderful and awful, good and bad. Or praising it. Or just disliking it. Just make sure that you keep the deeper potential for experiencing right here, and that you spend some time describing how you feel about it, good or bad, or both. Whether you tell how much you find it valuable or repulsive, the method consists of keeping it close enough to you to tell your feelings about it. The net result is that the relationship becomes more loving, accepting, and welcoming.

ADMIT AND DENY THAT THIS DEEPER POTENTIAL FOR EXPERIENCING IS A PART OF YOU

Do your very best to admit that this deeper potential for experiencing is a part of you, is in there somewhere. Force yourself to make a case for it being inside you. Be your own prosecuting attorney. Then, take the position that there is nothing at all like that inside you. That deeper potential for experiencing is not at all a part of who and what you are. Fight the charge. Make a strong case that you are innocent of having that deeper potential for experiencing. Deny the merest possibility. Be your own aggressive defense attorney.

Remember, no one is going to hear what you say. No one is going to roll their eyes when you admit that the deeper potential for experiencing is there inside you, somewhere. No one is going to roll their eyes when you mount a full denial that there is anything even remotely like that inside you. No one is going to accuse you of flip-flopping or being inconsistent when you shift from admitting it to denying it. You are safe.

Openly admit that there is something in you that enjoys blaming someone, accusing another person, making another person feel guilty and bad. It may be a terrible quality, but you have it inside you. Sometimes it actually shows, right? Or, maybe it is just a sliver, a tiny little glow, way down deep inside. Assemble the evidence. Remember those times, perhaps long ago, when you actually sensed that experiencing inside you? Find the evidence. Others may not be able to testify because it did not show publicly, but you felt it inside. Go ahead; admit that this potential for experiencing lurks inside you. Tell about all those times when you experienced it.

When you are done, switch over to denying that there is even a tiny whisper of that deeper potential for experiencing in you. Ask anyone in your world today. Ask people from your past. No one would ever think of you as someone who has even the slightest inner tendency to blame another person, be accusatory, make others feel guilty and bad. Not you. You are totally innocent. Make a strong case of pure denial. "I am not that way. There must be some big mistake. I am not a saint, but that particular quality? Sorry. You are looking at the wrong person. I deny it, and I am right." Tell how you have never felt it in your whole life. Not even a tiny whisper. Just make sure that you enjoy your vigorous denial. Have fun denying the charge.

Whether you are admitting or denying, the more delightfully and buoyantly you are engaged in the admission or the denial, and the better job you do of admitting and denying, you are, at the same time, keeping the deeper potential for experiencing close by. You are welcoming, appreciating, accepting, and even cherishing the deeper potential for experiencing.

PROUDLY PROCLAIM THAT YOU ALWAYS KEEP
THE DEEPER POTENTIAL FOR EXPERIENCING
IMPRISONED AND NEVER LET IT FREE

Suppose that the deeper potential for experiencing is that of nurturing, taking care of, providing for; being passive, gentle, yielding; owning, controlling, being in charge of; or the experiencing of hardness, toughness, coldness. This method consists of proudly proclaiming that you have kept in the past, and will keep in the future, this experiencing sealed off, imprisoned, never free, never shown, never let out in the open. You are so proud of your achievement. Belt it out with vigor, pride, and pleasure:

"I make absolutely sure I never feel it. I have never felt it in the past, and I never will in the future. Never. It will never even come close. Never.

"If I even came close to feeling it, I felt rotten, awful. It never felt good. When I came close to feeling it, it was bad, a problem, something terrible. I hated it. It never felt good. Never.

"It is my enemy. It is a problem. I want to make sure it is always hidden because it is a bad thing. It has to be sealed off. It is not good. It is evil. I will fight to keep it imprisoned for the rest of my life. Everyone in the world should fight it.

"I actively avoid it. I do what I can to not be that way, to never experience that. The kind of person I am will always make sure it never shows. I campaign to keep it inside and even to get rid of it. I would love to kill it, cauterize it, execute it, be rid of it. I fight hard to not ever be that kind of person.

"I would do almost anything rather than be like that, to let it ever be free. I am forever at war with it, against it. It is my enemy, and I battle it in every way I can. And God and good are on my side."

Deliver an impassioned speech proclaiming that you always keep the deeper potential for
experiencing imprisoned and never let it free. That is your mission, and you are proud of that mission.

Step 2. Welcome the Deeper Potential for Experiencing

ACCUSE YOURSELF OF BEING DISGUSTING BECAUSE
YOU KEEP THE DEEPER POTENTIAL FOR EXPERIENCING
IMPRISONED AND NEVER LET IT FREE.

Try to imagine how the deeper potential for experiencing feels about you. Think of what it says to its friends about you. You have a glorious case against it. Suppose it has an equally glorious case against you. The main difference is that you are the boss. You are in charge of thinking, feeling, doing, and being in the real world. You are in a position to keep the deeper potential for experiencing hidden, subjugated, kept down, imprisoned. It cannot do that to you.

For once, try to take the side of the deeper potential for experiencing. Try to be its voice. Try to say what it could say to you. Here is what might come out:

"Just who the hell do you think you are? I love rebelling, defying, standing up for myself, and you keep me imprisoned. You have no right to do this. And you have done this our whole life. You have never once let me free. Ever. You think you are better than I am? I think you are disgusting. You are a liar. You are a nothing. But you sure do a good job of hiding me. Who gave you that right? You act so innocent. But you are a dictator. You keep me in prison. What about fairness? What about democracy? You've spent decades hiding me. Now it's my turn. I want to be free. You are subjugating me. For the next 20 years, I want to see what it's like to be free. You be in jail for 20 years; see what it's like. You are bad. You are awful. How dare you? This is a war, and I am going to win. You are my enemy, and I hate you. And that's just for starters. I have a lot more to tell you . . .

243

"Oh, yes. You have spent your whole life hiding me, avoiding this wonderful quality. A whole life dedicated to not rebelling, not defying, not standing up. What a colossal waste. A real waste of life. You should feel guilty. And there's more. You are so hardheaded, so rigid. You see me as awful, and that is the way it is for you. You are inflexible. You are prejudiced. You have a mind that can't budge. You are sick. You are crazy. You are out of your mind. I hate you because you have imprisoned me. You are disgusting. Yech!"

In the previous method, you railed at the deeper potential for experiencing. You told it how you felt about it. Now the tables have turned. In this method, you are the deeper potential, or you stand alongside it, and you rail at you, at the person who kept you imprisoned and never let you free. Both methods help you achieve a greater sense of welcoming, appreciating, and cherishing the deeper potential for experiencing.

FIGURE OUT HOW THE KIND OF PERSON YOU BECAME
AND THE KIND OF LIFE YOU HAVE ARE GREAT WAYS
OF DISPROVING AND HIDING THE DEEPER
POTENTIAL FOR EXPERIENCING

This method consists of figuring out all the ways that the person you have become and the kind of life you have carved out for yourself, the kind of personal world you have built around yourself, are well-suited to disprove the deeper potential for experiencing, to deny and hide it, and to make

244

sure that it never has the chance to come forth and breathe. You don't even have to be correct. You may even be wrong. It really doesn't matter. Just play a game in which your whole life and the very person you have become are mainly to make sure that the deeper potential for experiencing is sealed off, hidden, kept down.

For example, you discovered a deeper potential for experiencing a sense of bursting energy, vibrant aliveness, boundless vigor. Take a look at the kind of person you are. What about the person you are thwarts the essence of bursting energy, vibrant aliveness, boundless vigor? Here is what you proclaim:

"Look at me. I am so slender, not wiry and tough, just slender, like a waif. No strength. When I talk, I talk with a kind of slow whine in my thin little voice. Never loud, almost a whisper. And this look on my face. Anyone can see I have a look. A little shy, a little withdrawn. Half-dead. I watch. I look out. I see little details. I walk slowly. I always wait a few seconds before I answer. My God. And I titter. I never laugh loudly. And I can't eat this and that. My body is weak, and I get sick a lot. I don't swear. And I am shy. Yeah. My God.

"And the life I have. There's no room to be full of boundless energy and vibrant aliveness. No room at all. My husband is so sweet and gentle. We are like little birds. We live in this little apartment. And my friends. They would think I went out of my mind if I screamed or even laughed loud. If I had a fit or . . . And the way we make love. It's so loving and . . . no energy. My God, even orgasms are quiet.

And I am an accountant. Little numbers. Columns. Everything is nicely organized and in its place. The car we have. It's nice. I have this old clunker of a bicycle. Where would I have boundless energy? Nowhere. I'd have to hide it somewhere. I work in this small accounting firm, and the whole office is quiet. No one yells. No one even laughs hard. I've got a great life, and there's no place to . . . It's like I have a life that makes sure I can never feel this. That's for sure."

If you look carefully at the person you became, the person you are, the life you had, the life you have, it is almost as if all of this was created in order to make sure that you hide, deny, seal off, disprove, and have no room for the deeper potential for experiencing that you have discovered. Proclaim all of this out loud. Figure out all the ways and tell what they are. Be appalled, be annoyed, be sad. When you do this method well, you are welcoming the deeper potential for experiencing, you are valuing and appreciating it.

CONFESS THAT THERE ARE AND WERE TIMES WHEN YOU ACTUALLY ENJOYED UNDERGOING THIS DEEPER POTENTIAL FOR EXPERIENCING

You may find the deeper potential for experiencing to be socially acceptable. You may not have felt it much, but some of these feelings are acceptable to you. You can admit that you might even have had times when you enjoyed an experiencing of caring for, nurturing, taking care of, or loving, being one with, being intimate. These are nice potentials. This method consists of confessing to times when you knew the potential for experiencing, when you enjoyed it, when you reveled in it. The method is put to the test when the deeper potential is not nice, when it is one you can easily find fault with or even disown, dislike, see as awful. Suppose that you discovered a deeper potential for experiencing blaming the other one, accusing them, making them feel guilty, bad, charged. Your job is to confess to actual times when you truly enjoyed undergoing this deeper potential for experiencing.

"All right, it is confession time. Think. When did I really enjoy blaming someone, accusing them, making them feel guilty as charged? Recently, sometime recently. Think . . . I felt it, inside. Ah, yes, Susan, my responsible supervisor. She never makes mistakes. Except that she never sent that memo around. And the big boss was asking why there was no plan available. Susan lied, in front of all of us. She looked at me, and I just looked at her, and I was cold to her afterward. She came to my office and tried to be so nice. Ha! I was polite. Yes, I was. And I was thinking all the time that she lied. I would never tumble. I blamed her inside, and she knew it. I liked blaming her. I loved watching her squirm. Oh, I was bad. It felt good. It did!"

Go back to the past. Confess to times when you knew that deeper potential for experiencing, when you savored it, when you loved feeling it:

"Dad left when I was 14, and Mom would always criticize him for leaving. I remember when Mom was depressed that day when we heard that he had cancer. I listened to her start criticizing him again, and I guess I was

247

mad at her. I told her that Dad was thoughtless and not a great father, but that she always was after him. I told her that she punished him for everything she could find. I told her, and I guess I was so excited. Yes, I loved blaming her. It was about time. I was quiet, but I loved making her feel guilty. That was the first time she let me say it. She just sat there. I loved accusing her of hounding Dad until he couldn't take it anymore and he left us. You were bad, Mom. Oh, I loved blaming her then.

"And when I was little, I remember yelling at Joan. She took my ring. I must have been about five. Six, I was six. I told Mom that Joan took my ring, and I loved it! Joan was always the big sister, the good one. But she took my ring. Mom took my side. Mom yelled at her. I loved watching Joan cry. I loved it! I accused her, and she cried. It was great!"

If you work hard and stop denying and lying to yourself, you can remember both recent times and times long ago when you savored actually undergoing the deeper potential for experiencing. Tell about those times. Go ahead. Confess that there were times when you thoroughly enjoyed that deeper potential for experiencing.

DESCRIBE AS WONDERFUL AND ADMIRABLE SOMEONE YOU KNOW OR KNEW WHO WAS THIS DEEPER POTENTIAL FOR EXPERIENCING

Ask yourself: "Do I know someone, from today or from long ago, who was like this, and it was wonderful? They could be this way, and they were good at it? They could blame someone, accuse someone, and make the person feel bad, charged, and on them it felt great? When they did it, it was fine. Everyone liked it. So who comes to mind?" The person could be from your current world. He or she could be from the past ten years or so. Maybe you have to go back to when you were a child. Try to find someone. It might be a friend, someone at work or in the family, or someone you met just once or twice. It might be a character from television, the movies, or a novel. Try to think of someone.

If you can find someone, someone who exemplifies this deeper potential in ways that even you can enjoy, can happily approve of, then you are allowing yourself to like this deeper potential, to welcome and approve of it, to appreciate and love it. And yet the method is a little safer because you are looking for some other person, not you. In a way, this makes the task a little easier.

"I remember! Uncle Stan! That guy was so funny. Well, he didn't laugh, but he would crack everyone up. He and Aunt Betty used to play cards with Mom and Dad. Every week. And sooner or later he'd get on Dad. He'd tease Dad. No one ever teased Dad. Dad was like God. Except for Uncle Stan. He would tell Dad he was the worst partner. 'I gotta carry you cause you are an amateur,' and he'd say 'amateur' like he was an English lord. He would tell Dad that he couldn't remember anything. He used to criticize the hell out of Dad, and Dad would just grin. He loved it. Everyone loved Uncle Stan, and no one could accuse Dad of anything, except Uncle Stan. He gave Dad shit, and

249

everyone laughed like hell. He was good; he could do it. I haven't thought of that in years . . ."

Try to think of one or two more people who exemplify this deeper potential for experiencing in ways that are so wonderful, acceptable, and surrounded by good feelings. Try to picture them being this way. Describe in detail how they were this way. As you do this, as you are allowing this deeper potential to be wonderful, happy, and loved by you, you are helping to make the relationship between you and the deeper potential for experiencing much better, more welcoming, and more accepting, even if the deeper potential is there in that other person, not in you.

Describe Someone Who Is Being The Deeper Potential For Experiencing In The Scene Of Strong Feeling In Ways That Are Outrageous, Silly, Hilarious, And With Cartoon-like Unreality

Remember the original scene of strong feeling? You started the session by finding a scene of strong feeling. For example, it was when you and your wife were once again arguing about the same old problems, only this time Agnes was here with you, and you and your wife were both trying to get Agnes on your side, even though Agnes is your wife's best friend. The strong feeling is not good. You are hurt, angry, frustrated, trying hard not to explode, disgusted that you are not putting on a good case in front of Agnes. Bad feelings.

Step 2. Welcome the Deeper Potential for Experiencing

This method is a challenge. The challenge is to go back to the scene, only this time you actually see, witness, and describe someone being the deeper potential for experiencing. You know what the deeper potential is. You are to imagine someone being the deeper potential for experiencing in that scene of strong feeling. Furthermore, that person is to be the deeper potential for experiencing in a way that is absurd, silly, hilarious, and free of all reality constraints. The scene is to be wild, crazy, and cartoon-like. That is the method. That is the challenge.

You know the deeper potential for experiencing. It is the experiencing of sheer freedom, nice, warm liberation, being free of it all, doing what you want. The challenge is to picture someone being this deeper potential for experiencing in that scene of strong feeling with your wife and Agnes.

Who is going to be the one who enacts the role of the deeper potential for experiencing? There are some options here. The person could be you, but that is usually hard. Are you able to see yourself in that scene, being the deeper potential for experiencing? Or, the person could be the one you admired, the person you know or knew who seemed to exemplify this deeper potential for experiencing. If, using this method, you found someone, you could insert that person in the scene. Or, you could use some actor, perhaps from television or films, an actor who easily and happily can enact the role of sheer freedom, nice, warm liberation, free of it all, doing what he wants.

You have the scene of strong feeling. You have selected the person who is to be the deeper potential for experiencing in the scene. Go ahead and visualize what can happen, and describe what happens out loud, with good, happy, enjoyable feelings:

"He looks at his wife. He looks at Agnes. He sort of floats over to them, puts his hands on both of them, and then drifts up. He floats around the room with his arms out, and then he floats away, out of the room and outside of the house. He is floating and drifting, and he is free, really free. They are gone. He left! He's history! He's out of there! He is floating over the countryside; then he gently comes to the ground. I see him! He is grinning, and he just dances around. He is free. He is liberated. He can do what he wants, and he is . . . I see him sitting at some outdoor place, having coffee, by himself. He's in Greece! He is liberated. He just watches the people go by. He is at a piano, composing music. What a life! Go for it, man!"

Suppose that the scene of strong feeling was from your boyhood. Your mother is trying to get you to write the alphabet. She is right next to you, yelling at you, demanding, pressuring. The deeper potential is the experiencing of showing her, getting back at her, driving her out of her mind, being a wicked little devil. Yes! Can you see some character enacting this deeper potential in that scene?

"That little kid has a swivel head. He turns and looks at her. He is the devil, a wicked devil. Too much for her. With his mean little eyes on her, he opens his mouth and hisses fire. She backs away. He takes a step. She backs up. She is scared. She starts running, and the mean little devil breathes

252

fire on her. She is screaming. He loves it! He is shrieking. Gotcha! Run! He slaps her ass and she runs faster. He screams in delight. She runs real fast. He's after her. She can't get away. I see her backing up against the wall, scared as hell. The mean little kid is laughing. He snaps his fingers, and she is surrounded by a thousand snakes. He is the devil! Then she collapses. Ha!"

It is important that you have loads of fun doing this. Do it with plenty of gusto and energy. See what you see in vivid detail. When you do this well, you are welcoming the deeper potential for experiencing. You are accepting it, loving it, and relating to it well. That is the goal.

I have given you about ten methods that you can use to welcome, accept, and cherish the deeper potential for experiencing. Know what they are. Learn them. You will probably come to rely on a few of them, but, every so often, review the ten and try to be able to use any of them rather than just relying on a few.

Make sure that you use the method of describing the nature and content of the deeper potential for experiencing. This is the essential method to use each time. Learn to do this one well.

Step 2 is done. When Step 2 is done well, you are ready to let go of being the person you are and throw yourself into the radical, wholesale, qualitative change of being the deeper potential for experiencing. This is the job of Step 3. Are you ready?

p. 254
blank

7

Step 3.
Undergo A Qualitative
Shift Into Being The
Deeper Potential for
Experiencing in Scenes
from the Past

You now have a description of the deeper potential for experiencing. You know what it is. In Step 3, you find scenes, times, incidents from your past, and then you become that deeper potential for experiencing in the context of that past scene. You throw yourself into being the deeper potential for experiencing. You let go of the person you are and literally become the deeper potential for experiencing in the context of that past scene from your life.

This is a remarkable change, a radical transformation. It is a qualitative shift, a quantum shift. Rather than gradually or progressively, it happens all of a sudden. Up until now, you have been the person you have almost always been. After the shift, you are living and breathing as this whole new being, a person who is the deeper potential for experiencing.

FIND RECENT, EARLIER, AND REMOTE LIFE SCENES

Start by finding scenes from the past. These may be scenes, times, incidents that happened quite recently, perhaps in the past few days or weeks. Or, they may have occurred earlier in your life, some years ago, 10 or 20 years ago, when you were an adolescent, an older child, or even a rather young child. Or, the scenes may be from that remote period when you were a baby, the primitive period from a few years before your conception to a few years or so after you were born.

Follow The Relatively Simple Way Of Finding A Past Scene

You know that the deeper potential for experiencing is the experiencing of being solid, stable, sound, grounded, or the experiencing of being open, honest, exposed, not hiding. Whatever the experiencing, you are going to find a scene from the past and then you are going to undergo the qualitative shift of being that deeper potential for experiencing in the context of that past scene.

The method is relatively simple. This section describes the method in some detail, but the general idea goes like this: First, you select a period from the past, such as the past few years or so, or when you were a child. Then you have a choice. You can use the nature of the deeper potential for experiencing to find a scene from the past. Or, you can use the general contours of the initial scene of strong feeling to help you find a scene from the past. Either choice will do.

Almost any past scene will be sufficient for you to be the deeper potential for experiencing. You do not necessarily have to find a special scene. You do not have to look for some time in the past when the deeper potential for experiencing first appeared, when it supposedly was caused in the first place, or when you actually underwent that deeper potential for experiencing. There are no past scenes that are the "right" ones to look for and use. Just trust and use the relatively simple method that is described here.

PUT YOURSELF IN SOME TIME FRAME FROM THE PAST

Get yourself ready to see scenes from the past. If you start with the recent past, you may say: "I want to start with today, recently, the past few years or so. I am ready to see times, scenes from today, from recently."

You may look for scenes from when you were grown up, in your 20s or 30s. When you get yourself ready to see scenes from this period, it usually helps to remember, to see some of the highlights of that period. If, for example, you are in your 50s or 60s, you may say: "I am grown, in my 20s or 30s. What do I see already? Ah! I see the house where we lived, that brick house in the country, and the kids. I see my daughter, Delani, and there's my husband, Rashmi. Handsome. Okay. I am ready, I picture some time from the past. I am ready."

257

You may prefer a time frame from when you were an older child or an adolescent. Keep that period in mind. Try to see some of the prominent features of that period to help you get in the proper mind-set and to be ready. "So, I am 10 or 12 or a teenager. I see the tennis courts and the place we all used to hang out, and I see my Mom, especially her hair. It always looked awful. And I see Claudia. We were best friends. I am ready."

You may select the time when you were a little child, almost as far back as you can remember. "We lived on Garfield Street, in that little apartment, and I had a room with my brother. I remember the clock. It was mine. My dad worked for the railroad till he lost his job. I must have been four, around there. I can remember . . ."

You may want to select the primitive period from about a year or so before you were even conceived to a few years or so after you were born. Look for scenes involving mainly your father and mother, not yourself. You probably have no memories of that period, but you may have some idea of what was front and center, or of importance, for your father and mother. Getting ready is trying to highlight what was relatively prominent then. "That's when Mom was living with Grandpa and Grandma on Delaney, and she was going to the University. She wanted to be an engineer, of all things, and she met Dad. She got pregnant right away, and they got married right away. I don't know if they got pregnant and then decided to get married, or if they wanted to get married anyhow. She never got to be an engineer . . . "

Once you pick a time frame, even if the time frame is rather general and loose, then you are ready to find a scene from the past, some past time that you can use to move out of the person you are and into being the deeper potential for experiencing. You can find a past scene by using either the deeper potential for experiencing or the general structure or context of the scene of strong feeling that you started with in Step 1.

USE THE DEEPER POTENTIAL FOR EXPERIENCING TO FIND SCENES

When you look for scenes and times in the time frame you selected, you can start with the deeper potential for experiencing and use it to find scenes.

KEEP SAYING THE DEEPER POTENTIAL FOR EXPERIENCING UNTIL A SCENE APPEARS

Your attention is on whatever time frame you selected. Keep saying, describing out loud, the deeper potential; a scene will appear. That is the scene for you to use. It is the first scene to appear. Use that scene no matter what it is, whether it seems related to the deeper potential or wholly unrelated. Use the scene.

The time frame is the past five or ten years. You are ready. You say the deeper potential for experiencing: "Letting go of it, giving it up, just being free of it . . . I see something . . . I remember talking with my mother about the guy she was living with . . . Justin. I wanted her to see that it wasn't going to last. I didn't do too well. She told me to leave her alone . . ." You can use this scene. It was the first one that came to you. Say the words again and see what appears: "Letting go of it, giving it up, just being free of it . . . being free of it . . . Daniel. After three years, he left. We didn't even have big fights. He just . . . Well, we had nothing together. First time I broke up and no fights. We decided, together, it was a mistake."

Suppose that the time frame is when you were a child. You are all set, and you recite the deeper potential for experiencing: "Just being a helpless little baby, held, being held and cuddled. Cuddled . . . I see Dad, and he comes running out of the house. I broke a window. I smashed the upstairs window. I was scared as hell. He was mad as hell. And something else. I see my Aunt Diane. Big lady. I loved her and Uncle Paul. When I stayed at their place, she always liked me to massage her toes. She'd be on the couch, and I would massage her toes, and she loved that. She really loved that, and Uncle Paul would kid me about it."

The time frame is your childhood, and you say the words: "Being like someone, wanting to be like someone, hero-worshipping, being like someone . . . I see Louise's older brother . . . Lots of big older brothers in the neighborhood. Her brother . . . I don't know his name. He'd mow the yard, and I saw his huge legs. He was on the high school football team. He was powerful. Chuck and Sandy and I would watch him toss a football with other guys in the street. I haven't thought of that in years."

The time frame is early childhood. Get ready to see things from when you were little. You start with the deeper potential for experiencing: "Fighting back, rebelling, defying, fighting back, defying . . . I remember I used to love to stick my head down between my legs and see things upside-down. The front of the house, seeing the house upside-down . . . And when Mom had those ladies over . . . I got yelled at. I did the same thing. Mom let me be with them in the living room, and I put my head down and kept watching them upside-down. I got yelled at. I must have been . . . what? Three, maybe?"

You select the time frame of being an adult, grown up, and you are ready to see whatever appears when you describe the deeper potential for experiencing: "Violence, being violent . . . smashing, destroying, breaking things up . . . sheer violence . . . I remember having this hoarse throat and the flu, and getting so furious at Ron that I broke things! I smashed his trophy! I smashed everything, and even tried to smash the chairs, but they were too heavy. I was yelling and screaming at him. I have no idea what drove me crazy. I went out of my mind, and I couldn't even make any sense because I had this sore throat and I felt so sick.. I went out of my mind!"

You try out a time frame from the primitive period, starting a year or so before you were conceived and lasting to a few years or so after you are born. Get ready to see your mother and father during this period. Not you. Focus your attention on seeing them. Start by saying the words, describing the deeper potential for experiencing, and then seeing the first scene that appears: "It's feeling alone, by myself, no friends, no one. Not fitting in, all alone . . . That's my mother! Sure. I can imagine her right after I was born. Dad's white and Mom's black. She's the only black woman around here. She left me, or something, and went back to Jamaica. That's how she must have felt. And Dad was like a lawyer. He got me. She made a baby for him, yet she must have felt so isolated, far from home, really black, with no friend in the family, not really. I see Mom sitting by herself at home—she must have—and finally deciding to go back to Jamaica. Something like that."

You probably will not remember these primitive scenes, but they will occur when you get in the mind-set to receive one and say the words of the deeper potential for experiencing: "So what comes to mind? That deeper potential, a real fighter, don't take that shit, tough and a real heart, courage to fight . . . Hey! I see Dad in Grandpa's clothing store. He caved in all right. That's right after that high school girl accused Dad of doing something sexual, and he got fired from teaching. Right away he went to work for Mom's dad in the clothing store. Great, Mom's pregnant with me when it happened. Dad just gave in. I see Dad in the store, cleaning up and selling. He must have hated that! He gave in, he did! That must have been the worst time in Dad's life! He's by himself in the shop, at night, doing inventory, all by himself, and working for Grandpa yet! He never fought back! Damn!"

Pick a loose time frame. Get ready to see scenes from that general time frame. Say the words describing the deeper potential for experiencing and see what scene comes to your mind.

PASSIVELY RECEIVE THE FIRST SCENE THAT APPEARS;
DO NOT ACTIVELY SEEK A PARTICULAR KIND OF SCENE.

The aim is to find any scene from the past, recently or from long ago. Any scene will do. Do not censor any scene that appears. Do not reject any scene. Do not look for a particular kind of scene. Just say the words describing the deeper potential for experiencing and passively accept whatever scene comes to you.

The scene may seem related or connected to the nature of the deeper potential, or it may seem wholly unrelated, disconnected. That does not matter. It may be an old, familiar scene, one you know well. Or, it may be a new scene, one you hadn't remembered in years. It may be a dramatic, painful scene, a veritable turning point in your life, or it may be a mundane, little scene, innocuous and seemingly without much feeling at all.

Sometimes it is clear that the deeper potential for experiencing was present in the scene. It may have been exceedingly present, occurring just a tiny bit, or even just hovering inside. Those scenes are fine to use. On the other hand, the scene may be one where even intent study could not find anything even distantly related to the deeper potential for experiencing. That is also fine. Just passively accept the first scene that comes to mind.

YOU STARTED THE SESSION WITH A SCENE OF STRONG FEELING; USE THE GENERAL CONTEXT OF THAT SCENE TO FIND SCENES FROM THE PAST

The session began with you finding a scene of strong feeling. Whether this scene was from your current world or from a while ago, you can use this initial scene of strong feeling to help you find scenes from the past. You can find scenes from the past by starting from the deeper potential for experiencing or from the initial scene of strong feeling. Either or both will do.

First, pick a time frame from the past. Once again, you may choose the time frame of the past few years. Or, you can take the past ten years or so. Or, go back to your later childhood and adolescence, or earlier childhood, or even the primitive period from a few years before conception to a few years or so after you were born.

Once you select a time frame, describe the general context of that initial scene of strong feeling. The general context is a simplified description of the context or structure of that initial scene of strong feeling. Keep the description general, not concretely specific. For example, suppose the initial scene of strong feeling is when you are standing in line at the store, with two or three people in front of you. You are scared inside, but no one can tell. As usual, you stole something. This is not the first time you have stolen something from this store. This time, you stole nail clippers, and the package is in your jacket pocket. You are terrified that someone, maybe a store detective, will grab you. It is frightening. Here is the way you describe the general context: "So, the time is when I took something, have something I shouldn't have, and I'm scared of getting caught." That is all it took. You were attending to a time frame of being an adult, in your 20s or 30s, and the scene pops into your mind: "It's when I worked at Pennypackers. I had a key and went into Heather's office. She was a knockout, and I . . . It was at night, and I snuck into her office and looked in all the drawers. I don't even know what the hell I was looking for. I was scared to death that someone would find me and ask me what the hell I was doing there. But I was . . . crazed. I wanted to find something. Something personal, I guess. That was not good."

The scene you found at the beginning of the session is when you awaken in the morning. You are in bed, lying on your back, and you begin to lift your head, neck, and upper body. But your body hurts, and you suddenly remember that you have cancer and you will die. This grips you, and you just lie back down, exhausted, weak, and almost resigned to being helpless, victimized, dying. You don't even cry. Quite aside from the nature of the deeper potential, you describe the large contours of the scene as you get ready to receive a scene from some time in your adult life: "Just the main things. All right, I am in bed, alone, in the bed, and I . . . remember something terrible . . . In bed, wake up, something terrible . . . It was when I was a kid. I woke up because there was something in my room. I was scared to death. It was the curtain, and it was blowing, and I was scared to death that it was some creature. There was a big noise. Something got knocked over. The curtains . . . I think my heart stopped."

The initial scene was when you were in the kitchen and your husband called, and you realized you had mistaken the time your mother-in-law was to arrive at the airplane terminal. Your husband was furious with you; you had left his mother at the airport for hours already! This was the scene of strong feeling that you started the session with. Another one of your stupid mistakes. No one can count on you. You are really irresponsible. You set the time frame for some time when you were grown up, an adult, and you try to get the general contours: "I am supposed to do something, but I forget . . . Supposed to do something. I don't do . . . My God, I remember I was about 17, and it was really late, dark. I snuck Bill in to the room in the basement, and he's on top of me, and we're going at it, and that's when my little cousin Marty starts running away. He was in the doorway and he saw! I almost died! What does this have to do with my forgetting to pick up Tom's mother? I have no idea." It doesn't matter. Just receive the past scene that comes to you.

The initial scene of strong feeling was when you knew that your husband had lied to you about money. He didn't tell you, but you figured it out. That's when something snapped in you, and you started screaming at him. Your body was galvanized. You grabbed the lamp and broke it, and then you threw the ashtray through the window. You broke a window. You grabbed the fireplace poker and swung it around as you ran after your husband, and he ran out of there. You went berserk. You were out of your mind.

The time frame you select was when you were a child, and you sketch out the general context of the initial scene of strong feeling: "I am in a room with another person, and I lose my mind, go crazy, violent . . . I see something! I see my mom on the couch, screaming. My dad is on one side, and my older sisters are there too. Mom's yelling. They told me it was because she was going through a change of life, menopause, something . . . Mom was screaming. And I see . . . I remember my Uncle George. He was the family drunk. I loved that guy. When I was little, I remember he'd read stories to me at night, and he'd act them out. I've got tears in my eyes! I loved him. He was . . . sweet . . . He was such a gentle guy . . ."

You are just using a way to poke around in the past to find a scene that you can use. You can find a past scene by starting from the general context or general contours of the initial scene of strong feeling that you began with.

266

Step 3. Undergo A Qualitative Shift

Passively Receive the First Scene That Appears; Do Not Actively Search for a Particular Kind of Scene

When you are passively attending to a time frame, like some time during later childhood and adolescence, and you say the words describing the general context of the initial scene of strong feeling, some past scene will appear. It will just appear. Use that scene. Be passive and receive whatever past scene appears. Whichever method you use, just take the first scene that comes to you.

Use Past Scenes That Were Cimactic Turning Points in Your Life, Those Catastrophic Times You Always Remember

Some scenes in your life are so powerful, so big, so important, that you can always remember them. They will probably always be with you. They are so compelling, yet you don't want to think of them. They are the turning points in your life, and they are filled with powerful feeling.

These dramatic scenes may come to your mind when you start with the nature of the deeper potential for experiencing and get ready for what past scenes appear. However, these types of scenes usually appear when you start from the general context of the scene of strong feeling from the beginning of the session. It is as if these big scenes stand ready. Just say a few words about the general context of those initial scenes from the session, and you will see the big scenes from your life. These are the times when you were a little girl, and you were outside with a bunch of others, and your brother fell from high up in the tall tree, hurtled down, smashed on the pavement, and was killed. It was when you were caught in the powerful undertow, drawn down into the surging, deep water, and you passed out. You came so close to dying. It was when you were walking around in the old, abandoned farmhouse, and the dog lunged at your face, tearing your flesh and leaving those ugly scars that are still there today on your cheek and forehead. It was when that friend of the old man, the old man who showed you how to tie knots with the big rope after school, took you in his pickup truck. He took you to his place and forced you to put your mouth all over his penis.

These compelling, powerful, climactic scenes may come to your mind in a number of sessions. They may come to mind in one session and again later in other sessions. Use them. They can be useful past scenes.

You have selected a scene or two from your past, from your recent life, from a few or many years ago, or from your earliest, most remote past. Now you are ready to undergo the qualitative shift, the radical shift, into being the deeper potential for experiencing in the context of the past scenes.

Undergo The Qualitative Shift Into Being The Deeper Potential For Experiencing

You know the past scene. You know the deeper potential for experiencing. You are now to *be* the deeper potential for experiencing in the past scene. You are to disengage from the person you are, to exit out of the person you are, to just let go of being that person and literally be the deeper potential for experiencing. This is to be your whole new personality. Here is the miraculous change, the complete transformation, the glorious shift out of being one person and into being the altogether new person who is the deeper potential for experiencing.

THERE ARE SOME IMPORTANT GUIDELINES FOR UNDERGOING THE QUALITATIVE SHIFT INTO BEING THE DEEPER POTENTIAL FOR EXPERIENCING

These guidelines are more than merely a little helpful. They are essential.

Have A Clear Picture of the Deeper Potential for Experiencing That You Are Going To Be

Start by saying over and over what the deeper potential for experiencing is. You should have a fairly clear picture of what it is so that you can actually be it, undergo it, experience it. Start by saying: "Exactly what am I going to be like? All right, I am going to be seductiveness, yeah, playful and confident seductiveness, getting what I want seductively. That's me. Right." Say it over and over until you know it clearly. "I am loving, loving, caring, caring for, nurturing. I take care of. I feel nurturant, succoring, loving. I take care of. I am the one who loves, takes care of . . . I got it. I got it clearly. Okay, I am ready."

Keep describing it until you have a clear idea of the person you are going to be. Keep describing it until you can actually start to experience it a little. Describe it well enough so that a fine character actor would have enough to go on to be that person in the scene, and the audience would be convinced that the person is really undergoing the experiencing.

You Are To Be This Qualitatively New Person Fully and Completely

You are not to talk about this new person. You are not to describe what this new person is like. You are not to see, watch, or observe this new person. No, you are literally to *be* this whole new person, all the way, fully and completely.

The person who is here is the whole new person, the person who is the deeper potential for experiencing. It is as if this whole new person has been inside of you your entire life, and now it comes to life. It is here, finally, in all of its full and complete being. It is not you in the guise, in the role of an actor who portrays this role. Not an actor at all, you are literally to be this qualitatively new person. The person who thinks, who looks out, who feels, who acts, and who behaves is this entirely new person. There is to be no shred of the old, typical you.

The person who is here is the deeper potential for experiencing seductiveness, playful and confident seductiveness, getting what you want seductively. The new person is the experiencing of being loving, caring, caring for, nurturing, succoring, taking care of. The person who is here is the live embodiment of wickedness, mischievousness, naughtiness, devilishness.

Step 3. Undergo A Qualitative Shift

The shift is qualitative, radical, a quantum leap into being this entirely new person who is the wholesale, full, complete, utterly genuine and real deeper potential for experiencing. It is a transformative change, and it takes place in an instant. The last person who was here, who talked, was you. The next person who is here, who talks, is the qualitatively new person.

The shift is not one in which you slowly and gradually evolve into becoming the deeper potential for experiencing. It is not a matter of little by little. It is not a matter of development. Rather, a whole new, intact being replaces you. You step out, and the whole new person steps in. Your entire personality disappears in a flash, and a whole new personality takes its place. Boom. It happens in an instant.

It is not a matter of the deeper potential for experiencing being added as an interesting new component to the person you are. It is not a matter of there being an injection of loving, caring, caring for, nurturing, succoring so that there is more to you. You are not you plus the new quality of the deeper potential for experiencing. Instead, the qualitative shift is one in which all there is to you is this potential for experiencing. You are suddenly the pure experiencing of loving, caring, caring for, nurturing, succoring. That is all there is to the new person whom you are.

When you are this qualitatively new person, your old voice and voice quality are gone. Your voice is the voice of the whole new person. What is eerie is that your friends would not recognize your voice. You sound like a whole new person because you *are* a whole new person. It is not your voice. It is the voice of the qualitatively new person. If you

271

were to listen to a tape of this whole new person, you might not recognize the person on the tape as yourself and, in an important sense, you would be right.

Are you ready to be this qualitatively new person, fully and completely? This is an important guideline.

The Experiencing Is To Be Powerful;
The Feelings Are To Be wonderful

The experiencing is right when it is powerful, vigorous, saturated, forceful, strong, and full. You are literally the experiencing of seductiveness, playful and confident seductiveness, getting what you want seductively, and this experiencing absolutely fills you. It bursts out with enormous force. It is probably quite loud, but it may not be. It is always saturating and full, oozing and radiating the essence of the experiencing. The experiencing is powerful, not moderate, half-hearted, or feeble.

The experiencing is right when the accompanying feelings are wonderful. You should feel absolutely ecstatic, joyful, and deliciously pleasurable when you are being seductive, full of playful and confident seductiveness, getting what you want seductively. The feelings are to be wonderful, so pleasant, so happy.

You may think that it will be difficult to undergo certain kinds of experiencings powerfully and with wonderful feelings. Consider the experiencing of being the poor victim, the abused one, the one who is maligned. Consider the experiencing of being alone, not part of the group, or the experiencing of violence, smashing, tearing apart, crunching, exploding, or the experiencing of being cold, hard, icy, uncaring. It is likely the ordinary you, the person you have been all your life, who draws back from being these kinds of experiencings with power and with wonderful feelings. Before you take the plunge, it helps to simply take the plunge. Go ahead; just throw yourself into the deep pit of these "bad" experiencings. You can experience them as being powerful and wonderful.

Even if the experiencing is acceptable to you, if you have done a good job in Step 2 of coming to welcome and appreciate the deeper potential for experiencing, it is still a deeper potential for experiencing. You have rarely, if ever, literally been that deeper potential. You have not spent 100 hours undergoing the deeper potential, and certainly not with feelings that are wonderfully delightful. Now you have to. Follow the guideline. Go ahead and throw yourself into undergoing the experiencing powerfully, fully, and with feelings that are simply wonderful. Keep being the deeper potential until you reach the point at which the experiencing is indeed powerful, and the accompanying feelings are indeed joyously wonderful.

Let Go of Reality Constraints and Be Absolutely Playful, Silly, Zany, Wild, Crazy

When you are being the deeper potential for experiencing, the emphasis is on sheer playfulness, silliness, zaniness, wildness, craziness. This applies to you, to the entire scene, and to everything in the scene. Let go of reality constraints. The context should be cartoon-like, burlesqued, farcical fantasy. Walls can split apart or disappear. Colors are wild and unrealistic. People can be instantly cloned, can become eight inches or eight feet tall, can have two heads and four arms, and can run up and down walls and around ceilings. Weird creatures can appear, play the harp, sing and dance, dissolve into pools of Jell-O, speak Spanish and Greek. You can run at the speed of light, go back in time, make things appear and disappear. Bathtubs can float in the air. Reality constraints are reduced, ignored, changed in an instant, washed away. You are being the deeper potential for experiencing in a complete comedy, in the context of sheer unreality.

The scene that you remember is when you threw the ball through the upstairs window, smashing the window. You are standing frozen in the driveway next to the house, and the door bangs open. Here comes Dad, furious. The deeper potential for experiencing is being a helpless little baby, being held, cuddled. You can instantly be transformed into a cute little baby. Snap your baby fingers, and the window is fixed. Dad arrives, and he is so caring, so nurturing of his wonderful little baby son. You coo. "Hold me, Daddy. I am just a wee baby." You are rocked and cuddled by the loving father. The whole family appears. They rock back and forth in rhythm with your father rocking you back and forth. You are now a big, big boy, but still held and cuddled by the whole family. Music appears, theme music for being loved, cuddled, and cared for. You are stroked caressingly. You purr in the sheer enjoyment of being so lovingly cared for and cuddled. The sun comes out, and angels surround you. There are such caring looks on everyone's faces, and everyone is looking at you, cuddled and loved by the whole family and all the angels. You sigh in sheer satisfaction.

In Being the Deeper Potential for Experiencing,
You Can Replace Yourself in the Scene or
Be An Additional, New Person in the Scene

Usually, you will be the new person who is the deeper
potential for experiencing, and you will simply take the place
of yourself in the scene. Take the scene in which you were the
little kid who had just thrown the ball through the upstairs
window. You are standing in the driveway, frozen in terror,
watching your furious father striding toward you in fierce
armor, ready to tear you limb from limb. You can simply
replace yourself in this scene. In a flash, the scared little kid is
gone, and here is the whole new child, the qualitatively new
embodiment of the experiencing of helplessness, the
experiencing of being loved, cuddled, and held.

Or, you can be an additional, new character in the scene.
There is a scared little kid. There is a furious father. And now
there is a whole new character, the pure embodiment of the
experiencing of being helpless, being loved, held, cuddled.
The choice is yours. Either option can work well. You can
simply replace yourself in the scene or be the added, new
person in the scene.

If You Start to Feel A Wave of Pure Terror,
Let It Pass By Staying in A State of Readiness
to Undergo the Qualitative Shift

You are poised to throw yourself into being the deeper
potential for experiencing. Up to this very moment, you
have probably never actually been this deeper potential.
Indeed, you have spent your entire life not being this deeper
potential for experiencing, and almost certainly not being

275

this deeper potential for experiencing in ways that are full and saturated, with joy and happiness. The person whom you are and whom you have been has managed to barricade, seal off, and push down this deeper potential for experiencing. Now, the person whom you are is entitled to keep you from hurling yourself into being the deeper potential for experiencing.

If you did a wonderful job in Step 2, the relationship between you and the deeper potential for experiencing may be friendly. If so, you may well undergo this qualitative shift with little or no problem. That is typically what happens when Step 2 was done well. Every so often, however, the person whom you are is entitled to get scared, maybe even to feel a little bit of pure terror. In wanting you to remain you, the person you have been can try to effectively induce you to stay you and not to undergo the qualitative shift.

The feeling is that of terror that you will lose your mind, fall apart, become deranged, be out of your mind, become crazy, become a complete lunatic. The wave of terror is that you will become evil, the devil, do bad things, do wickedly immoral things, violate religion, morality, and human goodness. The fear is that you will die, end your existence, enter the endless black void of emptiness. You will lose all control, do wild things, be completely disorganized, fragmented, uncontrolled. The wave of terror consists of being taken over by a maelstrom of the worst possible feelings such as dread, black depression, rage, violence, terror, destructiveness, complete loss, and absolute emptiness.

Is this wave of terror foretelling real and true possibilities? If you go ahead and cave in to the deeper potential for experiencing, are all these awful things going to happen? Should you pay attention to this wave? The answer is yes, provided that you are firmly lodged within the ordinary, continuing person that you are and have been. It is correct, accurate, realistic. Hold back. Stop. Do not throw yourself into becoming the qualitatively new person. Look at what terrible things would happen.

However, the answer is no if you are not lodged deep within the ordinary, continuing person you have been. The answer is no if you are the qualitatively new person. And the answer is no, provided that you can remain in the state of readiness to become the qualitatively new person.

If the wave of terror starts to envelop you, let it pass, let it come and go. Even a slight leaning into the state of readiness to become the qualitatively new person will let the wave pass by. The wave does not ordinarily occur if you have done a good job in Step 2. If it comes, expect it, and let it pass by remaining steadfast in the state of readiness to become the qualitatively new person.

These guidelines can help you undergo the qualitative shift out of the ordinary, continuing person that is you and into being the whole new person who is the deeper potential for experiencing. What remains is for you to take a deep breath and leap into being the qualitatively new person. Just do it.

UNDERGO THE QUALITATIVE SHIFT INTO BEING THE
DEEPER POTENTIAL FOR EXPERIENCING IN THE PAST SCENE

Your job is to get into the past scene and live as and be the qualitatively new person who is the deeper potential for experiencing. You can say the instructions out loud: "All

right, I know the scene. I'm about 17, and I snuck Bill down
into the basement with me. We are on the bed. I'm on top.
Bill's got his pants off, I am naked, and we're going at it. I
see, or I hear and then I see, my little cousin Marty. He saw!
And I gotta be this whole new person—just plain, nasty, evil,
wicked, a little devil. Okay. Here I go . . . NOW!"

What happens next is you become this whole new person
in the scene.

You are hissing through your teeth. The hissing is loud
and guttural, like a fire-breathing dragon with a sore throat:
"I am coming after you, little cousin. Thump, thump . . .
Zap! Ha! You cannot move. You are stuck there in the hall.
March back into the room, Marty. I am grabbing you by
your little penis. Now, in the room, take off your pants, little
Marty. I am making your penis bigger and bigger. See? Oh,
you are scared! Bill and I will take care of that. Take off all
his clothes, Bill. Now, little cousin, you gotta watch Bill and
me. Lie down, Bill. Watch, Marty! This is called fucking!
Ha! You are shaking! Well, here we go. YES, YES, YES! Oh,
that felt so good. Thank you, Bill, you were great! NOW
IT'S YOUR TURN, LITTLE COUSIN. I AM GOING TO
DRIVE YOU OUT OF YOUR MIND AND THEN
UNSCREW YOUR PENIS! Oh, you are on your hands and
knees? Crying? Forget it. NOW, HERE WE GO. DOWN
ON THE BED. I have long nails. I will make you bleed all
over. You'll be having orgasms and loss of blood . . . I will
watch you die, little cousin. Who's at the door? More at the
door? Brother Nicholas and brother Donald. Zap. I gotcha!
I am going to bring your girlfriends here to watch. Oh,
you're worried? Don't worry, I will keep you guys over
there, chained to the wall, and your girlfriends will be

chained to that other wall, and I will drive you all crazy with lust. Till you all scream! And little Marty will spit on all of you. By the way, I am getting all hot, so I am going to show you all what a great team Bill and I are. Okay, Bill, assume the position. NOW! THERE. YES. YOU ARE GOOD. OH, YOU ARE VERY GOOD. I am driving you all crazy, Well lookee here, here are the girlfriends! I feel so wicked! I am so mean! AND THE PARTY HASN'T EVEN STARTED YET!"

The deeper potential is fighting back, defying, rebelling. Be this person in the scene from when you were about three years old. Your mother had invited a bunch of ladies over to have tea and cake, and to play cards. Mother asks you to come in so the ladies can see you. Then, some minutes later, you do what you have started to do lately. You face away from the ladies, bend down so that your head is between your legs, and have fun seeing things upside-down. You believed no one could see you, but then you heard your mother say, angrily, "Glen! Stop that!" You are in trouble. That is the scene. You know the deeper potential for experiencing, and you know the guidelines. Go back into being the three-year-old in the corner of the room where all the ladies are sitting at card tables, and you undergo the qualitative switch into being the completely different, whole new person who is pure defiance and rebellion:

"NO, I WONT. NEVER! NEVER! All my blood will rush to my head, but I will never move, and no one can force me! WHAP! Oh, sorry, ladies! I didn't mean to let one go. I aimed it at the lady with the big hat, but I think I missed. All of you are passing out? I'm just going to stay here with my head between my legs. ANOTHER FART?

SORRY! You want me to stop, Mommy dear? NO WAY! NEVER! It's my will against yours, and I will always win. No one can ever get me to do anything! Just give up, Mommy dear! Here I go, wiggling my cute little ass! I'm going to get all my buddies . . . Yes . . . Here we are on the street, at the big church on the corner, thousands of people in the church, and we all walk in, bare asses; 200 three-year-old asses in the aisle. YOU ARE OFFENDED? YOU DON'T LIKE 200 BARE ASSES? TOO BAD! DINGA DINGA DOO, WE FART AND SHIT ON YOU. DINGA DINGA DOO. Our heads between our legs. We love driving you all out of your congregational minds! CHURCH PEOPLE! JOIN US! BEND OVER AND BARE YOUR ASSES! IT IS GOOD FOR YOUR SOUL! Everybody find a thing to defy! The church? No way! Defy it! All the damned church do's and don'ts! DEFY THEM! All the rules of polite society? DEFY THEM! These are the ways we should be nice to one another? NO WAY! REBEL! DON'T TAKE IT ANY LONGER! EVERYONE BEND YOUR HEAD DOWN AND SHOW YOUR BARE ASS! EVERYONE SAY IT TOGETHER, ' WE AREN'T GONNA TAKE IT ANY LONGER!' NOW EVERYBODY FART!"

The actual scene was when you and Daniel talked and talked. He wanted to end things and, after three years, he did. He closed everything out. He got up from the couch, patted your hand, and walked out. In the actual scene, some years ago, you were almost numb. However, the person you are to be now is quite different. You are to live and be in that scene as a whole new person, one who is the exemplification of pure giving it up, letting go of it, being free of it. First, take a deep breath, and then throw yourself fully into being this entirely new person. In a powerful voice you sing, and the singing voice is nothing like your voice:

"Take it all, take it all! It is yours, it is yours! Let it go, let it go. Dum de dum, dum de dum, dum de dum . . . If I have it, and you want it, it is yours. Take my nose, take my ears. Here, I gotta lotta fat around my belly, and it is gone. Snap, it is gone. Ah, Daniel, I am saying, 'So long.' It was great while it lasted, but I am ready to let you go. And my sister wants my cell phone. It is yours. I am giving you my car, too. It is yours. (Settling down into a happy whisper.) I am in my front yard now. Hello, weeds, I have waged a war against you each year. No longer. You want to take over the grass, I will help you. Here, I am spraying on you my new concoction, Weed-Grow. It works wonders. I am keeping my sandals and my shirt and jeans, and I am free of everything else. No more clinging. That was a lifetime's worth. I am letting go of everything. Hello, Nicole. Hello, Marie. If you want my time, it is yours. I have nothing I cling to. I will be with you for as long as you want. I will go with you to your brother's place. Do with me what you want. It is yours. Everything of mine is yours. Daniel, hello, Daniel. I think we tried to own pieces of each other. I give it all back to you. I think you are wonderful, and I think you are a great guy. And I am saying good-bye to you. So long. It is finished. I am giving up my job and my rituals. Good-bye, rituals. My God, I think I am starting to rise up, to float in the air. I am lighter . . . No more smoking. No more ritual prayers. No more family meetings. No more job. For the first time, I am free. Let it go! Let it go, let it go, let it gooooo!"

You have become the new person, the deeper potential for experiencing. You are living as and being the qualitatively new person in this past scene. The experiencing is full and complete. It is also accompanied by wonderful feelings. In a way, you have accomplished a miracle, a great feat. Are you ready to remain as this qualitatively new person?

THE MIRACULOUS QUALITATIVE SHIFT IS DONE; YOU ARE NOW THE QUALITATIVELY NEW PERSON FOREVER

The shift from being you to being the deeper potential for experiencing has occurred. You have done it. Congratulations! Here you are, the qualitatively new person. You began the session as the ordinary, continuing person you have almost always been, and right now you are the living, breathing, full-blown, happy, vital, qualitatively new person.

Furthermore, the qualitative shift was accomplished rather swiftly and painlessly. There were no melodramatic death scenes, no suicide of your self, no grand leaps into the black abyss of death. The heavens did not quake. The earth did not shatter. You did not take 20 years to withdraw from the world, probing inside yourself, and waiting for the years of painfully slow growth and development, study, and thought. You merely discovered the deeper potential for experiencing, selected a past scene, and underwent the qualitative shift into being the deeper potential for experiencing in the context of the past. The old you is now gone, and you are fully and completely being the qualitatively new person.

Why not remain as this qualitatively new person? You are being this qualitatively new person right now. There is no law that says you must return to being the ordinary person you have been. There is, however, a law that doing the experiential session well necessitates remaining as this qualitatively new person for the rest of Step 3, the rest of Step 4, and at least until the end of the session. This is the law, the strong guideline, the way to have a successful and effective session.

Isn't this interesting? Look at what you have accomplished. If you did your work well, you have left the old you behind, and you are now experiencing, thinking, feeling, and behaving as the qualitatively new person. It is a momentous achievement. Congratulations! Stay being this qualitatively new person. How about forever?

You Are Now The Qualitatively New Person As You Go Through Scenes From The Past

You have shifted into being the qualitatively new person. This part of Step 3 gives you some ways to remain as this whole new person, to lock you into being the person you now are. You underwent this shift in a particular scene from the past. It may have been a scene from the past few weeks, or one from childhood. Whenever the scene happened, you will now be using some other scenes from earlier in your life or from later in your life, all to help you become more solid and secure in being the qualitatively new person you now are.

How can you find these other scenes? The general idea is for you to use almost any scene from the past and then become the deeper potential for experiencing in those past scenes. You were already the deeper potential in one scene.

Just look for other scenes. This is the general idea. This section shows you some helpful ways to find these other past scenes.

Just know these methods well enough so that you can select two or three ways to find other past scenes. You can use different ways in different sessions, or keep using one or two favorite ways. You may use just a few of these ways, or most of them. What follows are helpful suggestions for finding other past scenes in which you can get practice being the qualitatively new person.

Once you find a scene, be the qualitatively new person in the scene. Be this new person with happiness and joy. Be this new person with power and strength. Be this new person with silly unreality. You are being the qualitatively new person in the past scene. You are being the person whom you weren't in the actual scene. This time, you have a chance to live and be in the scene the way you weren't in the actual scene. You are not reliving the scene. You are using the past scene as a useful context in which you can take opportunity after opportunity to be this qualitatively new person.

SOME PAST SCENES JUST SEEM TO APPEAR SPONTANEOUSLY

You are being the deeper potential for experiencing in one scene, the scene you found. Then, spontaneously, you see something else. You are in another scene. Go ahead and fill in the new scene, and continue being the new person in this new scene. You started with the scene in which Daniel finally left. He sat with you on the couch, patted your hand, got up, and left. You played out that scene as the deeper potential for experiencing, the letting go of it, being free of it, giving it up. While being this whole new person in this scene, you suddenly see a little glass horse. Just like that! You move over to this new scene:

"Where did this come from?. . . Mrs. Coates, from down the hall. She had that whole collection, and when she moved she gave it to me, 10 or 12 glass horses. So delicate. I loved them. I played with them when I was at her apartment. I was so little. I kept them in my room. My sister broke one . . .You like them? Here. They are yours. They really are! It's shocking, huh! Me, giving them to you? Sure. Here, Sis, they are yours. I hereby transfer the glass horses to you. I know you like playing with them, and you love them. So do I. But here's my chance to let go. Bye horsies! My sis will take care of you. They are yours. You should see that look on your face!"

USE SCENES WHERE YOU FELT THE DEEPER POTENTIAL FOR EXPERIENCING A LITTLE OR A GREAT DEAL

Now that you are being the qualitatively new person, actively look for times when you knew the deeper potential for experiencing. Perhaps there were times when you felt it a little bit. Or, you may have felt it a great deal at other times during your life. Find these scenes and then throw yourself into undergoing the deeper potential, fully, and with wonderful feelings.

The deeper potential is the experiencing of being the helpless little baby, being held, being cuddled. The first scene you used was when you were a little boy. You had tossed a ball through the upstairs window, and here storms your father out the door, his beady eyes staring at the child who broke the damned window. You are going to get it now. While you are being the qualitatively new person in this scene, actively look for another past scene:

"There must have been some time when I felt it. Some time when I felt cuddled, like a helpless little baby . . . held, being held, in someone's arms. With Annie? No. Sometime . . . How about just a little bit. In bed with someone . . . When I was little . . . I remember! I remember. With Mom. In my parents' bedroom. Before school. I didn't even go to school. Got sick. Threw up. I got so sick. Warm. I was warm. I remember Mom put me into their bed. She held me. She rocked me. She sat in bed with me. Oh, it feels so good. I feel you, Mom. Take care of me. I wanna sleep. I love this, Ma. Rocking me back and forth. You love me . . . Oh, God, I've got tears . . . Feels so good.. I'm a little baby. I want to stay here. Hold me. Ahhhhh.. This is wonderful. Mom, Mom, hold me. Ahhhhh!"

As the New Person, You Will Probably Find Past Scenes You Could Not Have Found Before

When the qualitative change happened, and you became the new person, you remembered a time when you actually had the experiencing of being cuddled, being held, being a helpless little baby. The experiencing may have been mild or strong, but now you remembered the time. When you actually switch into being the qualitatively new person, it is common to remember scenes that you were not able to remember when you were the ordinary, continuing person you were before the dramatic switch.

Step 3. Undergo A Qualitative Shift

It almost seems that each potential for experiencing has its own package of memories. When you switch into being the deeper potential for experiencing, you will likely find some memories that were not very accessible before the switch. This is so common that you can go ahead and search for past scenes, even though earlier in the session you had no memory of these past scenes.

USE SCENES WHERE YOU COULD OR SHOULD HAVE BEEN THE QUALITATIVELY NEW PERSON

The deeper potential for experiencing was undergoing sheer violence, smashing, bashing, and destroying things. The first scene you found was with Ron, when your throat was so sore and you had the flu, and you went berserk, breaking things. You even tried to break chairs. Now, as the qualitatively new person, you look around for other past scenes in which to revel in being this qualitatively new person. You start by saying out loud, with the voice of this whole new person: "Now I want to look for some times when I could have been like this, or I should have been like this. Some time . . . Could have been . . . I see the tennis courts. Oh, yes! I'm about 12, and we're waiting for them to finish their time on the court. We're waiting. It's our turn. And then . . . Shit! They finish, and we go out on the court for our two hours, and that's when those four older boys just come on the court and take over! We tell them . . . It does no good! We just let them! Shit!"

Go ahead and be this whole new person: "I grab that blonde guy and heave him over the fence! Ha! We've got

287

guns! Get the fuck off our court! We grab them and beat the crap out of them! I just knocked out your teeth! Now I ripped your head off! Hey, kids, let's use his head as a tennis ball! EVERY GUY ON THESE COURTS! WE'RE COMING AFTER YOU! SMASH! YOU'RE DEAD! Swing 'em around and toss them in a pile! We've got hands of steel, and we are gonna kick the shit out of all of you! Bam! There goes the fence! Hey! You're all running away! BAM. We gotcha! Pow! POW! POW! COME ON, GIRLS, LET'S KICK THE SHIT OUT OF THE WHOLE DAMNED TOWN!"

There are usually plenty of past scenes when you could or should have been the qualitatively new person. Find these times, and then be in those past scenes as the qualitatively new person.

You are being the deeper potential for experiencing true closeness, oneness, intimacy, and you say out loud, "I wasn't much like this. So when should I have been? More loving and close, intimate, really close. I wasn't much. When could I have been? Oh, I see Mom, in the bed, and she's going to die of cancer. She wanted to be home. Dad and Jean were with her the most. I liked Mom, but I always . . . I always felt like you thought I never measured up. Wasn't good enough. You're so weak, Mom. You're telling me stories about when you grew up, and I know I have to listen. Your voice is not like you. I'm looking at your hands. I'm holding your hand, Mom. Looking at your hand. It's almost like it's my hand. I . . . something's happening . . . God, I love you, Mom. I don't want you to die. PLEASE DON'T DIE, MOM. PLEASE. I'm healthy. I'm going to make you healthy. Oh, Mom, please . . . I can feel you. I don't want anything from you. Just let me be close with you. I am so close to you. I love you, Mom. Don't die. I feel you. Mom, I love you, Mom. Something's happening . . . Like peaceful. I know what you're feeling . . . You're ready to die. You are. You're ready. I can feel it. Mom, Mom, Mommy. I can know what you're feeling. It's all right. I can feel it . . ."

USE SCENES WHERE YOU WERE PRACTICALLY THE OPPOSITE OF THE DEEPER POTENTIAL FOR EXPERIENCING

You know what the deeper potential for experiencing is. Look for past times when you certainly were not the deeper potential for experiencing. In fact, it is almost easy to find plenty of scenes in which you were anything but that deeper potential. The likelihood is that you spent most of your life being practically the opposite. The kind of person you are and were virtually hid that deeper potential, showed yourself and the world that you were anything but that deeper potential, denied and disproved such a deeper potential. Now that you are being this qualitatively new person, it is rather easy to find such past scenes and, this time, to throw yourself into being this whole new person in those scenes.

As the new person, look for a past scene like this: "There must have been times when I was anything but the helpless little baby, held, cuddled. Oh, yeah. I wasn't like that at all! No way. The opposite. Not like that. Hell, I wasn't. I really wasn't. I wasn't like that at all. Ever! Let's see, some time . . . I . . . I was cool, confident, sure of myself. I was always the leader. I remember when we were in high school and that kid got it. The kid was in the hospital. He lost his eye. One of the guys . . . Joey . . . hit him with a board or something.

We were kicking the shit out of that kid. The teacher said there was trouble. They were with me at Sandy's place, and I told everyone what to do. Shit. I was like a cool lawyer. I calmed everyone down. They relied on me. Okay. So I am going to be this helpless little baby, cuddled and held. Boy, I sure wasn't . . ."

Go ahead and be this whole new person in that scene: "Listen, Len, can I put my head on your lap? (Whispering.) I'm just a little baby . . . I think we're in trouble. Help! Everybody hold me . . . I want to play with my toys in the bathtub. Please give me a bath. Bathe me. Put baby powder on me. I don't know what to do . . . Mummummummum. Cooooooo. Everybody hold me and take care of me. I'm just a little baby. Will you all please take care of me? Aahhhh. Yessss. Just hold me and cuddle me. This feels soooo good . . ."

The deeper potential is the experiencing of sheer violence, being violent, smashing, destroying, breaking things. "But that was not me. Oh, no. For my whole life, I was the quiet one. I've been sweet and gentle. I didn't do anything physical. I never did anything . . . sports . . . I was slender and kind of frail, and my voice was soft and whispery. I walked slowly. I tried playing tennis a little, but I was no good . . . I remember that everyone liked me. Confided in me. I remember when Kathy wanted to talk with me about Mark. She came to work, and we went for lunch, and she told me that they were having trouble. I really didn't know Kathy all that well, but everyone trusted me and confided in me. Because I understood . . ."

Go ahead and be this whole new person in this past scene: "Here I go! (Much louder voice, raucous, hard..) What? The whole restaurant will hear me! Mark? Mark? I lift up the whole table and everything crashes! Okay, Kathy, let's go straighten this out. I grab you by your wrists and drive you over to your place. Mark! Sit down! Listen to me! If you mistreated Kathy, I'm going to tear you apart! No man is going to mistreat my friend. Got it! I got your throat! Ha! You can't talk? Then listen. Kathy's going to stay with me for a week. If you bother her, I'm going to break your goddamned neck, you sonofabitch! Now I'm picking you up, high in the air. Say you're sorry! Go ahead! Kathy! Come with me! Yesssss! I love this. Stop sniveling, Mark. Be a man. I hate men! They are little boys trying to pretend to be grown up. Kathy! No more men! We're going to kick the shit out of every man we see! SHIT! KICK SOME SHIT!"

Now That You Are the Qualitatively New Person, You May Well Have a Whole New Perspective on the Person You Have Been Most of Your Life

What will likely become rather clear is how you became a person who definitely was not the deeper potential for experiencing. Not at all. You became a person who was in many ways the opposite of the deeper potential for experiencing. You became a person who served to hide, deny, and disprove that there was such a deeper potential for experiencing inside you.

This was probably not easily known nor seen during your life. But now you have switched into being this qualitatively new person and, from this new perspective, things can be seen differently. You see yourself in a whole new light. In one way, this is exciting. You get what seems like a clear view of the person you have mostly been throughout your life. In another way, you are entitled to be sad. What a waste. What a sham. How silly it was for you to have spent much of your life successfully being a person who is virtually the opposite of what the deeper potential for experiencing is.

What we have here is a kind of reversal of what is usually believed by most psychotherapies and in many attempts to solve problems and to be different. The common belief is that, if you can only see things differently, in a better way, if you could come to a better understanding or insight, then things would change, things would be different. Instead, here is a belief that, when you first undergo a shift, a significant change, you will see things differently, have a new insight or understanding. In the common belief, insight and understanding *lead* to change; in this experiential way, change is *followed* by insight and understanding.

USE THE CATASTROPHIC SCENES, THE POWERFUL TIMES YOU ALWAYS REMEMBER

The worst time in your life, the catastrophic scene that will always stay with you, is when you were little, and your older brother was high up in the tree. Everyone was at first terribly scared, but he seemed to make it all right, higher and higher. Then your eyes are riveted on his body falling through the branches and hurtling down to the hard ground. Bam. A broken pile of flesh and bones, blood coming out of his head. He was dead. Your memory stops there. That moment is seared into your memory.

Step 3. Undergo A Qualitative Shift

Every so often, when you have a session, go back to that catastrophic scene and give the qualitatively new person a chance to live and be in that scene. You can use that scene over and over again. As you do this, the very meaning of the scene can and will loosen, alter, change. Much of its catastrophic impact will soften. It can and will take on a gradually evolving new set of meanings.

This time, you are the qualitatively new experiencing of riskiness, taking risks, daring, adventurous. And you are quickly drawn to that childhood scene when your brother died. You are ready to live and be in this scene as the qualitatively new person:

"I'm going up there with you, 'cause I want to see what it's like! I try out new things. I take risks. You can hardly keep up with me. Up, Mike, up. Come on! Higher and higher. Yes. Up and up. I've got these gloves. Here, take a pair. Up and up! We're way up top! We did it. Now, let's start getting it to go back and forth! WAIT! YOU`RE FALLING! HERE I COME. WHOOSH! I GOTCHA, MIKE! HEY, MIKEY, LET'S FLY! HERE WE GO . . . WHEEEEEE! WAY UP IN THE AIR. CATCH ME IF YOU CAN! Let's go to Athens. Or Paris. No! I wanna go to Grandma's place. It's just a few blocks away. We'll drop down, swoosh her up, and then fly with her. And we can let go of our clothes and fly naked . . . With Grandma . . . Hey! Let's swoop down on Terry and Sam and Lisa and scare the shit out of them! Right through their place at the speed of light! Grandma would love it! COME ON, GRANDMA! BET I CAN BEATCHA!"

293

You are now fully being the qualitatively new person who is the experiencing of being captivated, wondrous, in awe. And you look for some catastrophic time in your life: "So was there some time when everything changed? Or at least when the feeling was so powerful? Well, yes. It's when that guy showed me how to tie knots with the big rope, and I'm with him in the pickup, and I'm in his place and . . . I hate even thinking about that . . . I suck him off. Jesus! That was the worst time . . . What do I gotta do?"

Go ahead and be this whole new person in any part of that scene. Just be in the general scene and be the qualitatively new person: "LOOK AT THAT! WHAT A GREAT THING THAT IS! I've got a weeny, too, but mine is so tiny. Look at that thing. It's so big . . . Can I have one like that? Here! Snap! I got a picture of that huge thing. It's so hard! And BIG. IT'S HUGE, MAN! I can' t believe it. Did you always have a big one like that? Can I look at it up close? How the hell do you pee? Here . . . Look at mine. It's nothing. But yours. Wow! WOW! HOW'D YOU GET A WHOPPER LIKE THAT? And . . . what do you do with it? Do people come over here to see it? Can I bring some buddies over to see? You don't know Brent or Charlie, but they are my best buddies. I'm gonna take some other pictures. Can you turn to the side? Snap. Wow. Look at that! I'm looking closer . . . Look over there, right there. See? Right here? What's that spot on it? I ain't got spots. You do. Where'd that spot come from? Can I play with this thing? Does it bounce? Yeah, it does. Christ, does it hurt? And how do you keep it in your pants? You don't talk much. Well, I ain't given you much of a chance . . . Can I see you pee with it? Is yours bigger than a horse's? I saw a horse once. His was massive! Is yours bigger? IT'S AMAZING!"

USE SCENES FROM THAT PRIMITIVE PERIOD
A YEAR OR SO BEFORE YOU WERE CONCEIVED
TO A FEW YEARS AFTER YOU WERE BORN

In each session, you may have found a scene from the primitive period of your life. Or, you may recollect a primitive scene from a previous session. Living and being as the qualitatively new person can mean living and being in these primitive scenes.

The scene is when Mom was pregnant with you. She is sitting alone on the bed. It is afternoon. She is black and Dad is white. Mom has no black friends. She and Dad met in Jamaica, and they lived together in Ottawa. Mom is lonely. But, worse still, she and Dad don't get along at all. Dad wants to keep the baby—me—and have Mom sent back to Jamaica. He's cold, and like a lawyer, and Mom is sitting there, crying. She is going to fly home that afternoon, and she did.

The deeper potential is the experiencing of tenderness, gentleness, softness. This is the way you are even as you describe the scene. Now you are to be this qualitatively new person as you live and be in this scene. To do this, you can take the role of your mother, or the qualitatively new person, the new you, can enter into that scene as the second person in the bedroom, here with your pregnant mother. In either case, you are the essence of the experiencing of tenderness, gentleness, softness. You are the other person in the bedroom:

"It's going to be all right, Mom. We will be together. I'm here on the bed with you. We'll be together. I know you are able to do this yourself, but I will kiss you all the way home, Mom. I know how bad you feel. Go ahead; put your head on my shoulders. Trust me, Mom. You are doing the best thing. You and your baby will be so happy back home. Your hair is so beautiful . . . I love stroking your face, Mom. You are such a good person . . . and you made a mistake with Dad. Leaving Jamaica. But I will be with you. And I will be your best friend. I know what you feel. Oh, are you ready to leave now? You sure don't have much to take with you. Two little cases, Mom; that is sad, you're right. You're looking right at me! You recognize me? I'm your daughter! Oh, Mom, I'll always be with you (A little giggle.) . . . 'Course you didn't go, did you? Not then . . ."

The important scene was when Dad and Mom sold the store. Grandpa had the store from when he was a young man, and Dad worked there all his life. It was a little hardware store, and then Dad made it much bigger. They sold the store to move to Toronto because Dad got a job as a reporter on the paper and Mom got accepted into the master's degree program in education. This was such a big move for them. The scene is in Toronto when they are looking for a place to stay. They are with their Toronto friends, Ed and Patricia. They are so excited, they can hardly sit still. The scene is in Ed's car, driving around to look at the places where they can afford to live. The deeper potential for experiencing is being the jewel, the precious one, exhibiting yourself, being admired. You are being your father, sitting in the back seat with Mom, feeling great:

"I sold the store . . . I got a great job. We made this big move. I am simply wonderful. We are . . . I am . . . You are, too, but I am mostly. Stop the car and tell me how wonderful I am, we are, I am . . . I will just lie back and listen. Tell me how wonderful I am. My first piece for the paper will be to let everyone know that I am here! And what I think! Ain't I great? Ask me all sorts of things about how it happened and what I think, and about my feelings. I was destined for great things from the day I was born. Now, here is the story of my life. Everyone listening? Anyone need pencil and paper to take notes? Ah, you all have tape recorders. Good. It all started when my grandfather started this little hardware store. He wasn't important, except that he had a son, and his son had a son, and that special baby was MEEE! Here I am, folks, the center of the world. Was I destined to run the most successful little store in town? Everybody say, 'NO. HE IS DESTINED FOR MUCH MORE.' Thank you, thank you. So, the great baby is born. Settle back, folks, this is just the beginning of the greatest story ever told: the story of MEEEE!"

Make sure that you are fully and delightfully being the qualitatively new person in these primitive scenes.

USE THE INITIAL SCENE OF STRONG FEELING FROM THE SESSION

Each session begins with you finding a scene of strong feeling. This is the initial scene of strong feeling in the session. As the qualitatively new person, the deeper potential for experiencing, you can return to this initial scene of strong feeling and be the qualitatively new person in this scene.

Here Is An Opportunity to Undergo the Magnificent Change of Finally Being Free of the Painful Scene and the Painful Feeling in the Scene

If the initial scene of strong feeling is painful, hurtful, unpleasant, accompanied by bad feelings, here is a chance to be the qualitatively new person in this scene. As this qualitatively new person, the entire painful scene changes. The scene should be much less painful. The scene no longer fits or is appropriate for the new person whom you are. As this new person, the painful scene should lack its painful punch. In other words, the qualitatively new person is essentially free of the painful scene that had been so much a part of the old person's world. By being this qualitatively new person, you are essentially free of the old person's painful scene and the painful feelings in that scene.

This will likely be the first time in the session that you can see what it can be like to undergo the radical change of being free of the painful scenes in your personal world and the painful feelings in those scenes.

As the Qualitatively New Person, Go Ahead and Live and Be in the Initial Scene of Strong Feeling

You are the living, breathing experiencing of merciless and relentless evil, utter cold killing, remorseless destruction. And you enter into your body in the initial scene of strong feeling. You are in bed, just awakening. Your body is weak.

Step 3. Undergo A Qualitative Shift

You are filled with powerful horror as you become aware, four to six seconds after you awaken, that cancer is in your body, a cancer that will certainly kill you. Except that you are this qualitatively new person. Your voice is the voice of this whole new person:

"I am breathing slowly, in and out. I have a mission. I slowly turn to that cancer . . . I see you. You picked the wrong person. Yesss. I am going to eradicate you. You are dead, little things. I am pouring acid on you. Zap. Zap. You are gone. I will track you down inside me. You can run, but you can't hide. I will track you down and kill you. You met your match this time, you little scrunge . . . This is the end of the line for you. You are dead meat. Acid. Special acid. I pour this acid on you, and that is all there is to you. It is all over for you . . . Yessss! Burn . . . I watch you die, die quickly. I would prefer watching you die slowly, little by little. You are finished. I have an endless supply of the corrosive acid that eats you up. And I pinpoint it right on you. There . . . You are gone. Yesss! I kill. I kill anything I want to kill. I am deadly. I just kill . . . Yes!"

You are the qualitatively new person, the experiencing of letting it go, no longer grasping it, being free of it, giving it space. You have experienced this in a number of past scenes. Now you are ready to be this whole new person in the context of the initial scene that began the session. You are in bed with your husband. He mentions that he doesn't suppose you want to have sex, and you are angered and hurt by the bitter tone in his voice. Soon he is again assessing the marriage, and he says he is just tired of it. He is going to get a divorce. What is seared into your head is the prospect of being at the bookstore all day, coming home to a small

299

apartment, and having no one to be with. You are angry, terrified, hurt, depressed, and you just cross your arms across your chest and pull tight. Now, as the qualitatively new person, you return to living and being in the initial scene:

"So, I turn and look at him. Hello, Denis. You are getting smaller and smaller. I am snapping my fingers, and here is the judge. Denis wants a divorce. I agree. There! Bye, Denis. Now . . . zot, zot, zot. Hello, Catherine. Come house-hunting with me. I want a small place with room for a garden. Denis is gone. I am free. Lord knows, I am free. Poor Denis. I cluunnggg to you, like a nut. You poor boy. I cling to everything as if I will die without it. Such crap! Denis, I am letting you go. Catherine, come fly with me. We are going to glide . . . I am getting rid of 30 pounds, a job I sort of like . . . Yes, I am letting it go . . . and a husband I made into an unhappy guy . . . Never mind, I am going to get on my bicycle and look for a place in Knottingham. That's where I want to live. No . . . better. I'm not looking for a house. I am getting rid of everything and going to Europe to just bum around. I can work anywhere. I will do what I want. I'll get a bike there and ride wherever I want. When I want. Denis, thanks! Thank God you took the first step. You can have everything. Well, I suppose some money for a ticket and food and stuff. Everything is gone. God, I am lighter, freer . . . When I come back . . . Hell, I have no idea <I>if<P> I'll come back. Hey, Denis. You are right! Thank you! Thank you! Whee! I am floating! DUMDEDUM . . . DUMDUMDUM . . . I AM FLOATING . . . Thank you, Denis. Go . . . YES!"

You started with an initial scene in which you felt just awful. You were crying, you felt like an irresponsible ninny, and once again your husband was disgusted with you. How could you be such an idiot, making that mistake, leaving your mother-in-law at the airport? Your husband had no use for you. You are like a brainless child. That is your life story with men. You were stunned, in the kitchen, letting his words strike you on the head, calling you a dunce, an idiot. You were crying. It was awful. But now you are the qualitatively new person, the experiencing of being a mischievous little devil, a nasty wickedness, a mischief-maker. And things are altogether different as you live in that initial scene:

"You are right! Her plane came in hours ago! I see it now in the note on the refrigerator! She is still at the airport! And she doesn't know where we live! HAHAHAHAHAHAHAHAHAHA! (Gales of laughter, cascading delightfully over one another.) But I am so sweet! Such a living doll! And I looooove your mother! (More laughter, only this time it is almost cackling.) Good for her! That'll teach the old bitch. But that's only the beginning. Wait till she tries to get into her bed. I fixed it just right for her, but don't worry, the snakes in her room are not poisonous. They just make her fart . . . I got my friend Elaine and Jack to pick her up. They'll take her all around the countryside and drop her off at the barn where the witches are meeting tonight. They are going to sacrifice her. Wanna go watch? Oh, this is delicious. Come on, we can drive the old bat batty. Heeheeheehee . . . I am going to get all my elves and goblins to come here when she finally makes it here. She'll remember this! She'll *never* be the same. I guess I just forgot to pick her up. Sure! HA!"

Step 3 is done when you have been the new person, the deeper potential for experiencing, in a number of past scenes.

You may have used only two or three scenes or perhaps five or six. In any case, you will reach a point where you are ready to move to Step 4, in which you will be even more of the new person in scenes from today, tomorrow, and beyond.

In Step 3, you found some past scenes. You went through the radical shift into being the deeper potential for experiencing. And you settled into being this qualitatively new person in a number of scenes from the past. You are ready for Step 4.

Stay Being This New Person From Now On

Once you achieved the switch, the quantum leap, the radical change, into being the deeper potential for experiencing, you actually were this whole new person in Step 3. You gained experience being this qualitatively new person in scene after scene. You know there is no law that you must revert to being the ordinary, continuing person you were before the grand switch, the person you have been throughout most of your life. Indeed, considering the goals of an experiential session, that would be a shame. You do not have to revert to the person you were before the session.

Consider the revolutionary possibility that you can continue being this deeper potential for experiencing. Consider that this deeper potential for experiencing can be an integral part of the qualitatively new person you are capable of becoming, of being. The simple suggestion is for you to stay being this whole new person as Step 3 ends, as you go through Step 4, when the session ends, and from then on. Perhaps forever.

8

Step 4.
Be the Qualitatively
Whole New Person In
Scenes from the
Forthcoming,
Post-Session World

This is the final step in the session. You completed Step 3 by being the qualitatively new person who is the deeper potential for experiencing. As you begin Step 4, and throughout this step, you remain being this qualitatively new person.

Following is a simple sketch of what you do in this step and what this step is for. In Step 4, you stay being the qualitatively new person, and you live and be in scenes and situations from today, tomorrow, and beyond. You experience what it is like to be the qualitatively whole new person out in your personal, real world after the session is over. First, you find or create scenes. Then, you live and be in these scenes in full-blown, playful unreality. Finally, you modify and refine the scenes and how you are in the scenes until you are ready to end the session and be the qualitatively new person in scenes from the forthcoming, new, post-session world. This is Step 4 in a nutshell. This chapter tells you how to do it.

In Step 4, You Are The Qualitatively Whole New Person You Are Capable Of Becoming

Scenes from the Past Are Replaced by Scenes from the Imminent Future

In Step 3, you were the qualitatively new person who is the deeper potential for experiencing. You were this new person in the context of scenes from the past. In Step 4, you exchange scenes from the past with scenes from today, the present, and from tomorrow, a few days from now, and perhaps forever.

The Deeper Potential for Experiencing Becomes An Integral Part of the Qualitatively Whole New Person

In Step 3, you went through the magnificent, radical shift into being the deeper potential for experiencing. In Step 4, you continue being the deeper potential for experiencing, but something even more dramatic happens. The deeper potential for experiencing becomes an integral part of the qualitatively whole new person whom you now are. More than merely being the deeper potential for experiencing, you are now a qualitatively whole new person, and this new person includes the former deeper potential for experiencing. In Step 4, you become the person you are capable of becoming.

You Are the Qualitatively Whole New Person For Now or Forever

Step 4 virtually guarantees that you will become the person you are capable of becoming. It will happen. It will happen in this step. You may remain as this qualitatively new person until the end of the session. Or, before the session ends, you may revert to being essentially the person you were at the beginning of the session. If you are this qualitatively new person when the session ends, you may leave the session as this qualitatively new person, the person you are capable of becoming. And you may remain as the person you are capable of becoming for a few minutes, a few hours, a few days, or forever.

When You Leave the Session as the Person You Are Capable of Becoming, You Enter into a World That Likewise Is New and Different: A Qualitatively New World

The world is the world of the person you are capable of becoming. It is no longer the world of the person you were at the beginning of the session. Becoming the qualitatively new person is one side of the magnificent, radical transformation. The other side, just as magnificent or even more magnificent, is that your personal world is likewise qualitatively new, changed, transformed.

A bonus of this magnificent transformation is that the person you become is free of the old painful scene and the painful feeling in that scene. The pain is gone, evaporated, washed away.

FIND SCENES FOR BEING THE QUALITATIVELY NEW PERSON IN PLAYFUL UNREALITY

You are to find scenes, times, situations from the next day or so. In these scenes, once you find them, you are to be the qualitatively new person whom you now are. Furthermore, you will be this qualitatively new person in sheer playfulness, full of whimsy and silliness, with comedy and raucousness, in ways that are zany, wild, and farcical. To do this, the scenes you find are to be outrageously unrealistic, playful, whimsical, silly, comedic, raucous, zany, wild, farcical.

There are at least two ways of finding these playfully unrealistic scenes that may occur in the next few days or so, or that can be made to occur in the next few days or so.

INVENT PLAYFULLY UNREALISTIC SCENES BY STARTING FROM SCENES YOU ALREADY USED IN THE SESSION

You can start with some scenes that you already used in the session to make up new, wholly unrealistic, silly, whimsical, crazy, far-out scenes that you can place in the next few days or so. Remember, these are not scenes in which you will really and truly be the qualitatively new person. These are playfully unrealistic scenes in which you can let the new person revel and wallow in being the new person. Starting from the scenes you already used in the session, what scenes can you invent that just might happen, or you can imagine happening, or you can arrange to have happen, in the next few days or so?

This can be easy to do. In Step 3, you are being the qualitatively new person in perhaps two to four past scenes. If you say out loud what you are going to do now, you may say something along these lines: "I am going to stay being this whole new person, and I am going to look for scenes like these that can happen in the next few days or so. Let's take the one I just finished. So where can a scene like that happen tonight, tomorrow, over the weekend? Even if the scene is silly, crazy, or far-out, when can something like that happen right away?"

You might start from any scene you just finished using in Step 3. You might still be drawn toward that catastrophic scene you used in Step 3, the dramatic scene that you can't get out of your mind. Or, you might start from the initial scene of strong feeling that you used to start the session.

START FROM THE INITIAL SCENE OF STRONG FEELING, ESPECIALLY A SCENE OF STRONG BAD FEELING

You began the session by finding a scene of strong feeling. Usually, the initial scene is one in which the strong feeling is bad, painful, hurtful. You can start from this scene and invent or extrapolate how that scene can occur within the next few days or so, or how you can arrange for it to happen.

The initial scene of strong bad feeling was when you were waking up in the morning or in bed and felt weak. For a few seconds, you don't realize it, and then it hits you. You have cancer. You are going to die. The cancer is going to kill you. The feelings are powerful and painful. You are hurt, depressed, invaded, agitated, terrified, and angry—a whole package of awful feelings. This scene is definitely going to happen when you wake up tomorrow: "Well, that is the scene! I wake up tomorrow, and the damned cancer is still here. It's going to kill me! It's not gone. The war is on again! Nothing funny about this! I am going to die!" You have an imminent future scene in which to be the qualitatively new person who is the full-blown experiencing of mercilessness, relentless evil, utterly cold killing, a killing machine, remorseless destruction.

In the initial scene of strong bad feeling, you are in bed with your husband. Denis says, in a distant, critical tone, almost sneering, that he supposes you don't want to have sex, and then he proceeds to give his usual, cold assessment of your empty marriage. You feel rotten, torn apart, like a rejected piece of meat. The qualitatively new person whom you now are is the full experiencing of letting it go, no longer grasping and clinging, being free of it all, giving it plenty of free space.

For one thing, you can almost count on the fact that Denis is going to do it again. That scene, or some variation, is probably going to happen again, even tonight. Or, you can help arrange for it to happen soon after the session. Here is the qualitatively new you talking in the session: "I know! I can ask Denis if he will cooperate. Dear Denis, I am trying to be a good wife, to get over my awful problems. But I need your help. I'll lie down here. Please ask me if I want sex, and please do your assessment of our disappointing marriage. Please! Then, just stop. I want to recreate the scene and then have five minutes to do something. Please? I will grant your wish if you do this for me. How about it? Five minutes? Oh, and during the five minutes, you gotta just let me do what I do. Promise? Please? I think he'll agree . . . Or, maybe I can do it with Sam . . . That would be fun. Well, I'll start with Denis. He might even like it!"

In the initial scene of strong feeling, you were miserable. Your husband called to talk to his mother, and you hadn't even picked her up at the airport. You were sure that her plane didn't arrive for some time, although it had actually arrived some hours ago. It did not take much from your husband to make you feel that miserable sense of being an idiot, unable to think straight, someone who can't be counted upon, a brainless little girl. As you look for imminent future scenes, you continue being the qualitatively new person who is the exciting experiencing of mischievousness, the wicked devil, the mischief-maker.

You could reenact the scene with your husband, provided that you are able to get his willing cooperation. If your mother-in-law is still here, you could enlist her too in the reenactment. But you have a better idea: "That same kind of thing is going to happen. On Friday there is a formal dinner for a couple. He's going to explain about the couple the dinner is for. She's coming to receive an award for her novel, a big award I think, and he is going to get an honorary doctorate for his work on something. So, I am going to get a lecture on why she's coming and why he's coming so I won't screw up. Ha! And he'll keep saying, 'You got it straight?' I know that'll happen. That's my big chance. Yes!"

These scenes can be made into playfully unrealistic scenes by loosening the reality constraints, by having them be scenes that will likely occur in the next few days, but without the necessity of grim reality. And, they will be the contexts in which you are going to have all sorts of playful fun as the qualitatively new person.

START FROM THE CATASTROPHIC SCENES YOU USED IN THE SESSION

You used a catastrophic scene in the session, a scene that tore you apart, that almost changed everything, a scene in which your feelings went off the scale. Starting from that catastrophic scene, find imminent scenes that duplicate it, or almost duplicate it, that can happen, will happen, or that you can arrange to have happen in the next few days or so.

"I can still see him falling from the top of the tree, hitting the big branches, and then just . . . falling. He's like a clump of flesh and bones . . . and all that blood. So, how the hell can . . . That's not going to happen tomorrow. No way.

Well . . . I can climb up that tree in Tom's front yard. Up maybe ten feet. I'm getting scared already. Or, we're supposed to go to the federal celebration, and there is going to be an air show. Yeah, planes in the air, doing scary things. Uh huh. That'll do it . . . Or, I can take a ride in that scary outside elevator that terrifies me . . . or a cable car. I can rent the movie where they are in the cable car in the mountains, and a cable snaps or something. Those are good. I can feel it already. Those are very good." You are saying all this as the qualitatively new person who is the experiencing of riskiness, daring, adventurousness, taking risks.

You had used the catastrophic scene with the old fellow who showed you how to tie knots in the big rope. The scene was at his place when he got you to put your mouth on his penis. You have shifted into being the qualitatively new person who is the experiencing of being captivated, in awe, wondrous, and you look for some playfully unrealistic scene from the next few days or so: "Well, for sure. David and me. In the shower. We go to the gym and run for an hour, and then we take a shower. Wednesday. He's got this huge cock, and I never really look at it, or say anything . . . I'm seeing Andy! That's sick! He's my own son, and he's only 11! No way! . . . 'Course, that would be kind of crazy . . . Naw, I couldn't do that."

START FROM ANY OTHER PAST SCENE YOU ALREADY USED IN STEP 3

You just finished using several past scenes in Step 3. They are still warm. Starting from a scene you just used, invent or extrapolate a scene that can happen in the next few days or so. For example, you just finished being the qualitatively new person in a scene from high school after a bunch of you had kicked the shit out of some fellow, and it was bad. He lost his eye. You all are in deep trouble. The scene is when you get together at Sandy's place to hash out your strategy, what you all can do to save yourselves and fix the bad situation. "So, where can something like this happen soon? Where we are trying to figure out what to do about the situation . . . Oh, that's easy. We've got to meet. We already started. It's about that press release. Herb did it because he is a little kid! What an asshole! It's a bunch of lies, and now we're all in deep trouble. We've got to do something. I can get us together Wednesday, in Tim's office, with Paul and Betty and Mercedes and Victor, and a few others. We've gotta figure out what to do!"

In Step 3, the scene you used was when you and your girlfriend Kathy are having lunch together. The two of you are at the restaurant, and she is so concerned. She is telling you about her problems with Mark. "So, where can something like that happen? At some place, talking . . . Why not? I want to call . . . I can have lunch with Judy. I could! I could talk with her about Ron. I went crazy with Ron. I could have killed him! I went out of my mind. Lunch with Judy! Right!"

In Step 3, you found a past scene where Mom is in bed. It is weeks before she goes into a coma and then dies from the cancer. She's quietly telling you stories about when she was a little girl. When you finish thoroughly undergoing the

312

sense of oneness, closeness, and intimacy in this scene, work with one other scene, and then turn to Step 4. Where can you find or create a similar kind of scene in the next few days or so? "Be with someone, telling me stories . . . Ruth . . . Ruth . . . I go see her about once a month, in Allentown. Mom's older sister. No one takes care of her . . . Sometimes I wonder if she knows who I am . . . But then she loves telling me the same old stories from when they grew up in Lebanon . . . I could do it. Sure. I'm in her place, and I'll take care of the bills, and she'll start with the stories . . ."

You went far back, in Step 3, to a scene that happened before you were born, a primitive scene in which your mother and father had sold the family store and moved to Toronto, Dad to become a reporter on the newspaper, and Mom to begin the master's degree program. Now, as you head into Step 4, you look for a scene by extrapolating from that primitive scene: "So, I have a new beginning. End everything here. I'm in Amsterdam, doing something . . . Whole new beginning. I am on the back of Wylam's motor scooter, and we're buzzing along. I got a great new job, took it on a whim, don't know Dutch, and I'm looking for a place to live. And all that is happening Friday. Why not?"

Look for imminent future scenes in which you can settle into what it can be like to remain being this qualitatively new person. One way to find, invent, create these imminent future scenes is to start from scenes that you have already used in the session and use them to find, invent, create playfully unrealistic scenes a few days or so in the future. But there is also another way.

313

INVENT PLAYFULLY UNREALISTIC SCENES BY STARTING FROM THE DEEPER POTENTIAL FOR EXPERIENCING

You are being this qualitatively new person. Let this deeper potential for experiencing have free rein in looking for and inventing scenes that can happen or be made to happen in the next few days or so. When you use this method, you open wide the doors of wholesale unreality, creativity, fantasy, silliness. You create scenes that are wild, weird, whimsical, nutty, free of reality constraints.

Ask yourself questions like these:

What Would Be the Ideal, Perfect Personal World for the Qualitatively New Person?

When you started the session, you lived in a world with a husband, Denis. In your world, Denis and you drifted apart; you spend occasional evenings during which Denis is snotty to you, chiding you about your dead sex life, lecturing you about your empty marriage. The deeper potential is the experiencing of letting it go, no longer grasping and clinging, the sense of being free of it, and this is the qualitatively new person whom you are. You say out loud: "What would be the ideal life for me? What would be the whole new, perfect world for me?" Keep asking these questions while peering into the imminent future. Let scenes appear. See what you see:

"I can be with friends and let go of my business. Have time for them. Listen to them . . . Always be ready and

available for them. Live alone . . . Not much stuff . . . No
dog . . . No 'I *have* to do this.' No rituals . . . I see
something . . . Living by myself, or with someone, or even
two or three. I see someone who is really free . . . No burden
on others . . . Simple life. Few possessions . . . And she . . . I
. . . am with a man . . . am by myself . . . Spend time sitting
by myself outside . . . This is so peaceful. No, wait. I see
things. It's clear. I see a place. In the country. A small place.
Simple. Few possessions. Just a few things inside. One room.
Simple . . . And I just have simple clothes. Now I see . . .
another life . . . a motorcycle. Going places. Living in this
small town for a while, months, years. Do what I want. Take
whatever job I like. For a while. Drift on when I want. And
the people in my life, they can come, or go, or stay. They let
me be free, and I let them be free. No using. Free. Simple. I
can live in my little cottage. It is a simple world. Wow, this is
really something."

When you began the session, the initial scene was of
waking up in the morning and, some seconds later, realizing
that you are dying of cancer. The deeper potential is the
experiencing of mercilessness, relentless evil, utterly cold
killing. This is who you are as you look for the ideal personal
world in which you can live and be. "I am the hired killer, but
I specialize. I kill people who are bad, who have done really
awful things, and no one has found them out or put them
away. No, not hired. I find out myself. I study newspapers
and then study them personally. Here is a marked man. He
did bad. So I carefully figure out the cleverest way to
eliminate him, and I do it. Pow. Gone. She has a plan, a nifty,

careful plan. Track him down. It can take years. That would be just wonderful. It would be delicious! I work by myself. I travel to Chile, Austria, Russia, and South Africa. But I live in London, and no one suspects that I am the merciless, cold-blooded killer. I am gone for ten days at a time, three or four times a year. And this time I'm after that scumbag landlord politician. He's the one that screwed my Dad. He kept raising the rent for all the storeowners in his building until no one could afford it, and then he sold the building to the city. That's what killed Dad. So, I am going to end that bastard's life. And I can do it!"

As the qualitatively new person, have fun inventing the ideal personal world that would fit. Let your fantasy roam free. Create the ideal world for this qualitatively new person, a world that is so very different from your own actual world. And make sure that you have some kind of scene that is to occur in the next few days. It may be the scene of plotting to kill that politician who owned the building. It may be just enjoying sitting in the simple cottage. Always find some scene that could happen in the next few days or so.

Setting Aside All Reality Constraints, What Would You Just Love to Be Like and to Do as This Qualitatively New Person?

You started the session with the scene in which you felt so childishly irresponsible, being criticized by your husband, scared that he would become thoroughly disgusted with you. You had forgotten to pick up your mother-in-law at the airport. Now you are being the qualitatively new person, the

experiencing of sheer mischievousness, being the wicked
devil, the mischief-maker. As this new person, ask yourself
these questions aloud: "So, where would I just love to be
like this? What would I just love to do? Forget about reality,
all reality constraints. Something wild, far-out, crazy, wild . . .
would just love to do . . ."

Here come the answers: "That husband of mine is so
tight and so goody-goody. Except he loves his convertible. I
would just love to suck him off on the way to work . . . No!
Better, I'm in the passenger seat, and I take off all my
clothes. I'm stark naked. Yes! I hate my pompous uncle's jet-
black wig. It's so obvious! No one . . . I'm going to lift it
off, in public, at a family party, a family dinner at his big
place with the big dining room. I'll remove his hairpiece.
Oh, yeah . . . I know! My mother-in-law tells such lies about
her ex-husband. He hated her so much that he went to a
business convention in Florida and hasn't returned—in 19
years! I'll get her to tell the stories. I'll secretly record them.
I'll find her ex-husband . . . this is going to be great, and I'll
get a recording of his answers about what really happened.
How that lady lies! And I'll get the whole family over at our
place and strap her to a chair, and then play the recording.
You lie! Oh, I'd love to do that!"

You are the qualitatively new person, the experiencing of
being captivated, wondrous, in awe. You are looking for
imminent future scenes where you would just love to be this
person, putting aside all reality constraints. "Forget about
everything. The next few days. I'd love to be just in awe,
totally captivated. So, what would I just love to do?

Absolutely love to do?" You find answers, and the answers are the scenes: "I'm a great photographer . . . I have wide, big eyes. See all sorts of things. I see that older lady at the place I get breakfast. She's the owner. I put my face near hers and stare. Wide-eyed. Full of wonder. She's got a great face, like she's been through everything . . . I am sitting on the grass at night. In the park, looking up. The stars. Amazing. Space. Incredible. Mouth open. Staring up. Can hardly believe it . . . And we're in the airplane, off the ground. Just wandering around the plane. It is so heavy. It actually flies. Unbelievable. Incredible. Shaking my head. It is captivating. I am in total awe . . ."

What Daydreams or Fantasies Have You Had About Being the Qualitatively New Person?

Sometimes, you have had daydreams or fantasies about being the qualitatively new person. The daydreams or fantasies may have been recent, or you may have had them long ago, when you were a child. Let these daydreams or fantasies paint scenes from the next few days or so. Begin by asking yourself, as this qualitatively new person: "Have I ever had daydreams or fantasies of doing risky things, really daring, adventurous things? Well, yes I have. I was a kid! I'd go . . . before sleep, before I fell asleep, I'd always, for years, fantasize about hanging from the ladder of a helicopter and saving people. Oh, oh . . . Like I could have saved my brother from falling from the tree. But I'd fantasize about rescuing people . . . all sorts of people. So, what about today? A daring rescue . . . That guy who was lost in the race across the Pacific. Boats. I hang from the helicopter, risking my life, and swoop him out of danger . . . And the terrorists got that president, so I'd hang from the ladder, swoop inside the room, grab him, and swoop out! Got him! And I read about those people on skis in the Arctic. Here I come, hanging from the ladder, and . . . I gotcha! I would be the daredevil who saves people from catastrophe. What a life . . ."

How Would This Qualitatively New Person Look, Walk, Listen, Talk, and Do All the Little Things of Daily Life?

Picture that qualitatively new person as if you were ten feet or so away, watching her or him doing the little, mundane, undramatic things of daily life, like reading a paper, drinking juice, walking along the street, driving a car, sitting at a computer, showing some ordinary expression, brushing teeth, or sitting on a toilet. Or, you can actually be this whole new person while doing these things. Get scenes from the next few days by asking out loud: "It's tonight, maybe tomorrow . . . So, what do I do if I am being this whole new guy who is a helpless little baby, loves being held, cuddled . . . How do I get ready for bed tonight? Can I see it? Ah, yes . . . Just holding my clothes, touching them against my face . . . putting them away so slowly. And the look on my face when I'm with Betty and Victor at work, having coffee. They're laughing. My look, my expression . . . Ha! I see it. A little boy look, cuddly little kid. They'd want to cuddle him. And the way he sits on the subway. Head tilted to the side. Same look. Curly hair. Little boy curly hair, sort of huddled up, toes pointed inward, sitting there. Harmless, inviting. Just a helpless little boy, shoulders hunched. You'd want to take him home. I see it!"

Pick any ordinary situation from your ordinary daily life and see the qualitatively new person in that situation. You probably brush your teeth every day. You probably talk on the telephone every day. Pay careful attention to the way the whole new person does these things. Notice the body posture, the way he or she holds the toothbrush, what he or she attends to while brushing their teeth. Notice the toothbrush. Is it a modern toothbrush? Does he or she move around while brushing their teeth? Notice the way he or she talks on the phone, the voice quality, the tone of voice.

In What Scenes Would Being This Qualitatively New Person Be Something the Old Person Would Find Too Difficult, Almost Impossible, Completely Out of Place, Absurd, Disastrous?

The deeper potential is the experiencing of sheer violence, smashing, bashing, destroying things. As this qualitatively new person, you say out loud: "In the next few days or so, there must be lots of places where the old me would just die if I were actually like this. So, where? She would go crazy! Places where she could never be this way. It would be much too hard for her, impossible, out of place. It would ruin her life. Where would it just drive her crazy? She just couldn't do it? But I could!"

And you find answers to these questions: "Aha! Ron is taking me to the symphony tomorrow. If some big, fat guy is hard to get over to get to my seat . . . Yep, that's one place for sure. I'd smash a few things . . . Or, at the restaurant where we go for lunch, usually there's this waiter. We can't get service. Watch out, fella! I'm gonna create a little fuss! And, and . . . oh, yeah, at work. Janine comes in every day and talks about . . . I don't know *what* she talks about. She just rattles on, and I listen . . . and yeah, yeah, the boss gave me a memo to write, and he told a couple of us to write it, but he never told us that he was asking a few of us. That bastard! He always does that! Yes! Oh, that would be fun!"

The discovered deeper potential is the experiencing of tenderness, softness, gentleness. This is not simply a part of the person you are; you are now *being* this whole new person as you search for scenes in which this behavior would be impossible for the ordinary you. "Next day or so, tonight . . . it would be just impossible. Never could be like this . . . impossible . . . shocking . . . It would shatter my world . . . Hardest place to be like this? Scare the hell out of me . . . total disaster . . . Hmm. There are loads of places . . . This is easy." And you find times that could happen very soon, even later today:

"There's this mean neighbor. What a bitch! I take my dog for a walk in the morning, and I will again when I get home today. She watches from her window so Max doesn't shit on her property. She is awful . . . Impossible with her. That would be impossible. And Mom's visiting with her white boyfriend. I can't stand him. She knows that. Tender and soft with him. Oh, sure . . . He met her in Jamaica . . . I want to spend time with Mom. Shit. Tender, be gentle . . .

321

And the whole office knows I am the best black lawyer in town, always tough, always well prepared. Look, I'm meeting with the government lawyers tomorrow, just to see what can be done on this case. It would be totally out of character . . . Hell, they'd pass out if I . . . That would be the acid test if the wrong person showed up. Yes, that would be the hardest place for sure . . ."

You have found or invented scenes that could happen in the next few days or so. Now you are to live and be in these forthcoming scenes. You are to be the qualitatively new person in these scenes. And there is a way to do this that makes it easier to do it well.

BE THE QUALITATIVELY NEW PERSON IN PLAYFUL UNREALITY

In a way, what you are about to do can be considered rather straightforward and simple. You found some scenes that will happen or could happen in the next few days or so, and then you go through those scenes as the qualitatively new person. It makes sense. On the other hand, what you are about to do, to build on, is already a kind of miracle.

You Are Making A Miraculous Change Even Greater

In Step 3, you underwent a miraculous change, I believe. You had the chance to step out of the person you have been for virtually your whole life and to become a qualitatively new person. You entered into and became the deeper potential for experiencing. If you did this well, the change was a wholesale, qualitative shift into being a radically new person. To make this shift easier to accomplish, the scenes were from the past. But the shift was a qualitative shift, a miraculous change.

You are about to raise the stakes. You will remain being this qualitatively new person, only now the context is the alive present, the imminent future, the world that exists when you open your eyes and end the session. These stakes are much higher. Being the qualitatively new person in the past is one thing. But it is a whole different world when you are this qualitatively new person in the immediate and enveloping present. You are making the miraculous change from Step 3 even greater.

HERE IS HOW TO DO IT WELL

You are not really going to be this whole new person in these scenes. In the session, you are just playing, nothing more. You can tell yourself: "Don't worry, you don't have to be this way for real. It is just playtime. You are not going to do this tomorrow, or ever." It is all pretend. It is fantasy. So you can relax. It is not for real.

You are going to be the whole new person in this scene with absolute silliness, craziness, zaniness. It is all burlesque, caricature, comedy, farce. It is complete whimsy. It is complete make-believe.

Pump up the sheer strength and power. Be the radically new person with high strength and power. Do it loudly. Do it with gusto. Yell, scream. Keep the volume high. Doing this with strength and power means that there you will experience bodily-felt sensations inside and out, all over your body. This is the way.

The voice and voice quality are those of the qualitatively new person. No one would be able to recognize that it is the old you talking. Continue the voice of the person you switched into in Step 3, but exaggerate it. Growl much more. Sing-song much more. Use the exaggerated voice of some character from a terrible movie or great musical comedy.

In the scene, there are no reality constraints. There are no limitations on the new person you are or on the scene itself. Anything at all can happen. You can move with the speed of light. You can move mountains. People can balloon up or contract. Dogs can speak fluent Greek. Rocks can turn into wine. The ordinary constraints of reality are given a vacation, replaced by a friendly, made-up reality.

Be the qualitatively new person with absolute joy and happiness, ecstasy and exuberance. Let the feelings reach their pinnacle of sheer pleasure. You feel wonderful, simply wonderful, buoyant, and exhilarated.

Be this qualitatively new person until it is truly genuine, until you truly become this qualitatively new person in the scene. The experiencing is to be real. It is to be as if you are really and truly undergoing the experiencing. Even in unrealistic scenes, the person you are is to be the real experiencing. If you watched a video of this scene, it would not appear as though you were acting. You really and truly were undergoing and being this experiencing.

Step 4. Be the Whole New Person in the Post-Session World

You are so much the qualitatively new person that there is no kernel of the old you left. There is no tiny part of the old you having thoughts, being aware. There are no inner voices or thoughts like this: "This is all make-believe. It could never really happen . . . But I am doing this kind of well . . ." Keep doing this until the old you is extinguished, replaced, gone.

These are the guidelines for how to do it well. These are also the indications that you are succeeding or have succeeded. Keep doing this until all the guidelines are met. In other words, keep being the qualitatively new person in the forthcoming scene well after you are being it with power and in absolutely playful unreality. Do not stop when you succeed. Do not stop after you have been doing it well for five or ten seconds. Keep doing it for at least five or ten minutes. You are not yet seasoned and experienced at being this qualitatively new person, and certainly not in scenes from the next few days or so. Allow yourself plenty of practice being this qualitatively new person.

As you finish with one imminent scene, you may find yourself pulled to go on to more scenes from the next few days or so. Go ahead. Once you are the qualitatively new person in the playfully unrealistic world of today and tomorrow, it can become easier and easier to live as and be this new person in the forthcoming world, even though the context is silly and zany, with few, if any, reality constraints. Just make sure that you keep going until the guidelines are all smiling and satisfied, whether you are living and being in just one imminent scene or you move from one to another and another.

Here Are A Few Examples Of Being The Qualitatively New Person In These Scenes

You woke up this morning and, after a few peaceful seconds, you realized with gripping terror that there is cancer inside of you, ravaging your body. The deeper potential is the experiencing of relentless evil, cold killing, mercilessness. In looking for an imminent future scene, you invented an ideal world for yourself, a world in which you track down bad people. You are so organized and careful in executing the plans for their elimination. You work alone. And you continue, finding the scene for today or tomorrow: "Now, who is my next target? Ah! Yes. It is that politician, the one who owns the block where Dad had his store. That man kept raising the rent and not fixing things, and when the storeowners finally gave in, he sold the whole building to the city. Dad's life ended then. I have my target. Oh, yes . . . Tomorrow I kill that bastard. My way. Oh, yes . . ."

You start by hissing, in and out, and your voice lowers to a menacing growl. You are the essence of relentless evil, cold killing, mercilessness. "I am going to track you down. I have access to anything I need because I am a computer whiz. Aha! You are in Mexico. Well, I am coming down this week, you fat old man. And I am waiting until the middle of the night. (Hissing is sounding much more evil.) I open the door and close it gently. Oh, yes . . . YES! I SLAP THE TAPE OVER YOUR BIG MOUTH! I am laughing, laughing . . . You have no idea who I am, do you? I don't say a word. I tie your hands and your feet to the bed. Go

ahead, make noise. See this knife! I RUN IT SLOWLY
OVER YOUR TOES. SEE? AND THEN . . . WATCH ME.
WHAP! THE TOE IS GONE! Look at the blood. I
SCREAM. I CACKLE! YES! . . . And now is the time. Look
at this picture. Yes, you got it right. It's the photo of the
building. See my Dad's store? Look . . . My thumbs are
pressing against your eyeballs. I roll my thumbs around your
eyeballs. AND . . . PLOP! A BOUNCING EYEBALL! I
PLOPPED OUT ONE OF YOUR EYEBALLS! IT IS
ROLLING AROUND THE BED! OPEN YOUR
MOUTH, LITTLE MAN. THERE. IN YOUR MOUTH . .
.YOU SPIT IT OUT? HA! I AM GOING TO TEACH
YOU ANOTHER LESSON! FEEL THE KNIFE ON
YOUR LITTLE PRICK? YESSSS. GUESS WHAT'S
GOING TO BE SLICED OFF? I am going to kill you bit
by bit. (The voice is low and menacing, and the breathing is
full, slow, and deep.) It will take all night . . . And then I am
going to take your fat and cut it into strips and make bacon
out of it. I am going to eat your body, bit by bit . . . I am
going to love this. I am all muscle . . . I am a killing machine
. . . I kill. I love killing. And then I go to the next person on
my list. I have a list. I have a little list . . .
Heeheeheeheehee!"

The session began with the strong feeling in you when
the wife of your best friend called from far away. Sam was
your best friend from the time you started high school till
you were in your 30s. When he moved away and remarried,
the two of you wrote only occasionally, but you still thought

of Sam as your best friend. You met Sam's wife once, some years ago. Now she calls and tells you that he is dead. "Kip, he's gone . . ." The deeper potential is the experiencing of being a helpless little boy, being held, being cuddled. The imminent scene, one ridiculously unsuited for this experiencing, is one that you and Betty arranged. You are going to meet tomorrow in Tim's office, with Tim, Betty, Paul, Mercedes, and Victor, the whole bunch. What are you going to do about that disastrous press release sent out by the boss? Herb, the big boss, wrote that error-filled, embarrassing, and vindictive press release. There is going to be big trouble. Still being this qualitatively new person, you throw yourself into the scene:

"Betty! Betty! (Your arms are outstretched and your voice is high and plaintive, like a wailing little child.) I wanna curl up in your lap . . . Hold me! Put your arms around me. I'm just a little boy. I want to be held. (You repeat the words in singsong.) You gotta put your arms around me 'cause I wanna be held! I'm just a little boy who wants to be held! I gotta be held! Ooooooooh . . . (You kick with your little feet.) You are all here just to take care of me. Everyone touch me . . . Oh, Betty. It feels so good with your arms around me. Hold me tight. Tell me everything is going to be aaalll right . . . I love the way you put your arms around me. I'm just a little kid. Rock me . . . Rock me . . . Dumdedum . . . Sing me to sleep. I'm rocking . . . I'm just a little boy . . . Could you all sing me a lullaby? All together. A nice lullaby for the little baby. And Betty, just hold me tight. I love you,

Betty. You take such good care of me. (Happy, big sighs.) I feel sooo good. I think I am going to sleep in your arms. Yesssss. Keep patting my head. Keep stroking me . . . I feeel sooo good! Goodnight . . . Hmmmmmmmmm!"

In the beginning of the session, you started with one scene and then moved over to another one. You started with the bad feeling when you were in bed with your husband, Denis, and he looks at you coldly, barely hiding a sneer, and says that you probably don't want to have sex tonight. Then he launches into his usual critique of your empty marriage. You are frightened, depressed, confused, angry, and hurt. You then move to a recent memory of the bus stopping in the foreign countryside. While you are having a beer by the side of the road, you see the bus way down the road, carrying your luggage, money, passport, everything. The deeper potential is the experiencing of letting go, letting it go, no longer clinging and grasping, giving it plenty of space. You have swung into being this qualitatively new person in scenes from the past, and then you replace them with a scene from tonight, when Denis is sure to deliver his lecture on your empty, desiccated marriage, except that you are a very different person now.

You are giggling, tilting your head from side to side, and muttering out loud: "Hey, Denis, you are getting smaller and smaller! You're just a wee little thing. I'm making you smaller . . . smaller . . . and now you are a few inches high. I've got you between my thumb and index finger here, and I am making you smaller and (almost whispering) smaller.

(Mock loud whispering.) Hey, Denis, I can't hear you! I just see your face. You've got a funny face. (She blows a puff.) Good-bye, Denis. You are gone . . . I think I still have that collection of glass horses, down in the dining room, on that big plate, and I'm going to give the whole collection to my sister . . . Something's happening! I'm floating! I am floating! Wheee! Above the apartment. I love this. Just floating, quietly . . . Relax. Take it easy. Just relaxing. Hey, Sis, you always liked that collection. It is yours. And I am getting rid of the apartment. Too big. Much too big. And Denis. Bye, Denis. Poor guy. I used to cling to you. What a ninny. I held on to everything. Even old grudges. Denis, it's all right. Good-bye. What's her name? Sally. From college. I forgive you. I always talked about our relationship. A little sex between girls. I clung . . . (Mocking herself.) That was dumb. I want to float away . . . Grudges and rituals and possessions. I can let them go. Denis, you are free. Maybe we'll even be friends. Maybe not. You are free. Take a breath. Me, too. A deep breath, in and out. (Giggles.) I think I'm starting to float again. I like this . . . And I'm going to go to bed when I am tired and eat when I am hungry and, here, the glass horses are yours . . . and Denis, you are free. Me, too!"

You began the session with a dream, and the dream yielded a deeper potential for experiencing being a jewel, the precious one, exhibiting yourself, being admired. You threw yourself into being this qualitatively new person in Step 3, and now you are going to live and be in a scene from a few days hence. You are going to Amsterdam, and perhaps you might even live there. In this scene, you are on the back seat of Wylam' s motor scooter. And you continue being the whole new person:

"I have on my new off-white suit. No one on the street looks as handsome as me. My hair is black, any patches of gray are gone, and I have a compelling smile. I am smiling. No one even looks at Wylam. Go a little slower, Wylam, I notice a few people who aren't admiring me. Hello, everyone. I am beautiful, right? Off-white suit, very expensive and casual, and I am a gorgeous hunk. Tall and lithe and with the most beautiful face in the world. Ladies, admire me! Ah, I see an old couple. I am smiling . . . and you both see me! Here I am. Smiling at you. Hello, ladies. Go ahead; eat your heart out. Now, Wylam, ask me questions about me. Can you stop at an outdoor coffeehouse so I can be admired by the passing throng? Yes. Good for you. Now here we are, sitting. You know the special coffee I love. Tell me what it is like being with me . . . How I affect you. You must have all sorts of questions about me. Go ahead. I will tell you all my thoughts. Have you read my latest? Tell me what you think of it. I poured out all my personal thoughts, and I know that the world is craving more. Oh, I am so special. Go ahead; ask me questions. Be interested in me because I am so fascinating, such a jewel. Hello, young lady . . ."

In the initial scene of strong feeling, you were distraught and torn apart when Ron and you were fighting. You went a little berserk with Ron. You lost it. The deeper potential for experiencing is sheer smashing, bashing, uncontrolled violence, and you sampled being this qualitatively new person in playful unreality in past scenes with a few girlfriends on the tennis court with those guys. This Saturday, you and Ron are going to a posh restaurant where, last time, you were so annoyed by the supercilious, snotty waiter. Then, you are going to the symphony at the national arts center. You begin with the restaurant:

"It's been 45 minutes, and the damned waiter hasn't taken our order! Ha! I am standing up. Hey, waiter! HEY, WAITER! YOU WITH YOUR NOSE IN THE AIR! I go after you. Lady, give me your fork! I stick the fork up your nose, and pull you toward me! I AM GOING TO TEACH YOU A LESSON. I yank on the fork and split your damned nose! I lift you off the floor! I grab your neck and shove you over to that table. SIT DOWN. BLEED ON THE TABLECLOTH! I ram your head against the tabletop. Forty-five minutes! You bastard! Bam, bam, bam! Now I rip off your fucking tuxedo! Here comes the manager! POW! Look at him sliding across the floor! So, I grab the two of you by the ankles and twirl you around. Faster. Faster! FASTER! FASTER! Then . . . THERE YOU GO! OOOhhhhh! WHAT A CRUNCH! NOW I'M GONNA GO BACK TO MY TABLE, AND I WANT SERVICE—OR I GO INTO THE SECOND ACT! Hello, Ron. Hungry?"

The dream offered you a grand opportunity to discover the deeper potential for experiencing pure tenderness, gentleness, softness. You come to the general vicinity of undergoing this experiencing with your dog, Max, but not much else. In Step 3, you were being this radically new person in very early, primitive scenes with your mother, pregnant with you, sitting disconsolate on the bed, thinking seriously about going back to Jamaica. The forthcoming scene you envisioned was the tight scene of tomorrow when you are walking with your dog past your mean neighbor's yard. She hates Max. She hates you. She glowers at both of you. There she is, picking weeds in her precious front yard. You and Max are passing by. You are black; she is lily white. You are a lawyer; she is a housewife whose husband died years ago. You are the qualitatively new person who is the experiencing of sheer tenderness, lovingness, gentleness, softness:

"I walk toward you . . . slowly. The only time we have been physically close is when you saw me on the street and put your nose in my face and yelled at me about Max and your flowers . . . (Slowly and softly, somewhat gingerly.) My head is down . . . I am in a submissive position. Now I kneel down, further, and kiss the ground at your feet. I wrap my arms around your legs . . . gently and slowly . . . and I move my head back and forth. Now we are in your dining room having tea together, and I look at your face. Gentle! You have a gentle face . . . Hello, Mrs. Day, you have a gentle face . . . Call you Jennifer? I will. What a pretty name. My God, I feel loving and tender with you. There is something soft and gentle about you. Things in your dining room are so . . . friendly and motherly. I pick up the cup . . . and the teapot cover . . .You made the cover? There is a whole other world of you that I never knew . . . I am looking at your face. (Spoken almost caressingly, with a soft touch.) You are kind, kindly . . . Now I am looking at you. Just looking at you. So tenderly . . . softly . . . I think I feel gentle with you. There is a softness and a tenderness between us. I am here all the time, and you are at my place all the time. We are soft and gentle with each other. I am bringing you flowers . . . We go to the cemetery with the flowers, and I hold your elbow as we approach your husband's grave. And you weep by his gravestone. I put the flowers down. We are quiet. I look at you, and I feel so tender. Tell me what you are thinking . . . I know there were good times and bad times. You have tears in your eyes. You miss him so. Tell me about him . . .You must have loved him so. I feel so tenderly toward you now. Here . . . One of these flowers is for you. It is yours . . ."

The initial scene of strong feeling is being in the kitchen when your husband calls. He wants to talk to his mother. That is when you are slapped with the horrible realization that you got the time all wrong. You were supposed to pick her up hours ago, not hours from now. You idiot. You brainless idiot. Both you and your husband are thoroughly disgusted with your childish irresponsibility. The deeper potential for experiencing is a galloping mischievousness, being a mischief-maker, a little devil. You have already selected a few scenes for the next few days or so:

"Tomorrow morning, as usual, you drive me to work, and you love your convertible. Right. I am sitting demurely

334

next to you, and I . . . (Purring like a sexed-up cat.) start taking it off. Yes! And you like this . . . Oohhh, you are getting hard . . . I love stroking your cock. You like this? Rubbing up against you . . . Just keep driving . . . It's getting harder. Here I go, down, down, down on you. I am taking it out . . . Just keep driving. I think I'll take off all my clothes and suck you off along the highway here . . . Oops, I think a couple of vans and trucks are coming and . . . by the way, so are you! Surprise! Now this formal dinner. Let me see. We are all dressed up at the reception, and everyone is dressed to the teeth. Yes, dear, I should not forget. She is getting the big award, from the government . . . very nice . . . for her novel. And he is getting the honorary doctorate. There they are. They are so handsome! Hello! Hello! Congratulations on the award and the novel! Now my husband tried to get it straight, but the poor darling is so easily mixed up. So I am going to make it clear: STANLEY IS GETTING THE HONORARY DOCTORATE BECAUSE HE HAS DONATED A MILLION DOLLARS TO THE UNIVERSITY OF HIS CHOICE. ANNABELLE IS GETTING THE BOOKHAM AWARD BECAUSE SHE IS SO MUCH SMARTER THAN STANLEY. I AM ON THE BOOKHAM COMMITTEE, AND WE WOULD DEARLY LOVE A FRIENDLY CONTRIBUTION FROM STANLEY . . . Well, I am not on the Bookham committee, but two of the members are here. Sam . . . Shirley, would you like $500,000 from Stanley? . . . Oh! Wait! I know what I would love to do. That mother-in-law of mine tells such whopping lies about her ex-husband. I know the real story. He was a contractor, and he went to a convention in Florida and never came back! He took all his money and left. It's the only way he could get away from the clawing bitch. So I am going to go to Florida and record his true story. Yes! Ah, yes. And then I am going to have a family reunion at our place. She tells such lies about why he left. There was no problem with taxes! That's a huge lie! We're all at our place, the whole family, and then I say: "Sarah, mother-in-law, I have a surprise. It is special, just for you . . . And I play the recording. I'll hide the recorder. There will be romantic music. I will hold her hand and smile. Listen, darling. This is for you . . . I am so baaad. I love this . . . Oh, I really love this. She'll just die . . . I love this. I really love this . . . YES!"

The scene that has always haunted you is when you were a child, and you actually saw your older brother, way up in the tree, plunging down through the branches and crashing on the hard ground below. He died instantly. The deeper potential was the experiencing of being risky, taking risks, being daring, adventurous. Actually, you have hardly even had a glimmer of that experiencing throughout your life. In stark contrast, here you are, having been this qualitatively new person in Step 3, and now you are ready to see what it can be like to be this way in your forthcoming, new, post-session world, although in playful unreality. You have already found a few delicious scenes:

"I couldn't even look at those outside glass elevators when I was standing on the ground. Now I'm supposed to

ride one for real. Aha. That'll be real fun. I will do it in steps.
First, I am going to ride from the ground floor to the
second floor. With all of you. Six or eight people in the
elevator, please. Thank you. Look, you don't mind if I move
kind of close to the door, do you? And put my arms around
your waist? Okay? Please? I'm not really used to this, though
I am such a daredevil. Then, skipping all the next steps, I
arrange with the manager to go it alone on Sunday. Here I
am in the elevator. Sunday. And it's raining. Not too hard.
In the elevator. (Singing.) I am in the elevator. Can you all
see me down there? Well, no one is down there. Way, way
down there. Up and down. I am traveling up and up, to the
112th floor, up here in the clouds. I cannot even see the
building. And now we plunge down, a headlong plunge. I'm
gonna get my black belt. Shit, I am going to get a black
coffin . . . I know! I am going to learn how to fly an airplane
and put on shows for people. I will become a stunt pilot . .
.Yes! That will be fun. I am at the controls of the plane!
Zoom! Not too close, buddy! I am the best stunt pilot
around! I just feel a little queasy in those outside elevators.
Down we go! Wheee!"

You are living as and being the qualitatively new person in
the context of playfully unrealistic scenes from today and
tomorrow. The context is sheer, playful unreality, but you are
being the radically new person. Now you are ready to remain
this radical new person, only you are going to shift the context
from one of sheer zaniness, silliness, and fiction to one that is
more real, more like something you would truly do.

BE THE QUALITATIVELY WHOLE NEW PERSON YOU ARE GOING TO BE

You are now going to be the qualitatively new person in the real world. Training is over. It is time to get ready for the real thing.

For one thing, you have been the live embodiment of the deeper potential for experiencing. You have been a caricature of a person, but not the whole person. Now you are going to be the whole person. What had been a deeper potential for experiencing is now an integral part of the whole new person you are. You are going to be more than just the exaggerated form of the former deeper potential for experiencing.

For another thing, the session will be over soon, and you will be living and being in a very real world. Not only will you be a qualitatively new person, but the world will also be qualitatively different. You entered the session as one person, and the world was the world of that person. Now, you are a qualitatively new person, and your personal world is qualitatively different from the world of the person who started the session. However, your post-session world is just as real.

Your job is to prepare yourself for actually being the qualitatively whole new person in the real, qualitatively new, post-session world. Your job is to try it out, do a dress rehearsal, and see what it can be like in the actual post-session world. It is reality time.

Step 4. Be the Whole New Person in the Post-Session World

Find The Post-Session Scene Or Scenes

You are going to be the qualitatively new person when you open your eyes, leave the room, and enter into the real world around you. You might be this whole new person everywhere, in every scene and situation, or you may not. However, you are going to be this qualitatively new person somewhere, in some context, in some scene or scenes, and the scene or scenes should be ones that occur as soon as the session is over, or at least within the next day or so.

The Scene Should Be Selected By the New Person and for the Experiencing of the New Person

You are the qualitatively new person, and your job is to select some time, some incident or situation, some scene where you can nicely and fully enjoy this wonderful new experiencing. You can literally say out loud: "I am the living, breathing sense of tenderness, gentleness, softness. I am now alive and well, and I am going to experience this wonderful sense out there in the real world. I have played, and everything was delightfully unreal. Now I am ready to step out into the real world. Where? Where do I look forward to undergoing this experiencing?"

You are going to step out into a world that was largely the personal world of the person you were at the beginning of the session. You have a dog named Max. You are a lawyer. You have friends. You have a neighbor. You are black. There is a world that you will enter, or carry with you, when the session is over.

This new-felt experiencing is inside you. You can experience it anywhere and everywhere. From the moment the session is over, you can undergo this new-felt sense of tenderness, gentleness, softness. What scene do you select? It is up to you.

It May Be a Scene That You Just Used in Playful Unreality

You were just the new person in scenes that were playful, silly, funny, outlandish, delightfully unrealistic, and free of reality constraints. Now that you have finished living and being in these scenes, perhaps you are ready and eager to be this new person in those playfully unrealistic scenes. Consider the possibility: "Would I really want to be this way here? Do I really want to do this, for real? I think I do!" These scenes started out as ludicrous and fictitious. However, now that you have actually lived in these scenes, you may want to be this new person in that very scene in the real world.

You just finished five minutes or so of being the new person who is the experiencing of letting it go, letting go, giving plenty of space, no longer clinging and grasping. Most of your practice was spent being this new person the next time Denis launches into his arrogant lecture of how empty your marriage is. You were playing, and the whole scene was draped in gross unreality, but something seemed so right about being this way with him. It felt just plain good, solid, sound. "I'm going to do it! With Denis! He'll be home tomorrow. We'll be getting ready for bed, and the

340

air will chill with that mood. That's when I'll move! That's it. With Denis . . ."

Just a few minutes ago you were the experiencing of pure tenderness, gentleness, and softness in the playfully unrealistic scene with the mean old woman next door, the one who hates your dog and probably hates you, too. As this new person, you did some weird and bizarre things with your neighbor, and by the end of the episode you are surprisingly ready to do something altogether new for you but in keeping with the new person whom you are. You are actually excited about being this way with your neighbor, even initiating things with her, going up to her. This is exciting to you. "I want to do it . . . I think I want to do it!"

You are being the new person who is the experiencing of being risky, taking risks, being daring, and adventurous. In the spirit of playful unreality, you went through the incremental scenes of riding glass elevators on the outside of buildings. They had terrified the old you. You also mentioned learning how to fly an airplane, and you spent some time in a zany scene of flipping the plane during your first lesson. Your instructor fell out of the plane, and you rescued him in a daring maneuver. But the excitement about what you could actually do came with your playful scene about learning how to ride in one of those gliders. "They always fascinated me. I remember getting a video of people aloft in one of those graceful gliders. And I used to build them when I was a kid. I think . . . I'm going to do that! I am! I am!"

This happens often. That is, you start Step 4 by having lots of fun, being playful and silly, living and being in scenes that are outrageously unrealistic, ludicrous, bizarre. Then, having done this for five or ten minutes, you find yourself surprisingly ready and even eager to actually be this new person in the playfully unrealistic scenes in real life. The scenes have moved from being playfully unrealistic to becoming appealingly attractive. The scenes start with, "This is going to be weird, bizarre, far-out, kind of crazy," and end with: "Why not? I think I like being this way in this situation! I think I'll do it!"

The Scene May Be Public and High-Risk or Private and Low-Risk

The important thing is for you to actually undergo this new experiencing after the session in the post-session world. The qualitatively new person undergoes the qualitatively new experiencing. You can use a context that is public, one that opens up the possibility of significant changes in your personal world. Or, you can use a context that is private and would have little or no genuine effect on your personal world, where you live, the things you possess, or the people who are around you.

You are a new person, a person with the new-felt experiencing of being a helpless little baby, of being held, being cuddled. The session started with the call from the wife of your best buddy. She said, "Kip, he's gone." Sam is dead. If you want, you can leave the session and, within an hour or so, undergo this experiencing in a way that is completely private. This scene will have little or no effect on your world, but it provides a safe "token taste" of this wonderful new experiencing. Angela will not be home for about four hours. You can get into bed, take off all your clothes, lie down on your side of the bed, and curl up like a little baby. Put Angela's old nightgown or housecoat on her side of the bed. Lean toward where she would be. Put your thumb in your mouth. Lean your head down on your chest. Rock back and forth. Make baby sounds and thoroughly undergo what it is like to be a helpless little baby, being held, and cuddled. Revel in it. Coo. Smell Angela's odor, inhale her presence enfolding you.

If you are the new person in private, with little or no risk, make sure that the experiencing is full and deep. Do it. Do it well. No one has to see you. What you do may not be with real people. But make sure that you do it so that you undergo the experiencing. Do not pretend to be the experiencing of being the helpless little baby, held and cuddled, by closing your eyes for a few seconds and imagining. A little friendly fantasy is not enough. Don't think about doing it. Go ahead and do it. Call your friend and be the whole new person, even though you do not actually dial your friend's telephone number. Say out loud what the new person actually says. Don't just think it inside. Private and low risk means that what you do will have little or no direct impact on your immediate world. If you are going to show your ass to the world, do it late at night when no one can see you. Don't bend over in front of the police

343

station at midday, pull down your pants, and show your bare ass. But do sit in your favorite chair, close your eyes, and spend a few seconds imagining that you are showing your bare ass at midday in front of the police station. You must follow the guidelines and undergo the actual experiencing of being the qualitatively new person, even if you do it in private and with low risk to your immediate world.

On the other hand, you can undergo this experiencing in public, with real people. This heightens the risk of effecting genuine changes in your personal world. You could carry out the actual experiencing with Angela tonight for real. You could be the qualitatively new person with her. You could be this whole new person with your close friend at work, especially around this mess with what to do about the vindictive, error-filled, embarrassing press release written by the boss. Or, you can even be this whole new person in the meeting you called to try and decide what you all can do about the press release, now that it is out. These possible scenes are much more high risk. So, too, are imminent scenes in which you are being this qualitatively new person on the airplane Thursday, when the plane screams down the runway, or when you have your ritual coffee in the morning with the boss or the attractive woman down the hall, the woman who has such an infectious sense of humor. When and where to actually be this whole new person can have profound effects on your personal world. Or, you can decide to keep the experience private and the effect minimal.

In any case, you have found a post-session scene, a place, a situation, where you can be the qualitatively whole new person whom you are. It will happen, or can be made to happen, very soon after the session is over, within the next day or so. Now it's time for you to try it out, to be this qualitatively whole new person in your whole new world. Stay being this whole new person. Get ready to live and be in the actual world outside the room where you are having the session.

REHEARSE ACTUALLY BEING THE WHOLE NEW PERSON IN THE WHOLE NEW WORLD

In the beginning of Step 4, you created, invented, or found scenes that might happen in the next few days or so, and you were the qualitatively new person in those scenes. But this was done in playful, whimsical, zany unreality, refreshingly free from reality constraints. You are now going to do it for real. You are going to live and be the whole new person in the whole new world out there. You are going to actually be the whole new person in the real world of the next few days or so.

It is try-out time. You are going to actually rehearse what it is like being the whole new person in the alive and real new world. You are going to see what it is like. You are going to modify and refine what you actually do. You are going to keep rehearsing it until it is just right.

Once you are done with the playful unreality part of Step 4, it can be a smooth and easy transition into trying it out for real. Just make sure that you are the qualitatively new person. You became this new person in Step 3; make sure to merely continue being this new person till the end of the session, and then beyond.

Use Your Bodily-Felt Sensations As A Guide

When you try out being the whole new person in the scene that is to happen after the session, when you live and be in the scene, carrying it out as the new person, stop and check your body. Pay attention to the bodily-felt sensations. Where are they? What are they like?

Suppose that the bodily-felt sensations are good and stretch over a fair proportion of your body. There is a lightness over your whole body. There is a kind of electrical tingling all over your skin. Your muscles feel nice and alive, supple. There is a light humming, vibrating sensation inside, all over. There is a pleasant coolness in your arms and legs. There is a general bodily sensation of vibrancy, aliveness, peacefulness, togetherness, and harmony, like everything in your body fits, goes together.

When the bodily-felt sensations are like these, it feels as though your body is saying: "Yes, you are doing it well. What you are doing is good, go ahead and actually be this way in that scene. You don't have to alter what you are doing. Everything is just fine. Be this way. Enjoy yourself."

Suppose that you try it out and rehearse being this way in this scene, but when you check your bodily-felt reactions, they are neutral, not there much, muted, barely present. It is hard to tell where the sensations are in your body. You may notice that your hands are warm, a little bit, maybe. Or, you are aware of your stomach, but you can't quite tell if the feelings are good or bad. Your nose might itch a bit. Your chest feels all right. There really is very little to notice.

When your body feels this way, the answer is "No." You are not ready to go ahead and be this whole new person in this scene. But that doesn't mean you should just forget the whole thing. You have more work to do. Revise what you actually did. Modify it, refine it. Change it to some other scene. Do it differently. Then go ahead and rehearse it again. Check your body. Keep on changing things, rehearsing, checking your body, and changing things again until the bodily-felt sensations are just wonderful and are present over most of your body.

Suppose that the bodily-felt sensations are prominently unpleasant or bad. The muscles across your chest are tight. Your whole body is heavy, dull, listless. You can feel blood coming from your nose. There is a dull pain in your upper back. Your right hand is trembling. Your feet are very cold. Your stomach is tied up in knots. There is a pounding in your head. Your neck feels so stiff. Your heart is racing out of control. The muscles in your thighs are clenching up. Wherever the bodily-felt sensations are in your body, they are painful, hurtful, unpleasant.

Accept this as your body's way of saying: "Absolutely not. No. Do not do it. Do not be this way in this scene. Stop." As this same person, this whole new person, find something quite different to be and do in this scene. Or, find some other place, some other scene, in which to do it.

Then, go ahead and rehearse being this new way in the scene, check your bodily-felt sensations, revise and modify your behavior or the scene on the basis of the bodily-felt reactions, rehearse it again, and keep going until the bodily-felt reactions are quite pleasant and spread over most of your body.

By using your bodily-felt reactions as a guide, you can find the most fitting way to be this whole new person and the most fitting scene or situation in which to do it. And there is a bonus. You are indeed becoming a whole new person. More than just experiencing what had been a deeper potential for experiencing, you are allowing other parts of you to add their reactions, to become pleased and welcoming toward you actually being this whole new person. You are, in other words, becoming a whole new person.

This May Be the Time for Other Parts of You to Voice Their Objections

You are actually rehearsing what it is like to be the qualitatively new person in a specific scene, one that is going to happen soon. Things are becoming quite real, quite imminent. You are very close to actually being this new person in the actual world. You have even checked out your bodily-felt reactions. Maybe your body said, "Yes, go ahead," or it said, "No, change things first." Or, perhaps it warned you to stay away from the whole affair. It is too dangerous. This may be the time for you to give other parts of you the opportunity to voice their objections. You don't have to do this. A good rehearsal does not have to include this step. But it can be exceedingly helpful to give other parts of you the room to have their say, to voice any serious and passionate objections to what this whole new you is so close to actually doing.

In Step 3, you threw yourself into being the deeper potential for experiencing. You were this newly discovered you throughout Step 3 and also in Step 4, when you were the qualitatively new person in playful, silly, zany unreality. You were essentially one sided, caricatured. But now you are seeing what it is like to be the qualitatively whole new person whom you are. You are not just rehearsing being the formerly deeper potential for experiencing; you are getting ready to be a whole person, a whole new person, a qualitatively whole new person.

This means that you are rehearsing what it is like to be a full person, a whole new person in whom the deeper potential for experiencing is an integral part. Back in Step 2, you did things that gave other parts of you a chance to welcome, accept, enfold the newly discovered deeper part of you. Now, in Step 4, when you rehearse what it is like to leave the session and really be this qualitatively whole new person, you have another chance, if it seems right and proper, to let other parts of you have a few words to say. It is as if you are saying to these other parts: "So, what do you think about this new part that has joined us? If you have any objections, now is the time to talk. Anyone have anything to say?"

You just might revert back to the person you were at the beginning of the session. If you become this old person again, if the objections are from this old you, and if they are serious, then you might as well stop the session right here. It can happen. It is as if you are saying: "I am the old me again. I am not ready to be this qualitatively new person. I can go along with this big change in playful unreality. It was fun. But no further. I am back in charge, and I say no. I stop here."

Deliberately give any and all parts of you the chance to voice objections. Encourage passionate objections. Take the hand of every part of you that has a right to object, bring it to the front stage, and let it voice its hearty objections to the qualitatively new person actually doing what it rehearsed or even daring to exist at all. Cajole each part into saying things like this: "Being that way is crazy . . . It would ruin my life . . . I'd end up in jail . . . Doing that is immoral . . . What would others think? . . . That's not the way I really am . . . Everyone would hate me for that . . .You can't be like that . . . I couldn't do that . . . I couldn't be like that . . . It would ruin everything I've worked for . . . It's against everything I believe . . . Being that way is wrong . . . It would make things worse . . ."

When you voice objections, let yourself go wild. Be passionate. State your objections with strong feeling. Parade around. Make up and embellish objections. You may voice objections with deadly seriousness. You may be torn apart and pained. You may be on a delightful high, in a happy rush. It may feel wonderful. Just give yourself the chance, if it seems proper and timely, to give all parts of you plenty of room to voice every objection they can possibly dredge up.

As long as other parts of you have an honest opportunity to voice their objections, these other parts will almost certainly have a better relationship with the new person who is doing the rehearsing. They have had their say. Relationships improve. Sometimes it can be fun giving voice to these other parts of you. You can say wild and nasty things about being this whole new person, but it feels free and good to be able to give voice to such objections. On the other hand, sometimes you revert to the person you were at the beginning of the session. Your objections come across with meanness, deadliness, hatefulness. Perhaps the objections actually kill the whole new person, get rid of it, seal it down under. Everything you had achieved in the session is gone. You are back to being the old person you were at the beginning of the session. When you invite other parts of you to voice their objections, you risk either having the parts get along better than before, which means the whole new person is truly present and well, or you risk losing this whole new person, who is replaced with the person you were at the beginning of the session.

A Critical Question: Are You Going to Stay Being the Whole New Person, Or Will You Go Back to Being the Old Person?

Which person ends the session and walks out into the world outside the session? When the session ends, will you still be the qualitatively new person, or will you go back to being the person you were at the beginning of the session? There is a moment, a point, usually in this last part of the session, when you either revert to the person you had been or you accept the exciting risk of staying as this whole new person, perhaps until the session is over, perhaps even after the session, and perhaps for the next few weeks or months or longer.

When you, the whole new person, invite all parts of you to voice their objections, something dramatic happens. The old you is practically invited to take over again. You can so easily switch back into the person you were. Will you? Or will you remain being the whole new person? This is a powerful decision because it is one of those critical moments in the session when you often revert to being the old you, or you remain being the whole new you, maybe for a long time, maybe forever.

I know that a magnificent change has occurred when the person becomes the qualitatively new person in Step 3 and continues being this qualitatively new person in the first part of Step 4. I also know that by the time the session ends and the person leaves the session, he or she has often reverted to being the old person. This happens often. I hope we will learn how to teach more people, more often, to remain being the whole new person until the session ends, until the new person leaves the session, and until the new person lives in the new world for some weeks, months, or years.

There is no law that you have to remain this magnificent whole new person throughout Step 4 and after the session. Neither is there any law that you have to revert to being the old person. Someone, someday, will solve the problem of how to continue the magnificent change to the end of the session and beyond, maybe forever.

Step 4. Be the Whole New Person in the Post-Session World

In the meantime, please make sure that when you rehearse actually being the whole new person in the world, you provide a little time for other parts of you to voice their objections. The risk is that you may fall back into being the old you. The other risk is that you just might remain being the qualitatively whole new person.

See If This Whole New Person Is Free of the Initial Painful Scene of Painful Feeling

Some sessions start with a dream. Some start with a scene of strong feeling, in which the feeling is so pleasant, so wonderful. However, most sessions start with a scene of strong feeling in which the feeling was bad, a painful scene of painful feeling.

You are being the qualitatively new person. You are rehearsing what it can be like to be this whole new person in the actual world after the session. You are ready for a test. One of the goals of an experiential session is to free you of the painful scene that was front and center for you at the beginning of the session. It is gone, as is the painful feeling in that painful scene. Now you can face the test. Are you really and truly free of that painful scene and the painful feeling in that scene? As this whole new person, go ahead and face the test. Face the painful scene. Face it for the rest of the day, or tomorrow, or very soon. Is the scene so painful? You are rehearsing, so bite the bullet and go ahead and rehearse what it is like to live and be in a world that had included that painful scene and painful feeling.

If you are well and truly the qualitatively new person, that painful scene may no longer be a part of your new world. It has little or no place in your world. The world of the whole new person has no need for, and places no importance on, the old painful scene. Therefore, the scene is gone. For the new person, there is no longer any need to have someone like your husband, Denis, to fulfill the role of the removed critic, assessing your shortcomings and failures, and leaving you with such painful feelings. It is no longer important for there to be something in your body, coldly killing you, being the cancer. There is no more cancer in your body. It is gone, finished, evaporated, no longer in your world or in your body. It is no longer important for the qualitatively new person to have a mean neighbor who considers you disgusting and not belonging here, who fills you with awful feelings. It is no longer important to have a world filled with significant people, like your father, who make you feel so painfully pressured, having to be nice, full of broiling, inner frustration and anger when they hand you tax forms to complete for them.

In your new world, the painful scenes may be missing. Or, they may be present but totally free of the painful feelings. Many scenes have a realistic way of remaining part of the real world, but they can be dramatically different because the old painful feelings are gone. The whole meaning and significance of the scene are radically altered. Your whole relationship to it excludes the old painful feeling. You are a whole new person in that scene or in that part of the scene. Your husband, Denis, has somehow apparently

changed. He may start his lecture, but the feelings in you are
now almost wonderful. The painful feelings are gone.
Perhaps the cancer is here, but everything is so different,
including your feelings. The painful feelings accompanying
the cancer are gone. There are neighbors, and some of them
are still mean, but so much has changed in you and your
world. Those old painful feelings are gone.

Now that you are rehearsing what it is like being the
whole new person, go ahead and accept the test. Face the
forthcoming painful scene of painful feeling. See if the whole
new person—and the whole new world in which this person is
and lives—is free of the initial painful scene of painful feeling.

Here Are Some Examples

You began the session with the phone call from the wife
of your best friend from when you were about 12 or 13 until
your early 20s. Sam moved away, got married, and now his
wife was calling to let you know that he had died. You could
hardly get the phone call off your mind for the past three
days, and you are not as sharp and clever as you usually are.
It was not Sam's death so much, but something about the
phone call. Working from that incident of the phone call,
you discovered a deeper potential for being a helpless little
baby, the experiencing of being held and cuddled.

You just finished being this whole new person in the
context of playful, silly unreality in a forthcoming scene in
Tim's office at work. The whole crew met to discuss how to
handle the problems stemming from the awful press release

written by the boss. It was an error-filled, vindictive, problematic document, and the whole department is in big trouble. Things are going to get much worse because the boss is still in a bad mood and denies having authored the embarrassing press release. You playfully and unrealistically wallowed in being the whole new person in the meeting tomorrow, being the helpless little baby, held and cuddled by one of your colleagues. It was fun. It was well done. However, when you turned to the possibility of really and truly being this whole new person, the meeting tomorrow did not feel like it would be the right place:

"Well, that was fun. But I couldn't really. How do I feel? Really do it? I can't even imagine . . . So, where could I? Lying in a woman's lap. Angela. It would work. When? Sometimes I wake up in the middle of the night. Must have had a dream. I'm scared . . .Walking around. Angie . . . Angie. Hmmm. In bed here. Would you put your arms around me? Please? I am panicked about something. Please put . . . This doesn't even feel right. My God. I should be able to do this. Try again . . . I'm tight, in my chest. Should I try again? I could tell her about Sam, and the . . . Could I tell her about the phone call from his wife? Angie, please, I want to do something . . . Talk to you . . . Let me put my head . . . I feel funny, Angie. Is it okay with you if I lay on your la . . .lap? (He is crying.) My God, I don't know what's happening. You smell so good . . . I told you about Sam . . . (Still crying.) His wife called, and she told me he died. I feel your hands on my shoulders. Angie . . . I want to tell you . . . I have no idea why . . .When she told me he died, something

356

about her voice. I felt like a baby. Like it touched something inside of me. I'm looking at you, Angie . . . I love it when you hold me. My God, I'm shivering . . . Angie . . . (More crying.) This feels so . . . natural . . . missing . . . I'm going to do this. Angie, please let me . . . Help me . . .

"You know what I'm seeing now? Mercedes hit me when . . . like when I have this great idea, and it's turned down at the meeting, and I get all pissy. She's great, she always nudges me, or hits me, friendly. Here. On the shoulder. 'Hey, they don't like me . . . Hold me close, Mercedes!' I could do it! 'They don't like my idea. Aaawww.' You'd let me. Like clowning . . . How does it feel? I feel it in my chest. Nice . . . Now . . . now I think of Nancy (his three-year-old daughter) and how tired you get when I read to you . . . when I tell you stories in bed. This time I take you in my arms and read to you, and you can see the pictures, and you fall asleep. My God, I'm crying again. Holding you. But you really are a baby. Oh, I like this so much, and it feels so good. It's . . . exciting . . . And new for me . . .

"And now for some . . . objections. I should not do this. I shouldn't be this way because . . . because . . . I've gotta think of some good reasons. Uh . . . being a little baby is disgusting. It's just trying to be cute. Uh . . . No one likes a little baby. I am not a helpless little baby. I am a person with real responsibilities. I'd get fired; Angie would leave me. I can't come up with any good objections! I ought to! Come on. Object. Object. Ah . . . Actually, I think I like being this way. With everyone. With the family. Aha! The family! Watch out family!

"Aunt Sylvie. She's a big woman. This weekend . . . the whole family. We all love you, Aunt Sylvie. I'm gonna do it. After the big meal, when we clean up and the old folks go into the living room to talk. Aunt Sylvie, is it okay if I put . . . my head in your lap here? Yes? It is? You like that! So . . . I just want to curl up here and feel your arms around me. Oh, shit. Maybe I could do this if we're alone . . . I'm . . . well it doesn't feel so good . . . But with Angie. Yes. I want to tell you all about that phone call, Hon, and . . . Yes. I'm going to do it."

He had found and rehearsed when and where and how enjoy this newfound experiencing of being held, being cuddled, being a helpless little baby. It was with his wife, Angela. He had given other parts of him the opportunity to voice their worries, their serious objections, if they so wished. That was taken care of. He began the session with a recent scene of strong feeling when the wife of an old best friend called. He had not begun the session with a scene of painful feeling, so there was no need to see if such a painful scene were truly absent from his world. He was ready to commit himself to actually carrying out his homework.

Let us turn to the older woman who knows she is dying of cancer. She began the session with a scene of bad feeling when her body was so weak that she could no longer get up out of a chair. An even more powerful scene was in the morning when she awakened. For a precious few seconds, she was not aware of the cancer. Then she knew. Cancer is all over the inside and going to kill her soon. The deeper potential is the experiencing of mercilessness, relentless evil, being an utterly cold killer, and she thoroughly reveled in this experiencing as she tortured and killed the mean politician who forced the storekeepers out of the building so that he could sell it for a huge profit. This was perhaps the first time in her life that she actually felt this experiencing so fully and with such wonderful feelings.

"But I can't even get out of this house. I wish I could, but I can't. But this is more me, more real. I think I wasted my whole life being the good German daughter and wife and sister. What can I do? It's too late. My father died years ago. Mother died before that. My husband is gone. The only one left is Kurt. Kurt. Oh . . . Kurt . . . Do I have the courage? I feel so evil . . . Like it's been stored up all my life. (She is almost growling, and talking slowly, menacingly.) I am going to talk to Kurt. I am 69. Kurt is 77. He's still tall and has all his hair, and he walks every day. Kurt . . . Kurt . . . The whole family was afraid of you . . . I will have you come here. I am dying. You will come. It's just a few hours away by train, and you love trains, don't you? I want to talk to you . . .

"I will ask Marie to call you to come here. You are here in my room . . . (Her voice lowers. It no longer sounds like her.) You have that superior look, as always. I am your little sister. And I am dying, Kurt. When Father died, you said he was a coward, he never fought back. Well, Kurt, in the whole family, you were the only strong one. We all feared you. When you came home, you told us about the camp and shooting those people, the Jews and the Slavs. You were so excited. It's one of the few times . . . I hated you. I listened; we all listened. Well, Kurt, tell me again . . . No, I am going to plan it carefully. I haven't ever talked with Kurt or anyone about what he did . . . I am going to do something I should have done. I am . . .

"Here you are, Kurt. You are going to listen. The family never talked about what you did. You beat your daughter and threw her down the stairs. That's what happened to her back, not those lies about her hurting her back when she was diving. But no one ever said anything. Not your wife or anyone. But we knew! We all knew! My God, I wish I had the courage to shoot you, like you shot all those people in the camp! And you gloated! You are worse than I am! I was the nice one all my life. Nice! . . . No, this feels terrible. My abdomen is locked up. My face feels like leather . . . And I feel . . . awful. Tired . . . so tired . . . But I am going to do something. I know . . .

"My friend Howard, the lawyer. He is Jewish, and he knows nothing about Kurt. He's so young . . . I am getting a plan . . . Yes. I am going to ask Marie to get Kurt here. Yes. And I will ask Kurt to tell me stories about our childhood in Germany. After all (a wicked cackle), I am dying. Tell me stories . . . He will . . . He will . . . I know you, Kurt. Tell me stories like you did at home. Kurt will tell me how he shot the Jews. They took off all their clothes, and Kurt was one of the young soldiers who made them dig the pits and then shot them. Go ahead, Kurt, tell me again. I was just a young girl . . . And Howard will have the tape recorder. We will arrange the recording. I will tell Howard about my brother. Good Kurt . . . I will be so innocent, and you, Kurt. You will incriminate yourself, and Howard knows of the Nazi hunters. You were a good Nazi, Kurt. It will be on the tape recorder, hidden in the room. Every word . . . And then I am going to tell you that I know what you did to your daughter. Practice . . . practice. Kurt, tell me stories about when we were children. In Germany. I remember when you came home from the camp and were so happy. Tell me those stories again. Yes. You will . . . Howard and two of the Nazi hunters will be in the next room. And . . . Nothing. I will just . . . I wish I could see them shoot you. You are an awful man. You sinned. You are more evil than me. But I love this . . . I do like this! I do! I feel alive again! My God, I feel alive! YESSSSS! I will do it! I will plan it tomorrow. With Howard. He will agree. Yes. YESSSSS! OH, MY GOD, I AM FINALLY ALIVE!

"I am not done yet . . . More to do . . . Objections. I should object. Let me see . . . This is wicked of me. I am doing something cruel. Kurt is my brother. What would Momma and Poppa say? I am being cruel and sadistic. This is not me. I am not really this way. I am being bad . . . How could I ever do such a thing? It is not so difficult. Sorry, I do not feel so bad! I do not!

"And what about me—my life? I am dying of cancer. Should I remember more quickly? Should I just remember that I am dying, stay in the chair all day, and not even try to get up? Well? I feel so different. Can I fight you? You, you cancer. You think you win over me? I do not! I know you. I am more evil than you. Ha! Maybe we could kill the old lady together. This is so strange. My body feels so weak. I am weak. And yet I feel strong. I feel wicked and nasty and . . . merciless . . .You know, I could kill that cancer, with acid. Squeeze the life out of it. I think you tried to take on the wrong person! I am going to kill you, my friend the cancer! And I won't even feel bad. Just good. When I finish with Kurt, you are next . . ."

The older German woman had indeed finished this part of the session. She was ready to actually commit to carrying out the homework she had rehearsed so well. And perhaps, just a perhaps, she was free of the initial scene of painful feeling, the scene involving the cancer.

It was the most dramatic incident in her life, being a child and watching with others as her older brother climbed higher and higher in the gigantic tree. And then he fell, hitting the high branches and smashing onto the hard ground. All that blood . . . He was dead. She knew of no direct ways in which that incident affected her life. She did not live in the desert, without trees. She was scared of heights, but she could still be in airplanes and on the top floor of buildings. The memory of the incident did not haunt her every week. It did not weigh on her chest, forever oppressing her. But that is the incident that came to mind when she started the session and opened herself to receiving a scene of strong feeling.

Step 4. Be the Whole New Person in the Post-Session World

The deeper potential was the experiencing of riskiness, being daring, adventurous, taking risks. At the beginning of Step 4, she has a great deal of fun riding up and down in the glass elevator outside the very tall building where she worked. She, like many people who worked there, wouldn't even step into that elevator. But she had great fun doing it in playful unreality. Furthermore, when she moved on to what she might do in the real world, it seemed inviting. She was quite willing to remain being this new person as she rehearsed what it would be like to cavalierly and daringly do it:

"Joe, I am going to ask you a favor. I want you to go with me, hold my hand, and tell me everything is going to be all right. I am going to get into that killer elevator and ride up to the top floor and all the way down to the ground floor. Just be kind to me if I press spread-eagle against the building or collapse on the elevator floor. You see, I am going to risk it. Without terror. This will be the beginning of the new me . . . So, here we go. Inside. I grab your hand. Three or four others are here with us. Up, up we go. I am going to be fearless. I am not terrified. I am not going to pee. I am becoming the fearless one. If anyone here is scared of this elevator, you can hold onto me . . . I will take care of you because I am fearless. Now we are at the top, and then down we go . . . One floor. Should I look out? Not this time . . .

"Okay, here come some parts of me objecting: Let me out of here! This is crazy! I don't want to read about my death in the paper tomorrow! I lived 32 years without this, and I can do without being crazy. I want to be safe. What

363

the hell am I doing this for? This is crazy! Wake up! I am scared of this elevator, and I ought to be. It's not a big tree, and I don't have to prove that I am not terrified of heights! So stop trying to prove something. All right, any more objections? Yes. Yes. Some other objection . . . Uh, uh . . . Joe will think of you as a fake, just trying to be with him. Oh, that's dumb . . . I think I'm going to do it. Yes, I will. Actually, I feel tingling all over. It feels good. Yes. And with Joe, too. I'm going to do it . . .

"And Joe, I am going to tell you about my brother. I will. I was a kid. He fell out of a big, tall tree and died. It stayed in my mind forever. There . . . No. Doesn't feel right. Ummm. Not much of anything. But I want to tell him. Someone. Bill. Bill! Listen, Bill. Teach me how to drive a motorcycle 'cause I want to get one. Uh . . . I want to . . . I think I do! I'm going to learn and then own my own motorcycle. Bill, now listen. I am going to learn how to drive one, and then I want to have my own motorcycle. Just that far. Teach me. YES! My dad had a Harley. I want one. Not a Harley, maybe. Bill, I want you to teach me. Teach me. I want my own motorcycle, and then we can ride together like you always wanted. I am the new Louise. Say hello to the risky one. I want my own bike! Damn. This feels so right. Bill, it's time we started living together! Think about it! You know that place by the river. Come on! We both love it. Let's live together. See what it's like! Try it! Oh, and by the way, I want a BMW. Yes, I do. Shiny and . . . black, I think . . . Oh, yes . . .

"Now for a few objections. That is dumb. Ummm. I can't think of objections. Ummm. There must be some . . . Let's see. Bill won't like you. He likes the more solid girl. The loyal one. That's it! Your friends will leave you! You are supposed to be someone to count on. Shit! I can still do that . . . I can't think of any objections! There must be some! I've never felt like this. It's like I'm waking up and . . . how I wasted my damned life. But I am going to do all this, starting with the elevator. Joe, I am going to give you such a surprise. Here comes me . . . and Bill, watch out, fella!"

Here are two things for her to do after the session. One is with Joe, riding in the glass elevator at work, and the other is with her boyfriend, Bill, learning to ride a new motorcycle. Both came from and enabled the new-felt experiencing of riskiness, being daring, adventurous, taking risks. She even voiced objections from other parts of her. Remember that her session began, not with some recent scene of painful feeling, but with a childhood scene that was catastrophic, a scene of the horror of watching her older brother fall from the tall tree to his horrific death. Louise was ready to commit herself to carrying out her homework.

You began the session with a rich and fascinating dream. Working from the dream, you discovered a deeper potential for experiencing tenderness, lovingness, gentleness, softness. No, you are not the polar opposite, a cold, hard, nasty woman, and there are times when you come close to this experiencing. You know what it is like to feel warm and affectionate with some of the men you have known, and with Lisa, a friend of yours, and with your great buddy Max, your dog. However, your life is virtually void of times of truly experiencing solid tenderness, lovingness, gentleness, softness, at least so it seems in this session.

In the first part of Step 4, you had a full dose of being this whole new experiencing in a forthcoming scene with your mean neighbor, Mrs. Jennifer Day, the busybody who eyed you from inside her home just in case Max shit on her lawn. You sailed through this scene in hilariously playful unreality, and you did it well. Now you are ready to see where you can really and truly be this whole new person:

"I know one thing. Tender and soft and loving as I am, no way with Mrs. Day. Sorry. My whole body feels heavy, and I can barely move. Not having tea with you, or visiting your husband's gravesite . . . Ah, I am a failure . . . My God, my hands are cold. And . . . rigid, and there's like a cannonball in my chest. Not with you, Jennifer Day . . . Now I'm thinking of Mom. Oh, Mom. Thursday. You're coming to visit. To show me your white boyfriend. Now, let's see. You came from Jamaica when I graduated from high school and then from law school, and when Dad died. And you wrote lots of letters. And I guess we at least correspond and sort of get along. Sort of. And I guess you want my approval of you being with this man. You sure do go for white men . . . All right, so you and this fellow will be at my apartment. Just at the door. You have that proud look about you, and I know you must have all sorts of feelings about me and . . . giving me up. I don't even like the sound

366

of that . . . You and the man are sitting together on the couch. I'm setting the scene here. You came from your hotel. Just to visit me and show me the fellow. So, I am holding . . . I actually sit right here, in front of you. And I (The voice quality is low and soft, flowing and tender.) am holding your hands in my hands. I look over at Gary . . . I know you because of the pictures Mom sent me. You two look something alike . . . You do . . .

"But I don't feel much. Like a little numb. I feel all right. Just all right. So, change it a little. Not with Gary. Bye, fella. Mom's fella. Alone with you, Mom. In the kitchen . . . In the living room. It's up to me. (The voice is lower, slower, and full of caring.) I want to know what you were feeling then, when you decided to have the baby—me—and later, to go back to Jamaica. I try to imagine being you, and I think of you as so scared. And . . . Why am I asking this? Mom? Mom? Look at me. I'm touching you . . . I always kept you away . . . friendly, but not really close. Like I wanted to keep the hurt . . . I did want to know how you felt. My God! It's like you had to have the feelings I wanted you to have. You were mad! You were really angry! You're laughing! All he wanted was the baby. So, here's the damned baby; now leave me alone! Right! I never thought of you as really pissed off. Just a pretty little girl from Jamaica. Mom, you know what I want? I want to lie on your lap and tell you all the crazy feelings I had about my mom all these years. And I want to hold your hand . . . Mom, I thought I wanted to . . . I just want you to know me . . . What I think . . . My

God, I have your nose. Exactly. Exactly!

"I want to make it different. Not on your lap. Just holding your hands, Mom. Yes! And touching your arms and face . . . What are you thinking now? No, I'll tell you . . . I am so sorry that I had to make excuses for you all these years. I used to excuse you. I got stronger. But I never touched your face or looked into your eyes . . . My God, your skin is so smooth . . . Mom, can you see me grinning? I have a fellow. I want you to meet him. But you have to know. He's black. So, excuse me . . . Oh, my God, you are grinning! I love touching your face. I want you to see something . . . Dad told me how you used to draw . . . He hated you, yet he so loved you . . . I want to show you my drawings. I spent my whole adolescence drawing. Secretly. Just the things I liked. Nothing special. I want you to see them. They're not good. Mom, I love just touching your face and hands. Just keep looking at me . . . Oh, I think I'm going to cry, but it's 'cause you have tears in your eyes. Mom. Hello, Mom . . .

"All right. Now maybe I should not be this way. I'll get soft . . . No, no . . . Come on . . . What's bad about this? The thing that I rely on is that I am fair and persistent. Yet I hold a grudge for years. That seems so hollow. I am looking for things about this that are bad! Last chance! Otherwise, I am going to be this way 'cause it feels so good. Objections, anyone? I have to have some . . . Ah . . . What? I can't think of any! All right, I sure feel different . . . I think something big happened. If I am this way with you, Mom, who knows?

My whole life . . . I think I missed out on a whole side of me . . . I am thinking of a baby! Oh, no . . . I think I've got to make sure this doesn't get out of hand! (A kind of lilt in her voice.) Make way for a whole new me! Mom, you are in for a surprise. And it feels so . . . natural. Like . . . I'm coming alive! I think I like being this way!

"And what about Jennifer—Mrs. Jennifer Day? She's going to be in my life. I'll take Max for a walk, and she'll be glued to the window or in her yard. Is anything going to be different? Let's see. I walk out in the morning to take Max for a walk . . . Where's the . . . Hello, Mrs. Day. I've got the bag . . .The thing is gone! I mean in my chest. I'm not scared! Well, well, well! Go ahead and glare. Hello! I've got the bag . . . You don't scare me! Maybe I can introduce her to Mom . . . No, I just like not being so terrified. It doesn't terrify me. Will it? I walk Max. There she is. My God, it feels all right! YES!"

An older man started his session with a recent dream that had two parts in which strong feelings were present. The dream showed him a deeper potential for the experiencing of being a jewel, being precious, being admired, exhibiting oneself. In the first part of Step 4, he played with riding on the back of his friend's motor scooter in Amsterdam, where he is going in almost a week. Wylam is his friend in Amsterdam, and the silly scene was that of acknowledging all his adoring admirers along the sidewalks, as he primmed and posed for the crowds who were stunned by his sheer good looks. Now, he moves from the playful unreality of the Amsterdam motor scooter to the sharper reality of what happens when he opens his eyes and the session is over:

"Yes! It feels so damned good. Me. Hello, everybody. Look at me! But what about here? People who . . . admire me . . . I think I've got it! It's the same thing. People who think I'm handsome . . . I am. I know I am. I'm nearly 53, six foot three, muscular and lean. I have thick black hair, and I am good looking. I've always been. And you know what? When I walk down the street, people really do look at me. I am better looking than those movie stars. I am, I am! People look at me. And maybe it's time to acknowledge it. Yes sireee! Walking down the street. With Annie or by myself. I know the girls are looking at me. Only from now on . . . I am going to pose. I grin. I turn my head. I look at the girls. Hello, girls. I am a sight to see, right? A beautiful silk shirt and my jet-black hair, with a sprinkle of gray around the ears. Hello, girls. I look back at you. I even have fun posing. Like this. I turn my head this way . . . You know, I think I am going to be like this . . . I am! I walk along the street. Even older women and men look at me. Hell, I am good looking! So I (There is a happy lilt to his voice, a jolt of excitement.) grin and look at you. This is me now. I know I am handsome. And when Annie and I go to buy a suit . . . Yes! That, too. I am going to go up to people. You think I am good looking? I am! I am! I hope it lasts. Look at me. I'm pretty! I go up to the couple glancing at me in the store when I find a suit and try it on. I should be a model, right? For an older man, I look great, right? I will walk along the street and grin back when people look at me. Men, women, girls. Boys don't admire me much. Girls do. Hello! I nod to you. I accept your admiration. I am pretty!

"How does this feel? Really? I am so excited. I feel it in my face and shoulders. I can't keep my feet still. They are full of energy. Damn! I want to do this . . . And more. I . . . I just thought of something. It's my birthday on Friday. I'll be 53. Annie and I usually go out for dinner to celebrate birthdays. Mine and hers. Quiet. Not a big thing. Well, I just figured out what to do. I am going to work it out with Annie. Here's what I'm going to do: My son's going to come over with his wife, Julie, and we're going to have Gregg and Ellen, our best friends. And Annie's brother and his wife. And here is what it's going to be. Nothing before . . . I will not tell them before. They are at our place. Here goes. I want something special from you. I want you each to tell me how wonderful I am. Just enjoy yourself, and everyone tell me about me. Oh, God, that feels so stale, and my heart's beating hard, and my feet are cold. No . . . Not right. Some other way . . .

"So, I've got to be honest. I am facing you. Look, I love you all, and something is happening to me. I want to see what it's like to be admired. Yeah, I mean it . . . To have you talk about me . . . I want to be the center of attention, even for just a few minutes. So, Lisa, you're Annie's sister. Please take a minute. Just a minute. And tell me something special about me. I want to hear some nice things about me. You don't even have to mean it. My God, this is getting real. You are going to tell me how much you trust me, that you can count on me. I am the one you can trust. Right? That's funny. I already know what you are going to say. I want to hear (He is quiet and serious, saying each word with meaning.) some good things about me. Just sort of honest. Tell me something nice about me. I want to be the admired one, even for just a minute.

"This is really serious . . . I've never done this . . . I like this. Not deadly serious . . . I am feeling my heart beat. Slowly. And my feet are not cold. Is this all right, please? Look, you don't have to. I just want to see what it's like to be a jewel. Tell me what you like about me. Just a little? Can you find something? Wait . . . This is going to feel better . . . I will join you. Here we go. (He is getting more animated now.) Lisa, your turn. I think I am solid, I mean, I am honest. You really can trust me. Do you agree, or not? Yes! And what? Louder. Aha! I am pretty! Yes, I am. I am a good person, not someone who would ever hurt someone else. Yes, I agree. That is a good quality . . . Go ahead, my son. You want to be like me? Yes? But I never knew that . . . And you think Annie and I should have a baby? Yes? All right. Maybe. I would ask Annie except that I am in the limelight. It's about me. ME. The center of attention, me! Oh, I just love this!

"What I am really going to do is nod and grin and acknowledge when people look at me on the street and in stores and at work, like in the elevator. I am pretty! And I'm going to ask people to tell me about me. I can do it. I love this! It's fun! It really is! But I haven't felt like this my whole life, so let me object a little. I am too old to be so . . . self-centered. Naaah. Doesn't do much . . . Better. All my friends like me 'cause I . . . I am always interested in them. That's who I am. I am the solid one. That's why I am a success and everyone trusts me and makes me responsible. I am responsible. It's true. But what the hell. I can't fight this. I should . . . Let's see. Suppose it got out of hand. I can't think of any real drawbacks. I am going to be this way. I think I like me! Yes, I do! Oh, I am such a marvelous person . . . and so handsome, right? Right? Say yes!"

When you started the session, there was an awful scene on your mind. It happened just yesterday. Your husband called to talk to his mother, who had just come in on the plane, and you were horrified to learn that you had mixed up the arrival time. You were still home, planning to pick her up soon, but she had been waiting in the airport for hours already. You forgot to pick her up. Your husband was disgusted with you. The feeling was so bad because you generally feel like an irresponsible idiot. Well meaning, but kind of dumb, irresponsible, can't be trusted. Your husband was attracted at first to that characteristic, but not for the past several years. He looked down on you, trusted the three kids more than you, felt he had to be the grown-up of the family. He often said that he had four children. That hurt so much, because he was right. When you described that painful scene in which he was so disgusted with you on the phone, you were almost crying.

The deeper potential for experiencing was something almost utterly new for you. It was the experiencing of sheer mischievousness, being a wicked devil, impishly malicious, nasty, a troublemaker. When you slipped into fully being this person, you were truly a completely new person. It started in Step 3, in the past, and you continued being this qualitatively new person in the first part of Step 4, where you had raucous and hilarious fun in two unrealistic scenes from the next few days. In one imminent scene, you and your husband are at a formal dinner for a couple who are being honored. The husband is receiving an honorary degree from the local university for his outstanding works and magnanimous contributions, and his wife is getting a prestigious literary award from the government for her latest novel. Your husband instructed you over and over again how to act at the formal dinner and to be quite clear about why the couple was being honored. In playful unreality, you clowned as the whole new person, being raucous and silly at the formal dinner, introducing the couple to the people at the event. In the second scene, you pretended that you had recorded a conversation with your father-in-law, who had, according to your husband, managed to escape from his wife by going to a convention in Florida and staying there. Your mother-in-law, now visiting in your home, had lied for years and years about the circumstances surrounding his leaving. In the imminent scene, you played the recorded conversation in front of your mother-in-law.

When you moved from being this whole new person in playful unreality to actually being this whole new person in reality, the next day, or soon thereafter, you decided to use these two scenes. You continued without a break:

"I am ready! I am. I am. I am going to do both of them. Why not? I am! You know, my voice even sounds different. I like it. Lower. More . . . natural. I like talking like this . . . I know that her novel is about the Norse expeditions to North America. It's about the village the Norse had in North America, long before Columbus. It's the story of people in the village. Ah, yes . . .

"So here I am, being introduced to you by my nervous husband, just the four of us, and I am off. Here I go. Watch me . . . Congratulations, Annabelle! I read your book up to page 167, because I wanted to ask you about the spanner on the boat. You must know the work of Professor Aarnhund of the Free University of Copenhagen, because he was the one who identified the problem in the readings that would account for the Norse boats ending up 200 nautical miles north of their destination. Right? Because the translation of the Dallaire tablets of Greenland, or Vinland as the Norse referred to the region, indicate that the native people on Greenland had already sailed at least 300 nautical miles south of where the village was situated in your book. Am I right? And I also wondered if you know of the carbon-dating system of Kozicki from Poland, and Donnelly from England. They worked together in dating the time of the tools found in Greenland and the village you wrote about, and the differences support your thesis. But you couldn't have known about their most recent findings because they were just reported in the *Hellenic Journal of Archaeology*, probably the most respected journal of its kind. I wonder if we can talk. I brought along a copy of your book, and if we can study page 167 . . . Oh . . . is this really of interest to you?

"And I am slowly turning to my left and looking at my husband's face. He will, of course, pass right out . . . He will be totally blown away. I am so wicked . . . And the worm has turned. Why does this feel so natural? I adore it. I think I have found me. I shall do it. I shall. I don't even have to go to the library. Just rehearse my spiel of complete lies . . .Will I really do this? I REALLY WILL! OH, YES. Hello, everyone. I HAVE BEEN BORN!

"However, I am not completely finished . . . I have a little plan for my mother-in-law. Now, let me see . . . I can . . . ah, yes . . . I am going to invite some friends over to meet good old Sarah. Now, how can I arrange this? Let me think . . . I know . . . Rose! She would be just great. A real practical joker . . . Oh, that doesn't feel right. I'm kind of tight . . . in my stomach. The whole idea. I was going to get Rose to make up a whole story about meeting this old fellow in Florida, Sarah's ex-husband. But that makes me tight. I'm not going to do that. But the other . . . Yes, yes! That feels so good! I am going to do it with the esteemed couple. I am going to do it for me! It is so right. Hey! The tightness is gone. I am so excited. I feel . . . wicked. Like a little devil. My God, I spent my whole life being the wrong person! Walter! Walter, my husband . . . can you deal with me? I mean the *real* me? Let's see. I shouldn't be this way. Right. It will ruin my life. Walter will freak out . . . He will divorce me . . . I will surprise everyone . . . Well, somehow I just feel like I woke up after a whole life . . . And I got my homework . . . But I feel so different! I love this. I love being like this. Good-bye, scared little Susan. I am a new Susan . . . mischievous, a little devil. I feel so . . . natural. This is so different . . . Oh, Walter. Oh, everyone! Enter the new Susan!"

Susan had found where and when and how to be this whole new person after the session. She had even given voice to objections from other parts of her. But what about the initial scene with which she started the session, when her husband called up and revealed her as the irresponsible dummy? This kind of scene happens almost continuously in her life. He thinks of her as a person who can't be counted upon, as just another child in the family, and she feels simply awful. She is continuously defensive, hurt, depressed, scared, and angry in scenes when he is critical of her, in the pauses when he pulls even further from her, in the look on his face and disgust in his voice when he finds, time after time, that she is deserving of his contempt. Susan is ready to explore these kinds of scenes:

"And what about Walter? Oh, you poor guy. What are we going to do? We will have to see. I am going to be me, and who knows? This afternoon, at dinner tonight. I think . . .Well, you're in for a surprise, husband, dear . . . I am ready for a whole new life. With you, maybe. I'll see . . . So, what is going to happen? Here you come . . .You will check around the house like usual, just to see if I did some massive screw-up . . . like forgot to pay the telephone bill or crashed the car or something. I think you'll get a surprise 'cause I am going to walk along with you and tell you, Walter, I smashed the car . . . and backed up into your boss . . . No, just follow you around . . . I feel so different . . . Walter, did you arrange not to go to Chicago in August so we can go to Pauline's wedding? You forget, you know. I will play with you, Walter. You know, it feels so different. And I just wonder. We are either going to have such fun together or . . . Or, Walter, we will see. I think I just became me. Do we fit together? It could be great. I think there are going to be some great changes! Hello, Walter, my man! Watch out! Here I come!"

You have spent some time being this qualitatively whole new person in the qualitatively whole new world. You have even rehearsed what it can be like to be this new person in the new world. Now you are be ready to remain being this whole new person and to actually do what you rehearsed doing. You are ready to do your homework

COMMIT YOURSELF TO REMAIN BEING THE QUALITATIVELY WHOLE NEW PERSON AND TO DO THE HOMEWORK AFTER THE SESSION

In Step 3 you did something that seems almost miraculous. You stepped out of the person you ordinarily were and leapt into being the deeper potential for experiencing, in the context of scenes from your past. From then on, you remained being this qualitatively new person.

And here you are, right now, still being this qualitatively new person. The miraculous shift has continued. Isn't this something?

You have become the deeper potential for experiencing. In other words, the deeper potential for experiencing has become an integral part of you. What had been a deeper part of you, the deeper potential for experiencing, is now an integral part of you. Even more, the other parts of the old you had the chance to talk to the new part, to welcome it, to voice their objections to it. Not only is there a whole new part to you, but the relationships among the parts are likely changed. What all this means is that you have become a qualitatively new person. The addition of the formerly deeper potential for experiencing has made for a qualitatively whole new person.

You Can Remain Being the Qualitatively Whole New Person for a Few Minutes or Forever

In this fourth step, you are being this qualitatively whole new person. The miraculous change has occurred. You have achieved the magnificent goals of an experiential session. That is, you are now the person you are capable of becoming. In addition, if you began the session with a scene of painful feeling, that scene and that painful feeling in that scene are now gone. This is close to a miracle.

How long will it last? It can last for two or five or even ten minutes here in the session. Or, it can last beyond the session so that you remain the qualitatively whole new person when you walk out of the room and into your own personal world. You can be this whole new person for some hours, some days, or even forever. Which will it be? Are you going to revert to the person you were at the beginning of the session? It can happen, and it can happen before the session comes to an end.

If you did a truly fine job throughout the entire session, the conditions are right for you to be the whole new person when you walk out of the room. Do a truly fine job in the session, and you make the conditions better for doing the homework. When you do the homework in a truly fine way, you make the conditions better for remaining this whole new person for the next hours, days, or months. The more you actually be and live as the qualitatively whole new person, after the session and in your personal world, the better you make the conditions for remaining as this whole new person for the next day and the next day and the next day, and maybe forever—or at least until your next session. In other words, you must do your homework.

The Qualitatively Whole New Person Must Leave the Session, Must Live and Be in the New Personal World, and Must Do the Homework

Here is the wonderfully exciting part. When the session ends, you must be the qualitatively whole new person who walks out of the room. You must be the qualitatively whole new person who walks into your whole new personal world. The world you are in is the whole new world of the whole new person. This is the world of the person you are now, not the world of the person who entered the session one or two hours ago. This world is different in so many ways. This world is different because you are different.

As this new person, you feel a kind of rush, a genuine rush, pull, or excited readiness and eagerness to be the whole new person. It occurs as you leave the room and as you live and be in your new personal world. It occurs as you do your homework. You are geared and programmed to carry out your homework. Do it. Do it within a few minutes or a few hours of ending the session.

The homework should be clean, clear, and explicit. You know what you need to do. You have rehearsed it. Therefore, the commitment is to carry out something explicit. It is not a dedication to being nicer to your mother, more understanding to your good friend, more assertive or showing feelings more, buying something for yourself, or starting a new venture. The homework is explicit, not mushy or vague. You leave the session as the whole new person and carry out your homework, which is clear, explicit, and defined.

You may have done a good job rehearsing the homework, but something is quite different when you actually do the homework in the real world out there. Mainly, there is a difference in the sheer experiencing. It is sharper, more vibrant, alive, and real. In-session practice is essential if you are actually going to carry out your homework. However, there is a huge difference between undergoing the new experiencing in the session and in the real world. There is a difference in the actual experiencing.

Experiencing is much better in the real world. Do your homework.

In the session, commit to doing the homework. Say something like: "I am going to do it! I want to do it and will do it! I solemnly swear that I will do my homework! I am ready and willing and eager to do my homework!" Then go ahead and do it.

The Session Is Completed When the Qualitatively New You Completes the Homework

In a very practical sense, the session is truly over, finished, completed when you do the homework. Furthermore, it must be the qualitatively whole new you who carries out the homework. Think of it this way: Step 4 ends when you do the homework.

Here Are Some Examples Of Those Who Did Their Homework After The Session

Kip started the session with a recent scene of strong feeling. The wife of his best friend in adolescence, Sam, called to tell him that Sam had died. Working from that scene, Kip discovered a deeper potential for experiencing the sense of being a helpless baby, cuddled and held, enfolded and cared for. Soon after the session, he carried out the homework he had rehearsed and rehearsed until it felt just right. Alone with his wife, in their living room, he was a quite different person as he told her about the phone call. With watery eyes, in a soft voice, he had the wonderful sense of being a helpless little baby, cuddled and held, enfolded and cared for, as he put his head on Angela's lap and quietly recounted times when he felt so safe with her, so cared for. In the same new state, he remembered and told her about times when he felt this way with his mom and dad, like when they both showed him how to tie the laces on his shoes. During the pauses, he reached up and stroked Angela's face, and he felt so good. It was quiet and peaceful, and the experiencing was so nice, so full. Being this way was new for him, and yet it seemed genuine and natural.

Something else happened the next day at work. The big boss had done an awful thing by writing a press release that created serious trouble for the whole government department. Kip and four or five of his colleagues set up a meeting to decide what to do; in the session, he played with how he could be this whole new person at the meeting. But something happened. When he went to work in the morning, he passed by the boss' office and, unusual for Kip, he went in. Even more unusually, he noticed that his boss seemed pensive, so Kip asked if he was all right. The boss told Kip that he had made a huge error in writing that vindictive, inaccurate press release. Did Kip see it? Kip, as this whole new person, quietly told his boss how scared he felt when he had seen the press release, that he had been so mixed-up because he trusted the boss and wanted him to make sure the department was all right.

"We're like your children . . . well, not really. But we wondered what happened to our 'Dad.' Is it okay to say this?" The boss grinned and seemed vulnerable and childlike as he asked if Kip thought it would be all right if he called in Kip and a few others to see what damage control could be done. Kip had never heard anything like this from the boss. He felt so good saying that the crew would help the boss, would take care of him. This was new territory for Kip. The boss laughed, and the whole atmosphere was warm, close, and good. Kip had done his homework well. He enjoyed living as and being this new person, and it seemed to open up positive changes in Kip' s own personal world.

She is a 69-year-old woman. Her opening scene of strong feeling was when she felt too weak to get up from the chair in her apartment. She slumps back, feeling cheated by her body and depressed about the cancer. The even more powerful scene was when she woke up in the morning; for a few seconds, she has innocent thoughts about whether her son will visit today and if it rained last night. Then the horror strikes: "I am dying of cancer . . ." This is when she has those horrible feelings: depressed, hurt, fatigued, trying to do my best, dying, dying, dying. The deeper potential is the experiencing of sheer mercilessness, relentless evil, being a cold killer.

She rehearsed and rehearsed her homework until she found the precise version that was accompanied by wonderful, bodily-felt sensations. That evening, as this whole new person, she called her friend Howard, the lawyer. Would he come over? He did. When he was in her apartment, she told him about her brother. Kurt was the oldest of four children. The family lived near Würzburg, and

Step 4. Be the Whole New Person in the Post-Session World

Kurt was a young soldier. He would come home on leave, and the whole family would be entranced as Kurt told stories about the camp, how he made the Jews and the Slavs dig trenches, and then he and his comrades would shoot them in the backs of their heads so that they fell into the trenches. She was this whole new person as she told all of this to Howard. She knew that Howard had friends who were Nazi hunters. What should she do to help Howard and his friends do whatever they wanted to Kurt? When she actually carried this out, Howard was impressed with how different she seemed, so much stronger, so tough, so resolved. Was she sure she wanted to go through with this? Yes, she did. Oh, yes.

A few days later, Howard called and told her what to do. She called Kurt and led him to believe she wanted to prepare him for her death. Would Kurt come for a visit? Kurt agreed, took the train, and showed up at her apartment. She was having tea with some friends, two of whom were really Nazi hunters. As she had rehearsed, she then told Kurt about the stories she remembered from Germany, stories about their father and then how everyone loved the stories Kurt told about the camps for Jews and Slavs. Would Kurt tell those stories again? Kurt just stared at her, hard, right in her eyes. He was glaring. The look said that he would not, that she should stop. She held his gaze. She stood her ground, fixed, looking him in the eyes. And she won! Kurt looked away. That is when she went further. She told Kurt that she and the family never mentioned those stories, and how she had acquiesced from then on. She said she hated herself for lying, hiding, pretending. And she almost forced Kurt to listen as she slowly, relentlessly recited the stories Kurt had told the family. The atmosphere was charged. Kurt bolted up out of his chair. "Sit down, Kurt!" He did. Kurt did not say a word.

She continued being this whole new person as she also charged Kurt with what had really happened to his daughter, how he had thrown his daughter down the stairs and the fall broke her back. Yet the family accepted Kurt's lie that she hurt herself while diving in a pool. "We all knew. We pretended. No more, Kurt. It is time to stop the lying, the pretending." She had carried out her homework, and she was being this whole new person.

There is more. The doctors had given her about six months to live after the cancer spread from her lung. Then, miraculously, the doctors told her that the cancer had stopped spreading. There is still more. She sent me a tape of another session, more than a year later. The cancer was gone! Gone! It was gone! I never found out about Kurt, but on the tape she mentioned that she felt like a whole new person, and she sounded so strong, so sure of herself, so tough.

I like to think that her sessions somehow helped free her of the cancer. Even if that was not the case, I believe that her sessions directly helped her accomplish the miraculous feat of becoming the whole new person that she was capable of becoming, finally, after so many years. The main point is that the session is not over until you are successful and effective in carrying out your homework as the qualitatively new person.

Step 4. Be the Whole New Person in the Post-Session World

When Louise began her session, the scene of strong feeling was from when she was a child. She saw her older brother plummet down through the branches of an exceedingly tall tree, and then she heard the thump as his body slammed against the hard ground. He died instantly. Working from this scene, the deeper potential was the experiencing of riskiness, being daring, being adventurous, taking risks. Louise figured that she had been completely insulated against this experiencing throughout her life. She had a touch of this experiencing at times, like when she and Bill started having sex, and when she went to conferences in foreign, exotic cities. But this experiencing was rarely present. The more she looked about, the less she could find this experiencing in her current world, even though she felt that she had not built a life that barricaded her from having such an experiencing.

Louise rehearsed two post-session scenarios for homework, and she was eager to do them both. The morning after the session, she left a message on Joe's telephone. Joe was a solid, responsible fellow at work, and he occasionally kidded her about avoiding the glass elevator in the massive inner courtyard of the building where they worked. The message asked for Joe to go with her on the elevator. Yes, she wanted to try it. Louise had already practiced being this whole new person in muted ways, like skipping her routine breakfast and going out for a special coffee and pastry, and like caressing and stroking herself sexually when she showered. But the delightful fun came when she and Joe took the elevator ride. She was bubbling with the enjoyment of the adventure. She babbled happily as the elevator went up to the top floor and then came down. "This is scary! This is fun! I'm scared of looking down. Joe! Grab my hand!" Others in the elevator kidded her about actually risking the ride, and she was giddy with excitement.

Louise had rehearsed and committed herself to another opportunity to undergo this new-felt experiencing as a whole new person. She was ready for her boyfriend, Bill, to show her how to drive a motorcycle. Bill had one, but she had been fearful of being the passenger on his bike. When she actually sat down with Bill and told him that she wanted to buy a motorcycle and go riding with him, Bill was taken with how different Louise seemed: more excited, playful, adventurous. They decided to try living together, but just for a while, to try it out. The sense of high adventure, of enjoyable risk, came to both as she told him she wanted to drive her own motorcycle and as the two of them, like kids, decided to see what it would be like to live together.

Louise had carried out her homework assignments. She left the session and lived in her new world as this whole new person. But the high points of experiencing came in the glass elevator and being with Bill as they talked about her motorcycle and living together. Do your homework. Be the whole new person in doing your homework.

What happened with the woman whose mother visited from Jamaica with her new boyfriend? The deeper potential was the experiencing of tenderness, lovingness, gentleness, softness, and her homework was to remain being this person alone with her mother, caressing her mother's face, and telling her mother little things about her life. Her mother was 17 years old when she delivered her baby in Canada, and soon afterward she returned home to Jamaica, leaving her daughter with the baby's father in Canada. The daughter corresponded with her mother, and her mother occasionally came to visit. She felt all right with her mother. There was no strong bitterness, and she talked with her mother about what it meant to her to have her mother leave her in Canada, to have given up her baby and returned to Jamaica.

This woman was not cold and distant, without friends, austere and aloof. However, when the deeper potential emerged from the dream, she acknowledged that there was little or no sense of genuine tenderness, lovingness, gentleness, softness in her present world. She was a lawyer who had friends, especially her close friend, Lisa, and she loved her dog, Max. She knew some men and had lived with a fellow for some months. However, she rarely felt a strong sense of softness, gentleness, lovingness, tenderness.

The day after the session, her mother arrived at her apartment with the man she wanted to marry. When they sat down, it was clear that her mother was shy, a little scared, and wanted her to come down to Jamaica for the wedding. From the time her mother arrived, she was this new person. When she held her mother's hands and looked deep into her eyes, there was a sense of lovingness, gentleness, softness. She merely grinned. She felt so different.

Her mother stole the show. For the first time, her mother started crying, quiet, peaceful, pleasant crying. Enfolding her mother in her arms, she rocked her mother, who just grasped her closer and closer. Her mother softly cried for a long time, and the sense of loving tenderness just seemed to glow quietly. When her mother stopped crying, she touched and caressed her daughter's face, talking nonstop about her whole life. Not bitterly or explaining herself, just in a slow outpouring of a contained caring, loving, softness, and gentleness toward her daughter. She did her daughter's homework far better than her daughter!

Judging from how the daughter began her next session, something quietly dramatic happened at work. She began the session by reciting all the little ways that people at work seemed to be becoming friends. More smiling. More light touching of her. Colleagues came into her office much more often, just to talk. The new young lawyer said outright, "You're nice to be with," and she seemed so comfortable smiling. She truly felt as if a veil had been lifted, and there was a muted, welcome, quiet, wonderful new sense of gentleness, lovingness, softness, and tenderness in her and with the people and things of her world. There was a change.

Do your homework. Be the whole new person who does the homework.

This older fellow began the session with scenes of strong feeling that occurred in a recent dream. In earlier sessions, he started with actual scenes from his real world, scenes that were filled with painful feelings. This time, he started with a dream, which yielded a deeper potential for experiencing something rather surprising to him, namely, a sense of being the jewel, being precious, being admired, on display. The homework assignment he set for himself was for a few days hence, at his birthday party. To celebrate turning 53, he and Annie invited some close friends, his son and his wife, Annie's sister and brother and their spouses. He had rehearsed deliberately asking these people to say a nice thing or two about him, even if they had to make it up. He would soak all of this up, being the center of attention. It would be fun, although the atmosphere would be a little contrived, of course.

After the session, he found himself posing in the full-length mirror. "Hey, Annie, look at this. Don't I have a great body? Just look!" Annie grins: "Well, you do have a great ass, and hair that some women would die for . . . and, well, you aren't fat. But how come you're posing?" He lies down on the bed, patting his full and wavy hair, and tells her what he would like to do at the birthday party. Annie kids him about getting old, but she thoroughly enjoys the idea, and they carry it out together.

At the party, he explains that he wants each of them to tell him something flattering about himself, while he basks in the limelight. The idea catches on, especially when Annie says she will start, kneels behind him, and drops bright red cherries into his mouth as he reclines on the couch. He asks his son to time her, because she will probably exhaust what she can say after about 30 seconds or so. Each person does say a few things in the appropriate way. The atmosphere remains light and kind of exciting; he laps it all up, posing and fawning on himself, playfully agreeing with each remark. The people are laughing, interrupting one another, telling stories about how wonderful he was and is. His son gets a little mushy as he tells what a great father he was: "I mean it, Dad. I really loved you and wanted to be like you. I even tried to imitate that big laugh of yours!" One of his friends said, "You know, you surprised us, 'cause you never were the kind of guy who wanted to be center stage. But this is a great idea. You deserve this. We were kidding, sort of, but we don't usually tell people nice things about themselves, do we? This was funny, but I must say, I like this idea . . ."

This scene was new for him, and the experiencing was also new for him. His life was not dramatically altered, but he was a new person in subtle and substantial ways. He did experience, here and there, in fitting and appropriate ways, a new sense of being a jewel, being precious, being admired, being the center of attention. Once again, the point is that you really should be the whole new person in carrying out the homework you selected, rehearsed, refined, and rehearsed until it felt proper and fitting.

When Susan finished her session, she was a different person. She even seemed to have a different look on her face. She walked out of the room as the living, breathing new person with a whole new part to her, a potentiality for experiencing a sense of mischievousness, a delightfully wicked devil, being a little malicious, feisty, a troublemaker. This was a spanking new element in who she was. Susan opened the session with the painful scene in which her husband called to talk to his mother, whom Susan was supposed to have picked up at the airport. Susan had not yet gone to the airport because she believed that her mother-in-law was to arrive a few hours later; in actuality, her mother-in-law's plane had arrived a few hours earlier. The painful feeling, one that Susan knew all too well, was being looked down upon by her husband, being dumb, irresponsible. She had even begun to believe that her three children were more mature and trustworthy than her. The feeling was all too familiar, and quite painful.

When her husband came home that evening, he met the new Susan. The highlight of the evening was when she rehearsed with two of her children what she was going to do at the formal dinner for the couple who was going to be honored, he by the university for his magnanimous contributions, and she by receiving the prestigious award for her novel. Susan was going to participate by making up a story about the Norse village in North America, which the wife had written about. Susan's son and daughter pretended they were the couple at the formal dinner, and Susan played by telling the daughter all about her "research" about the Norse village. Everyone in the family had great fun, and the husband laughed. He loved it. So did Susan's mother-in-law, who was visiting and whom Susan had managed to pick up at the airport, drenched in apology.

As it turned out, the husband and wife team did not arrive for the formal dinner party because the husband broke his leg in an accident that day. Susan could not carry out that part of her homework. Maybe playing out her speech to the wife with the family at home was sufficient. At any rate,

Susan was a different person. About a year later, I received another audiotape of Susan's sessions. She had been having her own sessions approximately every two or three weeks, and in the beginning of this session it was clear that her husband had left. They were still friends and still legally married, but Susan was living with the three children, and her husband was living elsewhere. In becoming the new person, Susan had apparently left behind that chunk of her personality involving the experiencing of being the one who was looked down upon, dumb, irresponsible, untrustworthy, as well as the external world that supported such painful experiencing. Mainly, that external world was her husband. There was no further need for the role of someone who was disgusted with her and frustrated and annoyed by her stupid irresponsibility. She and her husband were still friends, but she was a different person now.

There are two morals here. First, make sure that the new you does your homework. Second, you may well let go of some "chunks" in both your personality and the world, chunks that provide for and support the former who and what you have been. Becoming a qualitatively whole new person may well mean changes in your own personal world. Sometimes these changes are little ones, and sometimes they are big ones.

IN STEP 4, YOU BECAME THE PERSON YOU CAN BECOME

Here is a bird's-eye view, a simple summary, of what you did in Step 4. When you entered Step 4, you were already the qualitatively new person, but in the context of scenes from the past. In Step 4, you found scenes from the next few days or so and then simply had fun being the whole new person in those scenes. The context was sheer, playful unreality, silly fantasy. Then you changed the context to one that was more realistic, and tried out, rehearsed, modified, and rehearsed again what it could be like to be this whole new person in real scenes from the new, imminent world of the new person whom you are. The session really and truly ended when you actually carried out your homework.

Because you started the session with a scene of strong feeling, you could probe into that scene and discover a deeper potential for experiencing. In Step 4, you were able to be the whole new person you are capable of becoming, with that deeper potential for experiencing now an integral part of the whole new person you became. You became the qualitatively whole new person, whether it happened for just a few minutes during Step 4, whether it occurred as the new you doing the homework after the session, or whether the qualitatively new you is here from now on, in lots of scenes in your new personal world.

If you began the session with a painful scene of painful feelings, in Step 4 the qualitatively new person is essentially free of that painful scene and the painful feelings in the scene. The painful scene is no longer a part of the new person's world. Neither the painful scene nor the painful feelings are any longer a part of the qualitatively new person.

In a way, Step 4 is rather simple. It is also exciting and fun. And, it is slightly miraculous.

p. 396
blank

9

How Can You Get Better and Better At Having Your Own Experiential Sessions?

There are three times when this chapter will really talk to you. One is when you have finished reading Chapter 8 and you are thinking about having a session, or at least starting to have a session. The second time is when you have tried having a session or two, and you are ready to keep getting better and better. The third time is when you are already fairly good at having your own experiential sessions.

HERE ARE SOME HELPFUL GUIDELINES
TO GET READY TO LEARN
HOW TO HAVE YOUR OWN SESSIONS

Here are some guidelines that can make it easier for you to learn how to get better and better at having your own sessions.

It Usually Takes Some Time, Some Learning, Before You Can Go Through A Session Reasonably Well

I have known a few people who read Chapters 5 through 8 and then recorded a session that was fairly good. The ideas and methods of each of the four steps made sense, and these people then went ahead and had a session. They could do it. That happens, but rarely.

For most people, it takes some time before they are able to have a session that gets through the four steps. It seems to take practice, learning, and training. The purpose of this chapter is to show you ways to practice, learn, and train so that you can at least become good enough to have a complete session that goes through the four steps reasonably well.

If you learn reasonably well and you are geared to practice and learn, you can likely go through a complete session after about 10 to 20 hours of good practice. This chapter can show you how to practice, how to use these 10 to 20 hours well. If you study this book and practice by yourself, those hours will usually be enough for you to be able to complete a session. If you take advantage of the other ways of practicing described in this chapter, you can almost be assured that those hours of practice will be sufficient for you to be able to get through a session.

By 10 to 20 hours of practice, I mean 10 to 20 hours of studying, actual training, skill learning, and doing what this chapter says you need to do in order to have a good session. I do not mean 10 to 20 attempts at having an experiential session.

For many people, it is discouraging to face so many hours of serious learning, practice, and training just to be able to have a minimally adequate session. But being able to complete a whole session—and undergoing a radical transformation— takes more than just getting the general idea and then going ahead and doing it. It is not likely that half an hour or so of being told the general idea would be good enough for you to successfully pilot a passenger airplane from takeoff to landing, or play a piano concerto, or solve a problem in theoretical calculus. It does take time to learn and acquire the various skills required to go through a whole session reasonably well.

Once You Are Able To Go Through A Whole Session, You Can Keep Getting Better and Better

The first accomplishment is to get through an entire session, all four steps. You have to get through each of the steps well enough to progress to the next step. That is a fine accomplishment. Then the work begins.

You need to study. Think of yourself as a beginner who is barely able to go through the four steps. From now on, you are to dedicate yourself to getting better and better. This means that you are to learn more and more skills, and to become more and more proficient at the skills you learn. Think in terms of years of learning to be better and better.

It's Okay To Learn Little By Little, Step By Step; That Is Fine

There is a good reason to use the "little by little" way of learning how to have an experiential session: Each part depends on doing the previous part rather well. This is not a rule or law, but it usually makes sense in the context of having an experiential session. In fact, some people prefer learning this way. For example, it is easier to learn to play the piano by starting with the basics and moving on, at least for many people.

If this is the way you prefer to learn, you will be inclined to start at the beginning, that is, learning how to do the "warm-up," getting yourself ready to have strong feelings. Try this until you are able to do this fairly well. Then, try finding a scene of strong feeling. Here you may try using two or more ways of finding a scene of strong feeling. You may go over these a few times. All of this may comprise your first session. You want to get fairly good at the first few skills before tackling the next things to do.

In the next practice session, start with the warm-up, find a scene of strong feeling, and then fully live and be in this scene, going on to discover the precise moment of strong feeling. This is all you do in the practice session until you become reasonably skilled at getting this far into the first step. The spirit is one of learning little by little.

It's Okay To Learn By Trying To Go Through
The Whole Session As Well As You Can

Some people prefer learning by just throwing themselves into doing it. They read this book carefully and then go ahead and proceed through a whole session. They may record the session and then study the session to get better.

As a result, the next time they have a session, they manage to get through it a little better or perhaps even much better. They learn, not bit by bit, but rather by throwing themselves into trying to have a whole session each time.

These are the people who are inclined, for example, to watch others play tennis for a while before eagerly getting onto the court and just doing the best they can. In a way, this style of learning can be harder, because getting through an experiential session means that each part depends on doing the previous part adequately. It is hard to do Step 2 until you accomplish Step 1. Nevertheless, some people are geared to learn by just ploughing through an experiential session as best as they can, and then studying their performance so that each session gets better and better.

You Can Learn By Yourself Or With A Companion Or A Teacher

Or, you can combine all three. You can learn by yourself, with a companion, or with a teacher. A great deal depends on your own personal style and preference at the time.

I find that it is quite sensible and effective to study by yourself. I also find that a potent combination is learning by yourself and also working with a teacher, either in a tutorial or personal coaching sense, one-on-one, or in a small group or class.

Learning with a companion also works well, especially if you follow a few guidelines. One, your companion is a fellow learner. Two, your companion is not in the room when you have your own personal sessions. You may go over tapes of your session together, but you do the sessions by yourself alone. Three, you don't live with your companion or interact much with your companion in your daily living. Your companion should be free of having even the slightest involvement in the changes you undergo, the person you become, and the homework you carry out. The two of you should trust and help one another, but outside the session, your lives should not cross. Four, the two of you should take turns concentrating on studying your performance and then studying your companion's performance.

About The Only Special Characteristic Of Good Learners Is An Eagerness To Have Their Own Experiential Sessions

You have had a thorough introduction to what experiential sessions are and how to go through an experiential session. Are you eager? Are you passionately enthusiastic? If you are, that is about the only special characteristic I have found in people who are good learners. I am talking about ordinary good learners. There are always a few rare people who somehow read this manual and then have surprisingly proficient sessions.

People tend to think that other special characteristics are necessary. They seem to be important. They look important. But they are not important. For example, you do not have to be especially smart. You don't have to be inner directed, inclined to probe inside, to reflect about your insides and your personality. You do not need to have had experience looking inside, such as years of meditation, self-study, dream analysis, or examination of your own personal history. You do not need to be good at "mental imagery," or seeing things. You do not have to be in especially good shape and well put together. On the other hand, you do not need to be prone to bouts of craziness or horribly bad feelings. You do not have to be especially comfortable with emotions, with having a strong feeling. About all you really need is a passionate enthusiasm for having your own experiential sessions. That is all.

You Need A Room Where You Can Make Plenty Of Noise

When you have a session, you make a lot of noise. The noise level will probably be rather high throughout the session, and every so often there should be punctuated outbursts of extremely loud noise. You need a room where you can make plenty of noise without having any worries, and without muting the noise level because some part of you is thinking, "I hope they can't hear me!" It helps if your room is soundproofed. It helps if no one can hear you screaming, shrieking, yelling, and roaring.

It also helps if you cannot hear any noises from outside the room. Do your best to ensure that no one will knock on the door and intrude. You should not be able to hear telephones or doorbells. You should have a big chair in which you can recline with your feet up or on a large footrest. Or a comfortable bed to lie on. Your eyes should be closed throughout the whole session. Some people put something over their eyes so they cannot see. Make sure you have a tape recorder.

It is easy to talk about a proper room, but it is hard to have one handy. I have a soundproofed office in my home. Some people have access to a special room in a church, a hospital, a clinic, or an office building that they can use, especially when other people are not nearby. Some people use an isolated cabin or small house far away from neighbors. One woman told me that she called the local sheriff and two of her neighbors who lived more than a half-mile away just to let them know that she was going to have a session early in the afternoon. After the session, she found that a small bear always loitered outside her cabin when she had finished her session. So, in addition to warning her sheriff and neighbors, she put up a large sign on her cabin door! Although this practical matter is sometimes hard to arrange, you must use a room where you can make plenty of noise without being interrupted or worrying about someone hearing you.

HERE ARE THE WAYS TO LEARN AND TO GET BETTER AND BETTER

These are the guidelines I suggest you follow in learning how to have a successful and effective session, and to keep getting better and better from then on. Use each of the following ways, bearing two exceptions in mind: it can be helpful, but it is not necessary, for you to have sessions with an experiential psychotherapist-teacher, and/or for you to study the tapes of an experiential teacher's own experiential sessions.

404

Rely On And Use This Book As A Study And Training Guide

Once you have read this book, especially Chapters 5 through 8, try having your own session. Make sure that you record your session. You may spend only 10 to 20 minutes to start a session, or you may try to go through all four steps of the session. In any case, when you are done, use this book to help you find the first place, or stumbling block, where you did it wrong or could have done it better. For example, if you did the warm-up just fine, but had trouble finding a scene of strong feeling, reread that part of Chapter 5 to identify what you did not do, what you did wrong, or what you might have done much better.

This book can serve as your trusty study and training guide. Use it as a manual when you study the recordings of your session. Try to find the first big mistake you made in the session, the first place where you did it poorly, the place where you had to stop. Then, study the part of the manual that tells you how to do it well. In this way, the book can help you learn to have your own session. Make sure that you start with the beginning of the session and identify the first time you made a big mistake, the first time you went off track, the first time you departed from what you should do; then, return to this book and study what you could and should have done properly.

Once you are able to have a full session, use this book to help you get better and better. If, in Step 3, you are struggling to find earlier scenes in your life, Chapter 7 can help you use other ways of finding these earlier scenes and becoming more and more skilled at finding these earlier scenes.

You can rely on this book to help you learn to go through a session acceptably or even rather well and, from then on, to help you get better and better.

Have Some Actual Sessions With An Experiential Psychotherapist-Teacher

Experiential psychotherapists almost always serve as teachers because they show you what to do while going through the session. An experiential psychotherapist coaches and guides you, telling you what to do next and how to do it. You are the one who does the actual work in going through the session. You may have some experiential sessions with a psychotherapist-teacher as you start to learn how to have your own sessions, or you can have a session with a teacher every so often as you are learning.

If you just keep having sessions with an experiential psychotherapist-teacher, I doubt if you will be able to have your own experiential sessions. Even though the experiential psychotherapist-teacher shows you what to do, and you do the work, I have found that these sessions are not enough to prepare you to have your own sessions. They help, but they are not enough on their own. However, there are a few things you can do to best use these sessions in learning how to have your own sessions. Here are two helpful ways to use these sessions of experiential psychotherapy.

Record and study the sessions. This is what I do with people who want to learn how to have their own sessions by first having some sessions with me. I suggest to them that they bring a tape recorder and record the sessions. You can make such arrangements with your own experiential psychotherapist-teacher.

You can then study the recorded session. You can study the session by yourself, with a fellow learner, or with your teacher.

The psychotherapist-teacher gives you more and more responsibility in going through the session. When I am the psychotherapist-teacher, I invite the person to take more and more responsibility during the session. For example, when we are in our chairs with eyes closed, I may start by saying: "The first thing to do is free yourself of controls. Do the warm-up." I then show the person how to do this or, if the person is ready to try on his or her own, the person goes ahead and does it. Then I may say, "Now, find a scene of strong feeling." Again, if the person knows how to do this, the person does it. If not, I show the person how to find a scene of strong feeling. This is how I proceed throughout the session.

The idea is for you to gradually take on more and more responsibility for knowing how to progress through the session. In other words, the psychotherapist-teacher gradually gives fewer and fewer instructions as you gradually learn what to do next. The teacher's job is to give you more and more responsibility, and your job is to accept more and more responsibility.

It is interesting that the script of a session remains essentially the same over the subsequent sessions. However, the words increasingly come more and more from you, and less and less from the psychotherapist-teacher. For example, in the initial sessions it is likely to be the psychotherapist-teacher who says, "Now the thing is to find a scene of strong feeling." Later, you are the one who says, "Now the thing is to find a scene of strong feeling." In other words, the psychotherapist-teacher gradually recedes from the role of instruction-giver, and you increasingly take on the role of instruction-giver.

Even as the teacher says words and gives instructions, your attention should be out there, on the scene, and not on the teacher who is giving the instructions. The same holds true for the teacher. That is, even when the teacher says, "Now the thing is to find a scene of strong feeling," the teacher's attention is mainly out there, on the scene, and not on you. In other words, even as the teacher gives instructions, you and the teacher are mainly attending to the scene, not to one another. There is to be little or no conversation directly between the two of you; you and the teacher do not stop the session to attend to one another and have a conversation.

Study Tapes Of A Teacher's Own Experiential Sessions

If you are studying with a teacher, ask if you may listen to an audiotape of the teacher's own experiential sessions. Many people find it helpful to study these tapes. I have audiotapes of two sessions of my own. One began with a recent dream. The other starts with a scene of strong feeling that happened a few days before my own experiential session.

I use these two recorded sessions as teaching devices by interspersing some commentary on what is going to happen next so that people who listen to the tape can hear an actual session and learn about each step and sub-step.*

Study Tapes Of Your Own Sessions

This is essential. It seems to be the best way to learn and get better and better. When you are just beginning, try to study tapes of each session, whether the session was a complete one or you merely began to have one, whether you thought the session was all right or you knew it was a rotten trial. Later on, when you can actually get through a whole session, and as you aim toward getting better and better, study your tape once a month or so.

Go ahead and take the plunge. Make sure that your session is recorded, and then go ahead and have a session: your 1st, your 2nd, your 20th. You may just do the warm-up, in which you unwrap the usual controls and free your body of the typical numbness or state of mild feeling. That is all. You stop. It takes only a few minutes, and you have your first recorded session. Or, take a deep breath and plunge into a session, riding through Steps 1 through 4, perhaps even jumping over a step here and there. It may be a terrible session or a wonderful one, but you did a session and

---

*If you are interested in getting these two audiotapes, please write to me at School of Psychology, University of Ottawa, Ottawa, Canada KlN 6N5.

recorded it. Or, perhaps you look at the summary in Chapter 2, and then you begin. Then, still in Step 1, you open your eyes, check the summary, perhaps even read the relevant parts of Chapter 5, close your eyes, and continue with the session, stopping and starting a number of times.

All of this is fine. Just start a session or have a whole session. Make sure that you record it. That is the key.

Something special seems to happen when you have these first sessions. I have heard so many of these initial sessions, or I have heard from so many people who have had these initial sessions, that I can almost predict what their reactions will be when they finish or study these sessions.
Here are a few representative examples:

After just completing the warm-up, a woman in her late 60s said: "I never made noises like that . . . After a little bit, I stopped being so aware of how I was doing. Didn't think of it, of me . . . It felt so freeing. I just spent five minutes doing this exercise, and when I listened, it sounded so sexual. I was laughing. That's all I did! It seemed to free me up. I had never done anything like that. I like it."

A fellow in his late 20s told me, before we listened to the tape of his first attempt: "I didn't know what to expect. I cried. The funny thing is, I don't cry. That surprised me. I just started crying. It felt nice. I guess it hurt, but it was nice."

A woman in her 30s e-mailed me about trying to go through a whole session: "I know I didn't do it well, but when I thought I found something deeper and looked back over my life, it surprised me. I really felt that I had never felt anything like that, I mean feeling so close to anyone,

410

someone, feeling together. Not sexually, just accomplishing something with another person, together, the two of us. My whole life seemed like I had missed that. I was in analysis for three years. This was different. I think I'm still surprised."

In a way, these are testimonials. Yet they are so typical of what many people seem to think and feel after their first session or two. In any case, go ahead and try having a session, and make sure that you record it, no matter how long or short it is, no matter how well or how poorly you may have done.

Study your tape by yourself or with one or more companions. You can study your tape by yourself or with one or more trusty companions. Or, you can study your tape by yourself and also hold occasional study meetings with one or more companions who are also learning to have their own experiential sessions.

If you study with one or more companions, it is helpful to meet regularly, every month or so, to listen to each other's taped sessions. However, the most effective way is to go over your sessions by yourself, whether or not you also meet with a companion or two every so often.

Listen to the tape until you find the first place that needs improvement, the first place you did not do well. Keep handy the page in Chapter 2 that summarizes how to proceed through an experiential session. Read the part of this book that tells you how to do it well. This is an important and effective way to learn by yourself or with a companion. You are using this book the way it was meant to be used.

Study your tapes with a teacher. You may have private sessions with a teacher, sessions in which the two of you study tapes of your sessions. Or, you may meet in a small group of five to ten people, all of whom are studying tapes of their sessions. You may have sessions in a concentrated, set time frame, such as three to five days in a row, with just a teacher and you or as part of a small group. Or, you may have sessions every so often, such as every month or so.

As a teacher, I truly look forward to studying tapes with a person, either just the two of us or in a small group. I generally try to determine if the person is doing well enough to move on to the next sub-step. If so, I like to make some helpful suggestions for doing that sub-step even better. I listen for times when a person seems to miss or to skip a sub-step, or when the person seems to do a sub-step poorly.

You can progress by studying your taped sessions by yourself or with one or more companions. However, I hope that, every so often, you also study your taped session with a teacher, even if this happens only once or twice a year.

Concentrate On The First Thing That You Did Not Do Well

When you have an audiotape of your session, start from the beginning and find the first place where you did not do well enough to move on. Look for the first big mistake. Usually, this is something that you just ignored doing or did so poorly that you could not move on to the next sub-step.

Here are some common examples: You started, but you did not begin with a warm-up, or the warm-up consisted of only a few mild inhalings and exhalings. You found a scene, but it was a scene of mild feeling, or it was not a scene at all, but rather a general grouping of events: "I have trouble listening when I'm in a group and lots of people are talking. I feel bad when I am in a bad mood and don't sleep well . . ." You find a scene, but then you skip actually living and being in that scene. Most of the places you find are obvious and conspicuous. If you use the sheet in Chapter 2 that lists the steps and sub-steps of the experiential session, just look for the first place you skipped or did so poorly that you could not move on to the next thing to do.

First, find the first thing that you did not do well enough to move on. Then, study how to do it well enough to move on. If you are studying by yourself, look it up in this book. Look at Chapter 5, for example, for what you should have done. If you are studying with a teacher, the teacher will usually spot the first mistake and instruct you how to do it better.

When you have your own session, you may like going through the session bit by bit, step by step, sub-step by sub-step, until you can get through an entire session. Or, you may prefer a style in which you simply plunge through the entire session, whether you did each part well or poorly. In either case, studying and learning means identifying the first thing that you did so poorly that it needs work.

Each sub-step can be done better and better. Even when you are skilled enough to go through your own sessions, there are sub-steps that can be done better. This is why learning can continue for years as you do experiential sessions. However, in the beginning, your aim is to be able to get through all four steps, to have a complete experiential session. This means that you look for the first obvious and conspicuous error, mistake, or omission. Then, you find out what you should have done—not to be a virtuoso performer, but merely to be able to do it well enough to move on.

What are some of the more difficult skills to learn? Some of the skills are rather difficult. Please read those parts of Chapters 5 through 8 carefully and then practice doing them until you can do them well. One skill is difficult, not to master, but rather to keep up during the session. That is the skill of staying at a relatively high level of feeling, beyond your ordinary level of speaking and feeling. Talk with relatively strong feeling throughout the whole session. What is common, and needs to be fixed, is dropping to a low level of feeling and even having periods of silence. Throughout the session, the feeling level is to be high, unnaturally high, and there are to be no silences. Keep making sounds throughout the session.

Another common problem is talking about a scene of strong feeling instead of actually living and being in it. It is important to learn how to bring the scene to life, to literally live and be in the scene, and not to remain removed from the scene, talking about it.

One of the most difficult skills is locating the instant of peak feeling and knowing how to find the deeper potential for experiencing. Finding and living in the instant of peak feeling is hard enough, but it takes true study and learning—and a fair amount of concentrated practice—to be able to discover the deeper potential for experiencing. Carefully read this part of Chapter 5. Take time to understand the various ways of discovering the deeper potential for experiencing. When you practice, make sure that you spend plenty of time becoming proficient in each of these methods. Of all the skills in an experiential session, learning how to be in the instant of peak feeling and to discover the deeper potential for experiencing is probably the most unusual and difficult skill to master.

Another demanding skill is remaining the qualitatively new person once you undergo the radical switch in Step 3. From the moment you leap into being the qualitatively new person, you must remain being this new person throughout Steps 3 and 4. Do not return to being the old person.

The final skill that tends to be difficult to learn is how to play, how to engage in silly and playful unreality in the first phase of Step 4. It is common for people to move into Step 4 by skipping this first phase, choosing, instead, to consider where, when, and how to be this whole new person in the forthcoming, real world. Before you move into this second phase, this more realistic phase, it is critical to go through the first phase of playful unreality. Even if you do go through this first phase well, take time to learn how to be the whole new person in playful unreality. It is important to acquire the skill of living and being in the imminent, new, post-session world in a context of fantasy, outrageous silliness, and playful unreality.

These are some of the skills that people commonly skip, or must take extra time to learn, or that seem difficult to learn.

Practice The Skill Until You Can Do It Fairly Well

Being able to have an experiential session, to go through all four steps, means practicing some of the skills. It is the rare person who can have a session by just reading and carefully studying this book. You must practice the skills that you are not particularly good at. Learning means practicing. It means skill development. It is much more than merely "getting the idea" and then doing it. Reading and studying to get the idea help. However, you should expect that much of your work, especially until you get good enough to have a full session, involves practice: simple, repetitive, skill-developing practice.

You may practice by yourself. Even if the training session takes merely 5 to 15 minutes, it takes time to practice the skills you want to learn. You may practice that skill with one or more companions. If you study with a teacher, a fair amount of the actual session time may be spent on simple practice.

Suppose that you have trouble finding a scene of strong feeling at the beginning of Step 1. Or, suppose that you have had a number of sessions, but you always use the same way of finding a beginning scene of strong feeling. Look at the list of questions in Chapter 5 to help find a scene of strong feeling. First, you learn that, for example, it is helpful to start with a scene of strong feeling followed by looking for some time when that feeling was much stronger. Or, you see that you have neglected to start with scenes of strong feelings in dreams. Or, you have used only scenes of bad feelings and ignored scenes of good, pleasant, happy feelings.

Practicing can consist of taking each question and using it to find a scene of strong feeling. Go down the whole list. Actually try it out. Then, listen to the audiotape to see if you did it well enough. Or, go down the list, pick out one question that you did not use to find a scene of strong feeling, and use that question. Practice it. Listen to your recording. The key is practicing, doing it over and over until you can do it well enough to move on. I find that the people who learn how to have their own sessions spend some time each month in simple practice. They actually determine what they need to practice, and then go ahead and practice that skill. Unfortunately, too many of the people who cannot have their own sessions spend no time at all in simple practice. They have some sessions, but they do not practice skills to become good enough in the necessary skills. The key is practice. The key is critical.

Suppose you came to a point in the session where you found a scene of strong feeling, but you noticed that you had trouble living and being in that scene. Read about that sub-step in the book. Then practice it. You know the actual scene. Practice. It helps to record yourself practicing and to listen to the tape. Then try it again. Keep practicing until you are able to do it fairly well.

This chapter aims to show you how to get better and better at having your own experiential sessions. If there is a special way of accomplishing this, the answer is to use this book as a study and training guide and to practice, practice, practice. I still practice the skills every so often, doing a skill over and over to keep improving my skill level. Skill-developing practice is essential in the beginning, and remains helpful from then on.

WHEN YOU ARE GOOD AT HAVING YOUR OWN SESSIONS, ARE YOU INTERESTED IN BECOMING A TEACHER?

As you become better and better at having your own sessions, a time will come when you are good enough to teach others. Imagine showing a few acquaintances or fellow "practitioners" how to have their own sessions or how to get better. Or, picture a more formal arrangement in which you present yourself as a teacher to others who accept the role of students. They may even pay you. Are you interested in becoming a teacher? When you become good at having your own experiential sessions, you may—or may not—find yourself interested.

There Are Some Qualities Of A Good Teacher

Perhaps the most common quality of a good teacher, and the one that is most important, is to have a pool of excitement about teaching. The good teacher loves teaching. It is as simple as that. If you are destined to become a teacher, you probably learned from a good teacher, rather than all by yourself. You probably learned how to be good enough to have a session by studying and learning with a companion or two. You probably told friends and acquaintances about experiential sessions and offered to show them how to do it. When you became quite proficient at having your own sessions, you almost naturally found yourself teaching. If you are enthusiastic about teaching, go ahead and teach others how to have their own sessions.

The good teacher is a good role model. You have your own sessions fairly regularly, and you are quite proficient at having them. Furthermore, you keep on learning. You keep practicing the skills to become better and better, with more and more skills.

Some good teachers find themselves wanting to read more, to study more. They study *Experiencing: A Humanistic Theory Of Psychology and Psychiatry*. They study *Dream Work In Psychotherapy And Self-Change*. They study *The Complete Guide To Experiential Psychotherapy*. This is not characteristic of all good teachers, but it is characteristic of some.

Most good teachers become teachers when they are truly masters at having their own sessions. Achieving the status of a master practitioner does not mean that you will be a good teacher, but most good teachers have achieved that status.

For Now, A Teacher Is A Fellow Practitioner Who Teaches; There Is No Badge, License, Certification, Or Accreditation

It is only in the past five years or so that I have clearly understood what experiential sessions can be and how to have one's own sessions. I am hopeful that others can continue learning and teaching others how to make experiential sessions better and better. I am thankful that some people are not only good at having their own sessions, but are also inclined to teach others.

For now, teachers teach because they are drawn toward teaching, they seem good at teaching, and people seem to profit from what they teach. All of this seems fitting and sensible for now.

For now, the teacher has no special robes, elevated chair, diploma, license, certificate, or accreditation. The teacher need not have gone through training with me, or with someone whom I trained. There are no special training programs at universities or institutes. There is no formal body that approves of you as a teacher. There are only people learning how to have their own sessions and helping one another by taking on the role of teacher.

WHAT ARE SOME FOND HOPES FOR WHAT WILL BECOME OF HAVING YOUR OWN EXPERIENTIAL SESSIONS?

I have spent about 45 years trying to carve out experiential sessions, what goals they can actually achieve, and the means and methods for achieving them. Now, I have some fond hopes for what might become of having your own experiential sessions. This is where you come in. I can have fond hopes, but it is more up to you than to me to make these fond hopes actually come about.

At Least One Percent Of People Will Have Their Own Experiential Sessions

I know that I am being grandiose, but nevertheless, I have this picture of at least one percent of people across the world having their own experiential sessions, having them regularly, and having them throughout their lives.

This hope is so strong in me that I am embarrassed. On the one hand, I want to tell virtually everyone I see: "Read this book. Please. For your own good, for my good, and for our good, please read this book." Sometimes I want to tell everyone, "Just read this book!" I want to say this to the taxi driver, to all my colleagues, to people who live in my neighborhood, to people who pass me on the street, to the person I am talking to about a movie, or a leaky faucet, or how I feel, or their younger sister. "Please, read this book!" I really want everyone to read this book and have their own experiential sessions. When I am a little more serious, I do hope that at least one percent of all people will have their own sessions.

Yes, I am embarrassed. There is a part of me that says that one percent of people in the world do not do anything to attain what experiential goals try to attain. One percent of people do not even say serious prayers or do serious meditation regularly. That part warns me against trying to get others to do something just because I think it is good for them. That part laughs at me as a terrible public relations specialist or salesman or marketing expert. I listen to that part of me that makes some sense. Nevertheless, I still have a fond hope that at least one percent of people will have their own experiential sessions. Maybe even five percent.

Experiential Sessions Will Keep Getting Better And Better

Experiential sessions are made up of the two rather specific goals or aims for each session, the four steps in each session, and the specific means and methods of achieving each of the steps. None of these is hallowed. None is carved in stone. Although I do believe that the two goals are quite firm, and the four steps are almost as good as they can get, the means and methods for achieving them are marvellously open for improvement.

What I fondly hope is that some special people will love and honor the two goals, the four steps, and the means and methods, and then will work to make them better. Now that I have done a good job, the way is open for others to make experiential sessions even better.

It is exciting to listen to people who have such new and good ideas for how to make the sessions better. I have spent hours with special people who have mastered experiential sessions and who are exploring ways to make them better. This is exciting.

I am also saddened to see sessions misused and distorted out of shape by, for example, trying to force people to have experiential sessions to achieve altogether different aims than they were designed to serve. These sessions were designed to help you become the qualitatively new person you can become, and to be free of the painful scenes in your personal world. Experiential sessions will not improve when people try to use them to get other people to lose weight, to get along better with the person they live with, to stop getting in trouble with the legal system, or to sell more of a product.

It is also sad to watch experiential sessions change their shape, become amorphous, and lose their identity when they are swallowed by some other approach. About all that remains are a few of the actual methods in experiential sessions. The steps are gone, and the two goals are lost when experiential sessions are incorporated into a larger approach such as meditation; altering one's thoughts; expressing feelings through dance; studying one's past; studying the stars; exploring one's dreams; or talking things over with a professional psychotherapist. Incorporation into some other approach will not make experiential sessions better.

I hope that experiential sessions will keep getting better and better. I am counting on you to help bring this about.

An Ever-Increasing Number Of People Will Achieve The Two Goals Of Each Experiential Session

This is an important and magnificent picture. I can imagine more and more people becoming the people they are capable of becoming, undergoing qualitative changes as they become more and more integrated and actualized. This means that their potentials for experiencing increasingly love and cherish one another, and their deeper potentials become integral parts of the new people they have become. I can also imagine more and more people being free of their personal painful scenes and of the painful feelings in those scenes. I think this would be wonderful.

You can help bring this about by learning to have your own experiential sessions and getting better and better as you continue to use these sessions throughout your entire life.

I Can Picture Magnificent Social Changes Coming From Collective People Having Their Own Experiential Sessions

In my own way of thinking (Mahrer, 1989a), the social world in which we exist is the product of the collective personal worlds of collective people. We collectively create, build, and orchestrate the social world in which we exist. We are the ones who create things like guns and dams, income tax and cars, bathtubs and lawn mowers, computers and roads. We are the ones who create governments and organizations, industry and the military, religions and nations. We are the ones who create laws and regulations, rules and moralities. We are the ones who collectively create the social world in which we exist, for better or for worse.

According to this way of thinking, if enough people undergo their own personal change and keep achieving the two goals of each experiential session, there can be powerful, sweeping, grandiose, wonderful, and magnificent changes in the social world in which we exist. If you want to achieve powerful and wonderful social changes, one way is to have your own personal experiential sessions. If you have your own experiential sessions, you are thereby helping to achieve powerful and wonderful social changes, whether you want to or not.

By social changes, I am referring to you and the people with whom you interact. I am thinking of your family, the groups of which you are a part, the larger community, the nation and the state, the social world in general, and people in general.

I do not know what the social world will be like if collective people have their own experiential sessions. I cannot predict the nuts and bolts of what the social world will become. However, my guess is that the nitty-gritty, the real and hard, the tangible and actual social world will reflect what personal worlds can be like for people who have their own experiential sessions. That is, I picture the social world consisting of, accommodating and enabling, and reflecting collective people becoming the optimal people they are capable of becoming, and as being increasingly free of painful scenes and the painful feelings in those scenes. I can picture the social world becoming increasingly more optimal, as being the world created by increasingly more optimal people. And I can picture the social world being increasingly free of painful scenes and the painful feelings in those scenes. I can picture what the optimal social world can offer. I cannot picture whether they will have soccer fields or weddings, elephants or flying saucers, governments or guilds, religions or restaurants, pencils or paupers, experiential sessions or something better.

Parents Will Give Their Infants The Greatest Gift: A More Optimal Personality Structure

It is easy to say that, if parents can somehow feel better, can be less torn apart and unhappy, their infants will benefit. The experiential model goes much, much further (Mahrer, 1989a). It provides a picture in which the infant comes equipped with a relatively complete personality structure.

Who and what the infant is to become, the person the infant will be, is already present by the time the infant is an infant.

Using the experiential model, picture a kind of "field" that includes the parents and the physical infant. This field is present from the time the parents conceive the infant, or even the idea of an infant, as part of their personal lives. Usually this occurs a few months or perhaps a year or so before the infant is conceived. This field extends to some years after the infant is born, perhaps two to four years later.

In the experiential model, that field includes the parents and the physical infant. In the experiential model, that field literally is the infant. In other words, the personality structure of the infant includes the parents' relevant potentials for experiencing and their relationships. Whatever these potentials for experiencing are, whatever their relationships, all of this is also the personality structure of the infant. During this primitive period, from before conception to some time after birth, the personality structure of the infant quite literally includes the relevant potentials for experiencing and their relationships in the parents.

And there is more. During this period, the parents construct, conceive of, and build an external world that includes the infant. The infant is created and conceived to serve as the context, the right situation, the important external world, for the experiencing of the parents' potentials for experiencing and their relationships. Parents make the infant into the external world that can enable the experiencings that are important to them; parents make the

426

infant into the externalization of what is deeper inside of them so that they can relate to the infant in much the same way as they relate to their deeper insides.

The net result is that the infant is both the parents who create its physical being and itself, the being the parents created. The net result is that the primitive field of the parents and their infant includes all that is necessary to constitute the personality structure of the infant.

From then on, the personality structure of the infant simply plays itself out. The personality structure is already present in the infant, and it remains much the same throughout his or her life. If I know the parents well during this primitive period, I can have a good idea of the personality structure of that infant, and of the person that infant will become.

Enter experiential sessions. Imagine that the parents have their own experiential sessions before and during this primitive period. Imagine that the parents become more and more of the people they can become. With each experiential session, what is deeper in the parents becomes an integral part of who and what the qualitatively new parent is, and relationships between potentials for experiencing become increasingly integrative, welcoming, loving, and accepting. Here is the main point: By having their own experiential sessions, the parents are giving, are bequeathing, their infants the greatest gift they can, namely, the best possible personality structure the infants can have. The parents give this gift to their infants without even intending to do so.

Having experiential sessions can be fitting and wonderful for a person, whether an adolescent, a young adult, a mature adult, or very old. Having experiential sessions has an especially profound effect, a magnificently, powerfully profound effect, when the person is creating, conceiving, acting upon, constructing an infant as a part of the person's world. This is the main point: If you are going to have experiential sessions, this is one time when they can have a magnificent effect on more than just you.

The People Who Create, Organize, And Use "The Experiential Movement" Will Have Their Own Experiential Sessions

I have a naive faith that this world will turn out all right if enough people can achieve what experiential sessions are designed for. Whether experiential sessions remain somewhat the way they are or evolve into something different but better, I have faith that the world can be all right if enough people have their own experiential sessions.

I am sad when I see many different experiential psychotherapies being assimilated by a few people who want to be "king of the mountain," who do their administrative and bureaucratic best to incorporate all experiential psychotherapies into their own particular version of what they call experiential psychotherapy. It is as if they are proclaiming: " I am the king of experiential psychotherapy. All experiential psychotherapies will be absorbed into and incorporated into my experiential psychotherapy." I find that sad. I believe it is better for me to do what I can to help make my own experiential psychotherapy as good as it can be and to welcome others who want to make my experiential psychotherapy even better, whatever it eventually becomes.

I have spent many years trying to develop a way for people to have their own experiential sessions. This book describes what I have accomplished so far and invites others to keep making it better and better. Even now, people ask me about having conferences on the subject of having your own experiential sessions, organizing workshops all over the world, starting a journal, creating institutes, setting standards for those who teach how to have your own sessions, providing certificates, setting up licensing procedures, franchising the teaching, approving training programs, organizing "the movement," creating centers, and doing research to show that it works and that it works better than supposed rivals. These people raise all sorts of realistic issues about economics, power structures, organizational matters, and advancing "the movement."

I usually have two reactions, One is that, if you are excited by these things, if they are important to you, then I wish you well. For now, my own excitement is in helping to improve experiential sessions and to better understand experiential sessions and how they can help me and others. The other, more important reaction I have is a plea, a fond hope, that you will have your own experiential sessions. I have a naive optimism that experiential sessions will fare well as long as people keep having their own sessions. Please learn how to have your own experiential sessions and keep having them throughout your life.

How Can You Get The Books And Audiotapes
Mentioned In This Volume?

Throughout this volume, I mentioned Mahrer, 1989a, 1989b, and 1996. These books are for those of you who want to go beyond this volume, although you do not need these books to become proficient in having your own experiential sessions.

Mahrer, 1989a, refers to *Experiencing: A Humanistic Theory of Psychology and Psychiatry*. It was originally published by Brunner/Mazel in 1978, and then reissued by the University of Ottawa Press, 542 King Edward Avenue, University of Ottawa, Ottawa, Canada K1N 6N5. Their e-mail address is: .

Mahrer, 1989b, refers to *Dream Work: In Psychotherapy And Self-Change*. It was published by W. W. Norton and Company, 500 Fifth Avenue, New York, New York 10110. Their fax number is: 212-869-0856.

Mahrer, 1996, refers to *The Complete Guide To Experiential Psychotherapy*. The publisher is John Wiley and Sons, Inc., 605 Third Avenue, New York, New York 10158-0012. Or, you may contact Alvin R. Mahrer, Ph.D., School of Psychology, University of Ottawa, Ottawa, Canada K1N 6N5. Dr. Mahrer's e-mail address is (If you are interested in audiotapes of Dr. Mahrer's personal experiential sessions, including commentary and guidelines for going through your own sessions, please contact him at the above postal address or e-mail address.)